# The New Age Is Lying to You

## Eldon K. Winker

D0954955

CPH
SAINT LOUIS

Copyright © 1994 Concordia Publishing House
3558 S. Jefferson Avenue, St. Louis, MO 63118-3968
Manufactured in the United States of America

Library of Congress Cataloging-in-Publication Data

Winker, Eldon K., 1941–
    The New Age is lying to you / by Eldon K. Winker.
        p.      cm.
        Includes bibliographical references.
        ISBN 0-570-04637-8
           1. New Age movement—Controversial literature.
    2. Apologetics—20th century. I. Title.
    BP605.N48W   1994
    239′.9—dc20
                                              93-37610

2  3  4  5  6  7  8  9  10      03  02  01  00  99  98  97  96  95

# Contents

# Introduction

"May the Force be with you"—Dialing 900 numbers to hear a psychic give advice after casting a horoscope or reading tarot cards—Children in some public school systems in classroom sessions engaged in meditation, contacting spirit guides, and values clarification exercises—Environmental groups promoting the view that the earth is sacred, a goddess to be served—Reincarnation offered as an alternative to the Christian doctrine of the resurrection—Business seminars to improve employee productivity by teaching that individuals create their own reality through the mind—Political activities that support the concept of globalism and the development of a one-world government.

What do all of the above have in common? They are themes and activities that have become increasingly popular in American society in the last 10 to 15 years. Furthermore, they are all activities that are expressions of the New Age movement.

Aletheia Psycho-Physical Foundation (Grants Pass, OR)—The Aquarian Center of Universology (Sarasota, FL)—Association for Holistic Health (La Jolla, CA)—Association for the Development of Human Potential (Porthill, ID)—Astro Consciousness Institute (Denver, CO)—The Brotherhood of Eternal Truth (New Albany, IN)—The Brotherhood of the Followers of the Present Jesus (San Diego, CA)—California New Age Caucus (Los Angeles, CA)—Center for Spiritual Awareness (Lakemont, GA)—The Center of Light (Great Barrington, MA)—Church of Immortal Consciousness (Mesa, AZ)—Church of Ultimate Reality (Columbus,OH)—Church of Universal Light (Reno, NV)—Church Universal and Triumphant, Inc. (Livingston, MT)—City of the Sun Foundation (Columbus, NM).[1]

What do the above named 15 organizations have in common? They all promote the New Age philosophy. Note that the 15 organizations are located in 13 different states. While the preponderance of such organizations seems to be in the western states, New Age groups, associations, and churches are located in every state in our nation. Also note that this small sampling is taken from just the first three letters of the alphabet. The alphabetical listing for the letter "N" in the above source includes 18 listings that begin with "New Age." That section includes such organizations as New Age Action Group (Alexandria, VA), New Age Christian Church (Lakeside, CA), and New Age Institute (Champaign, IL). From Maine to Hawaii, from Alaska to Florida, the influence of the New Age philosophy continues to spread.

Of course, the New Age tentacles stretch out not only to the United States. The revival of its occult aspects can be traced to western Europe and to such individuals as Emanuel Swedenborg (1688–1772) and Franz Mesmer (1733–1815). The last decade of the 20th century is seeing the worldview of many Europeans shifting away from Christianity to what some European scholars describe as a New Age worldview. Since restrictions of religious activity have been eliminated in eastern Europe, reports indicate that New Age literature and paraphernalia are doing big business. Furthermore, since the roots of its foundational monistic and pantheistic concepts (cf. below, pp. 17–18) can be traced to Eastern mysticism, the fundamental worldview of the New Age is found in all parts of the world where the religions of Hinduism and Buddhism are dominant.

Even the southern hemisphere is not immune to the outreach of the New Age. "For the third year in a row, 40,000 people visited Sydney's [Australia] popular 'Darling Harbour for the Mind, Body, Spirit' Festival. Stalls were rented by representatives of the Grail Movement, Hare Krishna, Mind Powers, Astrology, Spiritualist Church, Tarot Card Readers, and other New Age, cult and witchcraft groups."[2]

The New Age movement with its concern for the evolutionary progress of the human race toward the quantum leap point that will usher in global harmony and world peace has, indeed, spread its philosophy worldwide. However, in this book I will focus on the subtle spread of its influence in this country.

A survey of the Princeton Religion Research Center found that in 1991 only one adult in four had heard or read about the New Age.[3] That might lead us to wonder why some in Christian circles are raising such an alarm about the New Age. If only 25 percent of adults in the country have heard or read about the New Age, a far smaller number would have experienced any direct impact of the New Age in their lives. Or so it would seem.

What is often not realized is that, dressed up in its humanitarian and Christianized forms, many do not discern that the New Age philosophy is nothing more than the age-old lies of Satan. The same PRRC survey found that, of those who were aware of the New Age, one in three felt that one could be a good Jew or Christian and accept New Age beliefs and practices as well.[4] When I spoke on the New Age for a Lutheran adult singles group, several indicated they could find little with which to disagree in Shirley MacLaine's *Out on a Limb,* a popular presentation of how the actress encountered and finally adopted a New Age worldview. Upon the unsuspecting, upon those who are not well grounded in the foundational teachings of the Christian faith, and upon those who are not discerning with regard to the spread of New Age ideas, the New Age exerts its subtle but deadly influence in almost every aspect of our society.

In an article identified as a "Special to Religious New Service," Rabbi A. James Rudin discusses the New Age movement. After a brief introduction to cults, Rabbi Rudin comments, "As dangerous to the American way of life as more clearly defined cults is the amorphous New Age movement. Its followers can choose from a wide variety of activities and beliefs, including some that have achieved a degree of acceptance."[5]

In his article Rabbi Rudin identifies numerous practices and occult tools available to the New Age practitioner—astrology, acupuncture, rebirthing, channeling, self-actualization groups, crystals, tarot cards, Shirley MacLaine's writings, and many others. Rudin warns,

> Cigarettes, movies, and alcoholic beverages contain clearly marked warnings for the public. But unfortunately New Age products and ideas do not. They should, because many of these practices and beliefs can be harmful physically, psychologically, and spiritually. In general, New Age groups use subtle manipulation techniques to soften up the mind, making people more vulnerable to mind control techniques used so successfully by cults.[6]

Rabbi Rudin writes from the theological perspective of Judaism. He obviously expresses great concern over the advance of the New Age movement in our society. Christians who have the full revelation of God's plan of salvation, brought to completion in the birth, life, suffering, death, and resurrection of our Lord Jesus Christ, should have even greater concern. They need to be concerned about the whole person. They need to speak out when New Age teachings and practices threaten people's physical and emotional well-being.

Of even greater concern is the threat which the New Age poses to a person's spiritual and eternal well-being. For Christians, following the teachings of the New Age as compared with the teachings of the God who has revealed his grace and mercy in Jesus Christ is the difference between death and life. To choose the light the New Age offers is to continue to walk in darkness. It is to continue listening to the old lies of Satan. It is to fall into the very practices which God has declared to be an abomination.

In these pages we will address primarily the spiritual dangers posed by the New Age. In so doing, we will also discuss the physical and emotional dangers which the New Age presents. Our hope is that the reader will become aware of the obvious conflict between the New Age philosophy and the Christian faith and, more important, that the reader will become more discerning and recognize the subtle ways in which the New Age worldview is influencing and modifying every aspect of life as we approach the 21st century. Our hope is that the reader will become better equipped to critique the New Age movement and to respond to it.

# 1

# The New Age Worldview

**Item:** In 1987 the employees of Pacific Bell, a San Francisco based utility company were required to participate in a "Leadership Development" program. They were instructed to give their attention to a speaker who addressed the topic, "A new context within which to think." This was but one of several topics in the program also called *Krone training*, after Charles Krone, the management consultant who developed material for the sessions. The stated purpose of this motivation and training program was to move employees toward greater realization of "end-state visions," organizational "alignment," and better management of "internal resources." However, some Pacific Bell employees complained that the training program subjected them to a form of mind control and promoted values that compromised their religious beliefs.

**Item:** In the year 1988, the Volkswagen Corporation sponsored a series of special advertising sections in *Time* magazine in which they invited "prominent figures in American culture" to share their views with future generations. One such prominent figure was Gene Roddenberry, the creator of *Star Trek*, a television program in the 1960s that led to a six-film movie series and a TV sequel, *Star Trek: The Next Generation*. Story lines for both TV programs and movies have done much to promote New Age concepts such as monism and pantheism. Apparently, Roddenberry also supported the concepts of evolution and globalism that are at the heart of the New Age. In his contribution to the special advertising section series he wrote,

> The present tumult in our world is the natural and understandable result of a vigorous intelligence moving out of the savagery of our life-form's childhood. Instead of humanity's demise, our era seems to be filled with evidence that we were meant to survive and evolve much further. . . .
>
> Rather than being unable to handle the complexities of today, the

9

combination of computer and brain appears to be doubling human knowledge every six or seven years, leading us toward knowledge and ability our ancestors would have considered godlike. . . .

Those who insist theirs is the only correct government or economic system deserve the same contempt as those who insist that they have the only true God.[1]

**Item:** Mission S.O.A.R. was introduced in 1990 into the Los Angeles public school district as a pilot program with the goal of reducing gang violence and building self-esteem. It was initially tested in 70 schools. The acronym *SOAR* stood for "Set Objectives, Achieve Results." While the goal was commendable, unfortunately some of the practices included in the curriculum material included hypnotism, the development of psychic powers, and contacting spirits of the dead. In one of the lessons the statement was made, "In this session you will experience communication with a deceased person. Deceased persons can be a source of valuable information for you." As the result of an information campaign by an organized citizen's group, the Mission S.O.A.R. program was removed from the Los Angeles public school district.[2]

**Item:** A national news magazine reports the growing popularity of an ancient Hindu method of medicine called Ayurveda. Translated from the Hindi language, Ayurveda means *the science or the knowledge of life.* Its basic tenet is that there is an essential oneness between the mind and the body. The brain controls the body and directs its actions through self-awareness and balance. Illness results when there is an imbalance in the mind-body oneness. Through Ayurvedic therapy a person can restore the balance that will lead to good health through such means as diet, meditation, massage, and yogalike exercises. One technique that is used is the slow pouring of herbal sesame oil on the forehead. Dr. Deepak Chopra, the physician instrumental in introducing the 6,000-year-old practice into modern medicine, says, "We slowly introduce them [patients] to procedures they find enjoyable and which give them a sense of comfort, self-power, and self-worth."[3]

**Item:** A co-worker at the International Center of The Lutheran Church—Missouri Synod sent me a copy of a letter which she had written to the vice-president for advertising for *Weight Watchers*

10

*Magazine,* protesting a full-page ad for a "crystal power ring." In her letter the co-worker indicated that she would not renew her subscription which expired with that issue. She also copied the full-page ad to me. The ad showed a woman's hand with the crystal power ring on the ring finger and with the hand holding a large, clear quartz crystal. The wording of the ad read in part, "The power of crystal. Close at hand. Energy at your fingertips. Captivating crystal aglow with New Age vitality. Capturing the spirit of well-being and inner harmony. Natural quartz crystal draws the power to you. Channeling prisms of light into positive energy."[4]

**Item:** A midwestern newspaper reported on a "summer psychic fair" held at a hotel in a large metropolitan area. More than 45 palm readers, advisers and extrasensory communicators were on hand to offer their services. One individual's card identified him as a "spiritual healer, psychic reader and home health specialist." The newspaper reported that for a $4 admission fee the fairgoer had access to palm, tarot card, and crystal ball readers, relaxation therapists, and sellers of various wares ranging from quartz crystals to "New Age" music.[5]

**Item:** The advertising section of an upper midwestern newspaper offered the following services:

> Spiritual healer and therapist. Therapeutic counseling sessions, psychic readings, and past life regressions.

> Professional astrologer offers 15 years' experience with specialties in newborns, transitions, addictions, incest.

> Psychic counseling for professionals and individuals. I channel specific steps you can take to make your work, relationships, and lifestyle more productive and enjoyable.[6]

The preceding items show quite clearly how subtle and how pervasive the influence of the New Age movement (NAM) is in modern American society. From business seminars to classroom exercises, from alternative medicine to body therapies, from entertainment media to advertisements in newspapers and magazines the New Age philosophy is being quietly yet forcefully embedded in the minds and lives of people in our culture. That is precisely what makes the NAM so dangerous. Like the temptation of Eve by Satan in the Garden of Eden, the NAM's influence is very deceptive, very subtle, and therefore very easily overlooked by those exposed to such influence.

## Satan's Old Lies

The third chapter of Genesis gives the familiar account of the temptation of Adam and Eve in the Garden of Eden. Here we discover that the tactics Satan used to deceive Eve are much the same as those used today by the leaders of religious cults as well as the leading New Age thinkers. We also discover that two of the most fundamental teachings of the NAM are as old as the original lies of Satan.

> Now the serpent was more crafty than any of the wild animals the Lord God had made. He said to the woman, "Did God really say, 'You must not eat from any tree in the garden'?" The woman said to the serpent, "We may eat fruit from the trees in the garden, but God did say, 'You must not eat fruit from the tree that is in the middle of the garden, and you must not touch it, or you will die.' " "You will not surely die," the serpent said to the woman. "For God knows that when you eat of it your eyes will be opened, and you will be like God, knowing good and evil" (Gen. 3:1–5).

Notice in these truths revealed in God's Word how Satan in the form of the serpent (Rev. 12:9) first leads Eve to question God's goodness and authority and to disobey God's wisdom. Satan, the father of lies, implicitly denies God's truthfulness and accuses God of lying in the matter of threatening Adam and Eve with death if they should eat of the forbidden fruit. Secondly, the devil confuses Eve in her understanding of what she previously knew to be right as far as what God had commanded. In her confusion she adds to God's command that they should not eat of the fruit of the tree of the knowledge of good and evil (Gen. 2:17) the idea that they should not even touch it.

In snakelike fashion, the devil twists God's Word to achieve his own ends. As his lies destroy Eve's ability to reason clearly, Satan also seduces her through her five senses—listening to what he said, opening her eyes, leading her to touch and taste the fruit. With such tactics Satan lures Eve into a different spiritual understanding.

Notice the false promises and lies (some would say half-truths)

12

Satan uses with Eve. He promises wisdom, knowledge, and understanding if she and Adam will eat of the fruit in disobedience of God's command. In other words, to disobey God, to ignore his word, to assert one's own will is the path to enlightenment and the gaining of secret knowledge. The first of Satan's lies, an outright contradiction of God's truth, is that Eve and her husband Adam will not die. In spite of rebellion against God, mankind will in some way continue to live. Implied in Satan's lie is that this continuation of life will be good and beneficial. The second lie is that when they eat of the fruit their eyes will be opened and they will be like God. There will no longer be any distinction between Creator and creature. Instead, they will have become as one.

One truth that is learned from the account of mankind's fall into sin is that there is not a duality of good and evil in the universe as though they were two separate but equal forces contending for supremacy. God created all things good. Adam, Eve, life in the Garden, the superior/inferior relationship between Creator and creature, a transcendent yet personal God who relates to his creation in a personal way—all was inherently good. Evil is a parasite that attaches itself to what God has created as good. As Brooks Alexander of Spiritual Counterfeits Project writes,

> [I]t is never evil in itself that tempts us. It is always a good that attracts us—one that we imagine, an even "better" good than which God proposes. Thus the archetypal pattern is struck: we cannot "do wrong" as the deceptive phrase leads us to believe, but we can "do wrongly" what we do with the gifts of God, including the supreme gift of our own being, created in his image. At its heart the lie is seduction to an idolatry of the image of God, a worship of the self and its powers, disguised as "secret knowledge" and presented as "god-realization."[7]

This lie, more than any other, is at the foundation of New Age teaching—man is God in himself. He has only to realize this and to strive to actualize the divinity residing within him. The first lie of Satan in the Garden is expressed in the NAM with reincarnation as its basic understanding of what happens in the death process. It is obvious that one's physical existence, the body of matter, ceases to exist at the end of any given lifetime. Nevertheless the soul, or mind, or spirit of a person continues to live on—according to the

NAM—to be reincarnated in body after body. The devil's false promise of secret knowledge or hidden wisdom is the carrot which the NAM dangles before lost souls searching for meaning in life. Channeled messages, psychic readings, meditation for enlightenment—all offer the promise of knowledge that will help a person achieve "god-realization."

Satan may not be very original in making up new lies. He is original, however, in how he brings the influence of his old lies into the lives of people. The NAM, perhaps more crafty than any religious blend mankind has made, is one of Satan's most powerful seducers of people today. With its deceptive teachings and attention-getting practices, its outright lies and its half-truths, its false promises mixed with expressions of genuine humanitarian concern, the NAM is a powerful tool in the hands of the Deceiver who prowls around looking for someone to devour. The New Age philosophy is nothing other than Satan's old lies for a new age.

## Definition

What is the New Age movement? There is no easy answer. There is no brief, one-sentence definition that will capsulize all that the New Age is. The New Age has a very broad base. It is very diverse in terms of participants, teachings, and practices. Its philosophy is very eclectic. As a result, many authors who write about the New Age often don't attempt to provide a brief definition of what he or she understands the NAM to be. An example of this would be the excellent work by Douglas Groothuis in *Unmasking the New Age* and *Confronting the New Age*. In his two books Groothuis has presented, in my opinion as well as the opinion of many others, as well-balanced an evaluation of the New Age from a Christian perspective as any author writing on the subject today. Yet nowhere in these two books does he have a two- or three-sentence paragraph that is intended to be a precise definition of the New Age. About as close as Groothuis comes to such a definition is in his second book, *Confronting the New Age*.

> *The New Age movement* is an umbrella term referring to a variety of people, organizations, events, practices and ideas. Sociologically speaking, it is not a centrally organized movement with one human

leader.... Rather it is a constellation of like-minded people and groups all desiring a spiritual and social change that will usher in a New Age of self-actualization.[8]

Instead of attempting a precise definition, Groothuis describes the basic themes of the New Age, how these themes are finding expression in our American society and culture, and how Christians might respond to the counterfeit faith of the New Age.

An exception to the observation that NAM authors seldom provide a brief definition of what they understand the New Age to be would be Elliot Miller in *A Crash Course on the New Age Movement*.

The New Age Movement then is an extremely large, *loosely* structured network of organizations and individuals bound together by common values (based in mysticism and monism—the world view that "all is one") and a common vision (a coming "new age" of peace and mass enlightenment, the "Age of Aquarius").[9]

Others define the NAM in terms of its basic principles or teachings. In the 1990 Cult Catalog of its official newspaper, *Watchman Expositor*, Watchman Fellowship, Inc. included the following in a boxed area:

## New Age Definition

Because the New Age is simply an umbrella term which covers a myriad of groups, with scores of authors, it is impossible to identify all its doctrines. The following, however, is a brief overview of the basic teachings of the majority of New Age groups.

1) All is one: all reality is a unitary whole;

2) Everything is God (god) and God (god) is everything;

3) You (as an individual) are God. You are divine; God is within you;

4) You will never die; You have lived before and you will live again (reincarnation);

5) You can create your own reality or transform your own consciousness;

6) All religions are true and, therefore, one;

7) A new world is coming; a New Age is dawning.

(*Belief Bulletin: New Age Movement*, Southern Baptist Home Mission Board, p. 1).[10]

As indicated above, the primary reason for not providing a brief definition is that the NAM draws upon numerous sources, is highly varied as to its teachings, and is so broad in its applications, that it is almost impossible to define the NAM in a sentence or two. However, I believe it is important for readers of this book to know the author's definition of the New Age. Therefore, like the proverbial person who ventures in where angels fear to tread, this is my working definition and the springboard for what follows in the rest of the book.

> *The New Age movement is an eclectic, occult-based, evolution-promoting, man-centered, self-deifying, pervasive worldview (philosophy of life) that seeks, through the transformation of individuals, to bring about a transformation of society in order to achieve the ultimate goal of a new world order of complete global harmony.*

This definition attempts to summarize the basic concepts and goals common to the various expressions of the NAM. The key idea is that the NAM is a worldview, a philosophy of life that influences one's daily decisions and actions. It is its own religion, which, like all religions other than Christianity, centers on the individual's efforts to transform himself, to make himself right with God, yes, even to achieve the status of godhood.

In this the New Age is not new. It has been preceded by religious teachings and practices of almost every stripe and color that have promoted the same man-centered, self-deifying philosophy. What sets the NAM apart from its predecessors and its modern day competition with other false religions is that, as previously mentioned, it is perhaps the most crafty, most subtle, most deceptive religious blend the human race has ever produced. It is simply a clever reproduction of the old lies of Satan.

## The Basic Principles of the New Age Movement

Attempts to summarize the basic principles of the NAM are about as varied as the multifaceted quartz crystals that have all but become synonymous with the New Age. Some authors and publications summarize New Age teachings in four or five concise statements. Others identify ten or more salient features of the New Age philosophy. Walter Martin devotes a chapter of *The New Age Cult* to the "Ten Key Doctrines of the New Age Movement."[11] However, it seems that many authors (e.g. Philip Lochhaas[12], Russell Chandler[13], Douglas Groothuis[14]) identify six summary principles that underlie the New Age philosophy. While the six principles may vary slightly in the wording of each author, they closely parallel what follows.

# 1. All is one; therefore all is God

While some would divide this thought into two separate principles, it combines two aspects of New Age teaching with regard to God. The idea that *all is one* is the core teaching of the New Age. It is the foundational principle of the mysticism in Eastern religions and in turn of the New Age philosophy. Both the humanistic and occult aspects of the New Age embrace the oneness of matter and energy, divinity and humanity. This same New Age principle is expressed in science, medicine, politics, education, environmental concerns and the entertainment media. Russell Chandler writes, "The New Age bottom line can be stated in three words: 'All is One.' The cosmos is pure, undifferentiated, universal energy—a consciousness or 'life force.' Everything is one vast, interconnected process."[15]

*Monism* is an alternate expression of this same concept. Monism is the belief that all is one in complete unity with a continuous unbounded and undivided reality. This relates closely to the New Age teaching that ultimate reality is only what one perceives in the mind. Things that seem to be different and distinctive—e.g. good and evil—have no real existence, for all is one. The *oneness* that pervades all things is described as Divine Mind, Universal Energy, or the Force. In effect, there is no difference between God, a tree, or a human being.

On the other hand, if all is one, then all must be God. All that exists—rocks, plants, animals, people—is part of the divine essence, the dynamic force, the ultimate reality, the universal energy. The God of the New Age is thus an impersonal energy force or field that fills the universe. This is *pantheism*—that God, the universal energy, is in all things and therefore all is God. Douglas Groothuis comments,

> The One does not have a personality; it is beyond personality. God is more an "it" than a "he." The idea of a personal God is abandoned in favor of an impersonal energy, force or consciousness. Ultimate reality is god, who is in all and through all; in fact, God is all.[16]

Walter Martin, when identifying ten key doctrines of the New Age, quotes without additional comment what New Age writers have said or written. On the doctrine of God, Martin quotes from *The Seth Material* by Jane Roberts, who channeled the spirit entity called Seth. The quotation clearly identifies the New Age idea of God, often attempting to blend with the biblical teachings about God.

> He is not one individual, but an energy gestalt ... a psychic pyramid of interrelated, ever-expanding consciousness that creates, simultaneously and instantaneously, universes and individuals that are given—through the gift of personal perspective—duration, psychic comprehension, intelligence, and eternal validity.

> This absolute, ever-expanding, instantaneous psychic gestalt, which you may call God if you prefer, is so secure in its existence that it can constantly break itself down and rebuild itself.

> Its energy is so unbelievable that it does indeed form all universes; and because its energy is within and behind all universes, systems, and fields, it is indeed aware of each sparrow that falls, for it *is* each sparrow that falls.[17]

## 2. Mankind is divine and has unlimited potential

Logically, using the foundational New Age principle that all is one and all is God, the human race must also be divine in its essential nature. Dr. Philip Lochhaas explains this New Age error: "Any human being may say 'I am God' in the same sense that 'the man from Nazareth' said it."[18] A corollary to the divinity of mankind is that in being one's own god each person creates his/her own reality. "Humans are nothing but 'congealed energy,' the seeming solidification of thought. Hence the oft-quoted New Age slogan: 'You create your own reality.' "[19]

A prime example of how this dictum is actually applied can be seen in Werner Erhard, the founder of *est* and its offspring, The Forum—human potential training seminars. Although lawsuits and a variety of other accusations caused Erhard to sell Werner Erhard & Associates, which had run *est* and the Forum, and also led to Erhard's reported disappearance in 1991, his story still illustrates well how the eclectic (cafeteria-style) New Age philosophy can affect a person's life.

Werner Erhard, originally John Paul (Jack) Rosenberg, was a used car salesman from Philadelphia with a wife and four children. In 1959, in the midst of an extra-marital affair, he moved to the San Francisco area. Here, in order to evade his former wife's efforts to locate him, he changed his name to Werner Hans Erhard. Erhard became involved in scientology and mind dynamics, Zen Buddhism, hypnosis, yoga, encounter therapy, and transpersonal psychology. He was active in Silva Mind Control, a forerunner of his own training seminars. He also spent time in India with several Hindu gurus.[20]

As a result, Erhard came to believe that he was god in his own universe. Est (Erhard Seminars Training) was begun in 1971. In 1985, with some changes and modifications, est was repackaged into a new self-improvement seminar called The Forum. A goal of Erhard's seminars is to lead an individual to give up false belief systems, to accept that each person creates his or her own reality, and to experience the reality of being god in one's own universe.

This New Age principle states that each one of us is God in disguise. J. Gordon Melton summarizes this "good news" in an article on rebirthing in the *New Age Encyclopedia, First Edition*. He refers to Leonard Orr, the developer of the rebirthing technique: "According to Orr, human beings are a reservoir of the fullness of divine power. That is to say, each person is God."[21]

## 3. Mankind's basic flaw is the ignorance of his divinity

Since ultimately all is one, part of the divine essence and sharing in the universal energy or force, and since humanity is God, it would seem that there should be no problems. All things should flow smoothly and harmoniously. At the very least, nation should not be warring against nation. According to New Age teaching, the human race is the most highly evolved life form on planet Earth, the life form most capable of achieving the realization of its divine status. Therefore, humanity should be at peace with itself and all else that exists, especially because everything else, even the earth, also participates in the energy that flows throughout the universe.

However, although the NAM tells us that reality is only that which people create in their own minds, the news headlines tell us there are problems in our world. What is our problem? Why do nations war against nations? Why is man's inhumanity to man the focus of television and newspaper news reporting? The NAM answer is not a conflict between good and evil, for the reality of such conflict doesn't exist. Good and evil exist only in the reality each person creates in the mind. The problem is not sin, for there is no personal God to whom we are held accountable for our faults and failures. God is an impersonal energy force that is in all things.

What then, according to the NAM, is mankind's problem? Simply stated, it is that we are ignorant of our status as gods. We are walking in darkness, not the darkness of sin, but the darkness of ignorance. We have forgotten our true identity. We need to be enlightened again to see who we really are.

Tal Brooke is the president of the Spiritual Counterfeits Project which is devoted to offering a biblical perspective on new religions and spiritual trends. In his early adult years, before his conversion to faith in Jesus Christ, Brooke spent two decades following the New Age and its occult practices . On the basis of his previous personal involvement and his research and study of the New Age, Brooke in *When the World Will Be as One* summarizes what he envisions to be the birth of a New World Order. He provides a concise statement of the second and third principles of the New Age.

> The mystery of man's ultimate identity is finally revealed as his divinity within. It is the basic tenet of pantheism, the core belief of Hinduism: All things are One, since all energy is divine consciousness "frozen" into matter. Since all things are made of God, man in his deepest self is none other than God. But without "enlightenment," he does not know this and, in effect, lives as an amnesiac. The purpose of man is to realize that he is God, thus ending the "illusion" of separation.[22]

In *West Side Story,* a hit musical of the 1960s, a song by one of the street gangs has the line, "I'm depraved on account of I'm deprived." The lyrics of the New Age song would change that to read, "My actions are depraved because I remain unenlightened." The "illusion of separation" to which Tal Brooke refers is *maya*, another of the many Hindu concepts that form the mix of the eclectic NAM. "*Maya:* A Hindu teaching that the only reality is the deity Brahman, the Supreme Absolute, and that all else in the material world is an extension of Brahman's thoughts and therefore illusory or transitory."[23]

## 4. Mankind's basic need is personal transformation produced by consciousness-altering techniques

Since for the NAM sin does not exist, mankind doesn't need a Savior. Instead, mankind needs enlightenment. To bring to an end living with the "illusion of separation" each person needs to pursue personal transformation to levels of higher consciousness that will lead to full "god-realization."

Douglas Groothuis writes, "To gain this type of transformation, the three ideas that all is one, all is god, and we are god, must be more than intellectual propositions; they must be awakened at the core of our being."[24] He describes how the est and Forum seminars of Werner Erhard are designed to awaken these ideas within us. He writes,

> And what are we to do? We are to look within. As one New Age ad put it, "The only way out is in." All is perfect, says Werner Erhard. The trouble is we don't *see it*. Humans are not depraved or dependent on any outside source of deliverance or strength. The answer is not reconciliation with a God different from ourselves, but the realization that we ourselves are God. The self is the cosmic treasury of wisdom, power and delight. . . .

> Once the true knowledge (or *gnosis*) of reality is realized, higher powers are activated within. The limitations of a supposedly finite and imperfect being fade into the limitless potential of the truly enlightened being.[25]

The New Age path to achieving such transformation centers in various consciousness-altering techniques—participating in human potential seminars similar to those of est or The Forum; sensory deprivation by spending time in a flotation tank; meditation accompanied by physical and breathing exercises; engaging in creative visualization in which one's mind pictures the reality of what one desires life to be—all intended to raise consciousness levels. The body, like the mind, is also considered both a receiver and transmitter of cosmic forces. Tuning the body through yoga, reflexology, iridology, acupuncture, the martial arts, and Therapeutic Touch will, in New Age thinking, help to achieve higher consciousness. If one is not successful in achieving higher consciousness by such practices, then perhaps using various objects whose energy patterns resonate with those of mind, body, and spirit—such as rock crystals, pyramids, colors, and flower essences—will help.

One can hardly write about the New Age without referring to Shirley MacLaine and her writings. She certainly ranks near the top of a list of popular and well-known entertainment personalities who have actively promoted the NAM. In a later chapter we will devote more space to what she has written. Here a quote from one of her books will demonstrate yet another technique for raising one's consciousness levels—meditative chanting and speaking affirmations.

> The ancient Hindu vedas claimed that the spoken words *I am*, or *Aum* in Hindi, set up a vibrational frequency in the body and mind which align the individual with his or her higher self and thus with the God-source. The word God in any language carries the highest vibrational frequency of any word in the language. Therefore, if one says audibly *I am God*, the sound vibrations literally align the energies of the body to a higher atunement.

> You can use *I am God* or *I am that I am* as Christ often did, or you can extend the affirmations to fit your own needs. . . .

> Before performing I always did them [affirmations] during the overture and continued right on through my entrance. I felt the alignment occur all through me and I went on to perform with the God Source as my support system.[26]

If all else fails, certainly individuals will be in touch with the divine energy or force when they allow themselves to be used as channels for a spirit guide, or at least learn from the teachings of such a spirit guide. Again, Shirley MacLaine serves as an example of how powerful a spirit guide can be. Although her interest is no longer what it once was, MacLaine at one time totally committed herself to the teachings of Ramtha, who supposedly is a 35,000-year-old ascended master channeled through a woman named J. Z. Knight. Through Mrs. Knight, Ramtha has issued a book. Some of Ramtha's quotations are found in *The New Age Rage*, edited by Karen Hoyt and J. Isamu Yamamoto. Robert J. L. Burrows, one of the authors, quotes from the teachings of Ramtha:

> God . . . . has never been *outside* of you—it is you. God, of itself, is holy without goodness or evil. . . . God simply is. I am here to help you realize that you are an ongoing immortal essence. There is no voice that will ever teach you greater than your own. . . . Who you are this day is the answer to *everything* you have ever wanted.[27]

If you feel that you need to experience personal transformation or spiritual enlightenment, the NAM will almost certainly have some technique to help you reach your goal. However, one needs to ask, "If I pursue a New Age technique or teaching to find spiritual enlightenment, will I end up dancing in the light or walking in darkness?"

# 5. Personal transformation is the springboard to global transformation

Why all the concern about personal transformation? Why all the effort through consciousness-raising techniques to enlighten people to the divinity within them? The answer—to elevate cosmic consciousness on the part of a "critical mass" of people so that the goal of global transformation may be achieved. Shakti Gawain, a noted spokesperson for the NAM, author of the best seller *Creative Visualization*, writes in another of her books, *Living in the Light*, about a radical spiritual transformation taking place on a worldwide level as the human race lets go of its present way of life and builds a new world in its place. She explains,

> The new world is being built as we open to the higher power of the universe within us and consciously allow that creative energy to move through us. As each of us connects with our inner spiritual awareness, we learn that we can create our own reality and take responsibility for doing so. The change begins within each individual, but as more and more individuals are transformed, the mass consciousness is increasingly affected.[28]

In other words, the world's future depends upon people being willing to accept their role as creators of reality. As more and more people strive toward a higher consciousness, eventually the NAM will achieve its goal—a new and better world of complete peace and harmony, where all people and things exist side-by-side in the oneness they share with the divine essence.

Not all who identify themselves as Christians are deeply committed to living the teachings of the faith. Many dabble with being a Christian—with occasional church attendance, sending children to Sunday School, having a kind of generic belief in God, but really knowing little about the teachings of the Bible and caring little about the mission Christ gave to his church on earth. Likewise, many in the NAM are dabblers, reading their horoscope, wearing a crystal necklace for good luck, chanting their mantras, or attempting to create their own reality through visualization. They do not take seriously the deeper meaning of the NAM. However, like many Christians who actively strive to live the teachings of the Christian faith and who work to promote the theology and doctrine of that faith, so many New Agers seriously promote the NAM's deeper philosophical concepts and actively strive to achieve the New Age agenda.

For the serious movers and shakers, the New Age agenda is a new world order, globalism, a "global village." "All is One also applies to nations. National boundaries are obsolete, according to the New Age worldview. Thus, the New Age agenda calls for an emerging global civilization."[29] While written from a literalistic and millennialistic approach to Scripture, particularly in regard to the Book of Revelation, Tal Brooke's *When the World Will Be as One* nevertheless provides an interesting and insightful overview of what those who are serious about New Age concepts have in mind for planet Earth.

What is needed, say the leading New Age thinkers, is a major paradigm shift for the living of life. Initially the concept of "paradigm shift" was applied to scientific theories, but New Agers have applied it to planetary consciousness. Marilyn Ferguson wrote what some have termed the "bible" of the New Age. While not directly connected with all that has become associated with the NAM, particularly the faddish aspects, her book, *The Aquarian Conspiracy*, has probably done more to initiate and promote the popularity of the NAM than any other book. Ferguson "paints a broad picture of New Age activities and inroads into our culture, and suggests that this signals a transformation so radical that it may amount to an entirely new phase in evolution."[30]

Keeping in mind that *The Aquarian Conspiracy* is pushing for the acceptance of those ideas and activities that will result in a global transformation, listen to what Ferguson says about paradigms.

> A new paradigm involves a principle that was present all along but unknown to us. It includes the old as a partial truth, one aspect of How Things Work, while allowing for things to work in other ways as well. By its larger perspective, it transforms traditional knowledge and the stubborn new observations, reconciling their apparent contradictions. . . .
>
> New paradigms are nearly always received with coolness, even mockery and hostility. Their discoverers are attacked for their heresy. . . .
>
> But the new paradigm gains ascendance. A new generation recognizes its power. When a critical number of thinkers has accepted the new idea, a collective paradigm shift has occurred.[31]

Ferguson strongly asserts that what is needed is a radical shift in the worldview of the inhabitants of planet Earth, a major paradigm shift, that in spite of its seemingly heretical claims will nevertheless establish the model for a global transformation that will be the savior of the planet.

# 6. All religions are one and lead to cosmic unity

A sixth summary principle of New Age thinking is that all religions are one at their basic core and teach the oneness of all things. This teaching is identified as *syncretism* (a fusion of religions). Again, it seems quite logical to assume that if all is one, all is God, and we are God, then the enlightened teachers and masters of the great religions of the world—Jesus, Muhammad, Buddha, Krishna, and others—would themselves have experienced the higher consciousness of divine oneness. The various religions may have different teachings, "but the vital experience of 'the god within' is common throughout the world."[32]

Of course, the syncretist principle requires that the distinctive and exclusive nature of Christianity be denied. In an effort to reconcile the teachings of Christianity with the teachings of the New Age, the NAM goes to great lengths to reveal the supposed secret and hidden teachings of Jesus that were excluded from the Bible. Furthermore, the Christ of the Bible is reshaped and redefined in order to make him a spokesman for the NAM. For the undiscerning or somewhat biblically illiterate Christian, the result is a version of the 1950's television game show *What's My Line?*—"Will the real Jesus please stand up?" "Christ as the mediator between God and humanity is replaced with the idea of 'Christ-consciousness,' which is another word for cosmic consciousness."[33]

The NAM's syncretist principle seeks to combine Christianity with other world religions to form a one-world religion—the New Age religion. Those in the NAM who had an earlier Christian background will frequently refer to Jesus as a great teacher. They will use the title Christ, not in its biblical meaning, but to express the divine nature that is in each individual. In *Unmasking the New Age*, Groothuis quotes New Age futurist Barbara Marx Hubbard. In *The Evolutionary Journey*, Hubbard explains her concept of spiritual futurism. She writes, "At this moment of our planetary birth each person is called upon to recognize that the 'Messiah is within.' Christ consciousness or cosmic consciousness is awakening in millions of Christians and non-Christians."[34]

Because the New Age of today can be traced back to the 19th century, writings from a much earlier period laid the foundation for the present New Age view of Jesus Christ and the move toward religious syncretism. An example is *The Aquarian Gospel of Jesus the Christ* by Levi. In his chapter on ten key doctrines of the New Age, Walter Martin includes several quotations from this book.

> As a child Jesus differed but little from other children only that in *past lives* he had overcome carnal propensities to such an extent that he could be tempted like others and not yield. . . .
>
> In many respects Jesus was a remarkable child, for *by ages of strenuous preparation* he was qualified to be an avatar, a saviour of the world, and from childhood he was endowed with superior wisdom and was conscious of the fact that he was competent to lead the race into the higher ways of spiritual living. . . .
>
> Jesus: "Then hear, you men of Israel, hear! Look not upon the flesh (i.e., the person of Jesus); it is not king. Look to *the Christ*

*within who shall be formed in every one of you, as he is formed in me"*(emphasis added).[35]

Among that which makes up what Marilyn Ferguson identified as the "old as a partial truth" is the historic Christian faith. Its traditional knowledge must be reconciled with the new observations. However, Christianity lays exclusive claim to the path to spiritual enlightenment, truth, and life, for it confesses the One who said, "I am the way and the truth and the life" (John 14:6) and "I am the light of the world" (John 8:12). The exclusive claims of Jesus the Christ, apart from the distorted pictures of him painted by those in the NAM, cannot be denied by those who would be his disciples. Therefore Christians will be excluded from the new world order; for the old, never-changing truth they confess cannot be reconciled with the new, ever-changing observations of the New Age. Christianity cannot be blended into a one world religion and remain Christianity (see the biblical worldview, chapter 12).

2

# A Historical Review

**Item:** "So here we are in the New Age, a combination of spirituality and superstition, fad and farce, about which the only thing certain is that it is not new. Nobody seems to know exactly where the term came from, but it has been around for several decades or more, and many elements of the New Age, like faith healing, fortune-telling and transmigration of souls, go back for centuries."[1]

**Item:** "When you enter the land the Lord your God is giving you, do not learn to imitate the detestable ways of the nations there. Let no one be found among you who sacrifices his son or daughter in the fire, who practices divination or sorcery, interprets omens, engages in witchcraft, or casts spells, or who is a medium or a spiritist or who consults the dead. Anyone who does these things is detestable to the Lord." (Deut. 18:9–12a)

**Item:** "Buddhism, like other major world religions, is not one monolithic system of belief and practice; neither, of course, is the New Age philosophy. But Buddhism's influence on New Age thinking is indisputable. So is that of Buddhism's parent religion, Hinduism, which predates Buddhism by at least a thousand years. Both traditions stress reincarnation and *karma*."[2]

When did the "New Age" begin? The answer is almost as varied as the eclectic philosophy of the NAM. To answer we must first ask other questions. Do you mean the modern spiritual movement called the New Age? Do you mean the relatively recent (in terms of human history) development of the spiritual, theological, and philosophical foundation of what has become identified as the New Age religion? Do you mean the very foundational roots of the subtle, deceptive, occult-based, man-centered, self-deifying New Age philosophy?

Some would answer in terms of the modern development of the Age of Aquarius. "The New Age Movement can best be dated from circa 1971. By that year, Eastern religion and transpersonal psychology (the key new elements needed to create the distinctive New Age synthesis) had achieved a level of popularity, and metaphysical leaders could begin to articulate the New Age vision."[3]

Some would move contemporary New Age beginnings back another decade. "The turbulent sixties provided the perfect atmosphere for what we now recognize as the New Age movement or the New Age Cult. The neoorthodox theologian Nels Ferre correctly predicted the influx of Eastern and Indian philosophy and theology that characterized that decade, and concluded that the imported ideas would be a major challenge to historic Christianity."[4]

From yet another perspective the beginning of the New Age could be associated with the mid-1980s, the time when the influence of the NAM began to spread widely and rapidly as a result of a sudden and voluminous media interest.

> Credit for this goes to actress Shirley MacLaine's bold use of the media for New Age proselytization; to the "Harmonic Convergence," a supposed "cosmic event" which in August 1987 brought roughly twenty thousand New Agers to "sacred sites" all over the globe; and to the massive popular interest in such New Age fads as "channeling" and the occult use of crystal. Such a large and varied assortment of "true believers" in the psychic and the occult provides just the kind of journalistic color the national media is always looking for. And so, one article or program on the movement after another began to appear, including a cover story in *Time* magazine (Dec. 7, 1987). Suddenly, the general public was well acquainted with the label "New Age."[5]

Others would trace the origins of the New Age to its historical, theological, and philosophical roots in the 19th century. Tal Brooke points to a key event in Chicago in 1893, the World Parliament of Religions. Speakers there included Buddhist monks, theosophists, Shintoists, and "persuasive mystics." One was Swami Vivekananda, a leading disciple of Ramakrishna Paramahansa, who had died in 1887. Ramakrishna is considered still today one of India's most enlightened godmen. Through Vivekananda, Ramakrishna's revival of Indian mysticism came to the West. Brooke points out that Vivekananda's inspired oratory and pleas for world unity proved irresistible to those attending the World Parliament of Religions. He brought to the Western world the religious syncretism of his guru, Ramakrishna, and Westerners fell for the romantic imagery of God as an ocean of being and infinite bliss. Brooke also writes,

> The cardinal Vedantic truths are that the soul is eternal and divine and part of the godhead. It keeps evolving through reincarnation after reincarnation until it rejoins the impersonal godhead. Life is merely an illusion, sucking us all in with its sensualist pleasures and pains that deny the underlying unity of all existence. The dualisms of sweet and sour, light and dark, and good and evil, are two sides of ultimate unitive reality, like light coming out of a prism and breaking into colors. All reality is composed of consciousness. . . .[6]

This quotation makes clear that the New Age certainly is anything but new. Its pantheistic view of God, its theme that reality is what one creates in one's mind and all else is illusion, its teachings of reincarnation and karma—all can be traced to the ancient Eastern religions whose influence began to be strongly felt in the West in the 19th century. Indeed, as was demonstrated in chapter 1, the old lies of the New Age can ultimately be traced to the Garden of Eden.

## Old Lies in the Past— The Old Testament Scriptures

The false promises ("you will be like God"), the half-truths ("your eyes will be opened. . . . [you will know] good and evil"), the lies ("you will not surely die") that Satan used with Eve are at the heart of the New Age philosophy as demonstrated in chapter 1. The Bible clearly indicates that these core New Age teachings have been deceiving mankind ever since. When it comes to the spiritual folly of the human race, truly "there is nothing new under the sun" (Eccl. 1:9).

However, unlike the fool who says in his heart that there is no God (Ps. 14:1—and there are many such fools around), the New Ager says, "I am God." But that is nothing new! Early in human history egotistical men undertook the building of a tower in order to make a name for themselves. Not content with the limitations the Creator had placed upon his creatures, the crown of God's creation attempted to assert its independence of God. These ancient temple ziggurats were intended to be staircases to heaven, steps by which rebellious men could elevate themselves to positions of supreme power and authority. It was a blatant, man-centered, self-deifying effort to replace the rule of God with the rule of man (Gen. 11:1–9).

The Bible records other efforts at self-deification on the part of sinful men. Some 700 years before the birth of Christ, the prophet Isaiah was given by God the vision to see a human king (Is. 14:4) who would say in his heart, "I will ascend to heaven; I will raise my throne above the stars of God. . . . I will make myself like the Most High." Yet this king would find himself "brought down to the grave, to the depths of the pit" (Is. 14:12–15).

The same prophet addressed a portion of his God-breathed message to the Virgin Daughter of Babylon, a personification of Babylon and its inhabitants. This "Virgin Daughter" is described as a "wanton creature" who made the same claim to godhood as do many New Agers today, "I am, and there is none besides me." Like New Age practitioners at the end of the 20th century after Christ, the Virgin Daughter of Babylon six centuries before Christ trusted in her own wisdom and knowledge. She looked to magic spells, sorceries, and "stargazers who make predictions month by month" to save her but to no avail. "[T]here is not one that can save you" (Isaiah 47).

## Old Lies in the Past—
## The New Testament Scriptures

As one reads the biblical accounts of such man-centered attempts at self-deification, it is not surprising, then, to find St. Paul describing the ultimate sin of man as being that of worshiping the creature rather than the Creator. At the pinnacle of that worship is the indulgent serving of self. Again we hear echoes of Eden and see a prologue of the New Age. "They exchanged the truth of God for a lie, and worshiped and served created things rather than the Creator. . . . [S]ince they did not think it worthwhile to retain the knowledge of God, he gave them over to a depraved mind, to do what ought not to be done" (Rom. 1:18–32). In his second letter to his co-worker Timothy, St. Paul describes New Agers then and now as "lovers of themselves ... having a form of godliness but denying its power" (2 Tim. 3:2, 5).

# Gnosticism vs. Neo-Gnosticism

We find further allusion to New Age teaching in the Scriptures when we compare the Gnosticism of the New Testament period, to which St. John and St. Paul provide veiled reference in their writings, with the Neo-Gnostic representation of Jesus espoused by those involved in the modern New Age. "The New Age [Neo-Gnostic] view of Jesus Christ involves a separation of the human Jesus from the divine Christ spirit (or office), which New Agers believe dwelt in Him and other great religious teachers."[7]

In one of his latest books on the New Age, Douglas Groothuis writes that Jesus Christ is viewed in many New Age circles as being one among several advanced human beings who realized and actualized the divinity within and so became trailblazers of the New Age message. Groothuis devotes a chapter to the connection between the New Age view of Jesus and Gnosticism. He writes,

> Many conceptions about Jesus, now current and credible in New Age circles, are rooted in a movement of spiritual protest. Until recently, the Gnostic movement was the concern only of the specialized scholar or the occultist. Yet Gnosticism provides much of the form and color for the New Age portrait of Jesus as an illumined Illuminator who serves as a cosmic catalyst for others' awakening.[8]

A more complete discussion of the New Age Jesus will be found in chapter 11 on the subject of New Age "Christianity." Here we want to compare briefly the Gnosticism to which Paul and John allude with the Neo-Gnosticism of the New Age.

"The Gnosticism addressed in the NT was an early form of the heresy, not the intricately developed system of the second and third centuries."[9] In his letter to the Colossians, St. Paul addresses several heresies or false teachings that apparently were circulating in the Colossian community and distorting the gospel of God's grace. Included in these heresies were (by inference from what St. Paul writes) a deprecation of the person of Jesus Christ, that he was not fully God (1:15–20; 2:2–3, 9); a special or secret knowledge along with the worship of angels or intermediary beings (2:18); and a reliance on human philosophy and wisdom (2:4, 8; see also 1 Cor. 1:18–25).

Both in his Gospel and in his letters St. John, writing later than

St. Paul, addresses a developing Gnosticism in the church. At the root of ancient Gnosticism was the concept of a duality of matter and spirit, with matter being evil and spirit being good. The goal of life was for the spirit to escape the evil, material body. This "salvation" was to be accomplished by acquiring special or secret knowledge (Greek, *gnosis*). Part of the Gnostic worldview was also that there was a single eternal principle or being (God) who was so transcendant that there could be no direct contact between God and finite creatures. Therefore, this God placed a series of emanations of the divine, intermediary beings, through which contact is made with the world of mankind. It is one of these intermediary beings, Yahweh, the God of the Old Testament, who created the world. The soul of man, caught up in the evil of a material world and a material body, must be delivered from such bondage. In *The Counterfeit Christ of the New Age Movement*, Ron Rhodes states that, according to ancient Gnosticism and New Age Gnosticism, this deliverance was provided by a special emissary sent from the kingdom of light. The emissary appeared either as a celestial being in a phantom body or as a higher spirit who temporarily entered the body of an earthly being. Rhodes writes,

> The Gnostic Christ allegedly came to earth to provide a Gnostic redemption for humanity. Ronald Nash tells us that, for the Gnostics, "Christ came into the world, not in order to suffer and die, but in order to release the divine spark of light imprisoned in matter. The Gnostic Jesus was not a savior; he was a revealer. He came for the express purpose of communicating his secret gnosis."[10] This gnosis (knowledge) encompassed an understanding of what we once were (divine) and what we will return to (divinity). Those who became enlightened by this gnosis were believed to escape from the prison of their bodies at death and eventually become reunited with the God from which they originally sprang.[11]

Rhodes describes the probability that Cerinthus was the first Gnostic of note who attempted to reinterpret Christianity through the worldview of Gnosticism. Cerinthus taught that at Jesus' baptism in the Jordan, or after, the Christ spirit descended upon Jesus. In other words Jesus became the Christ and was then endowed with supernatural wisdom and powers so that he could reveal to mankind the way back to God. It was against such heretical Gnosticism that

33

St. John wrote, "In the beginning was the Word. . . . The Word became flesh and made his dwelling among us" (John 1:1, 14); "This is how you can recognize the Spirit of God: Every spirit that acknowledges that Jesus Christ has come in the flesh is from God, but every spirit that does not acknowledge Jesus is not from God" (1 John 4:2–3); "Many deceivers, who do not acknowledge Jesus Christ as coming in the flesh, have gone out into the world. Any such person is the deceiver and the antichrist" (2 John 7).

This same Gnostic view of Jesus is found in the Neo-Gnosticism of the New Age.

> The Christology of Cerinthus is notably similar to that of Rudolf Steiner (who founded the Anthroposophical Society in 1912) and contemporary New Age writers such as David Spangler and George Trevelyan. These individuals all say the Christ descended on the human Jesus at his baptism. But they differ with Cerinthus in that they do not believe the Christ departed from Jesus prior to the crucfixion.[12]

Indeed, there is nothing new under the sun. The following is provided as but one example of the Gnosticism that is at the root of the New Age teaching about Jesus. The excerpt is taken from *New Teachings for an Awakening Humanity*. The author is simply identified as The Christ.

> In the historical epoch prior to my birth on the planet earth, the spiritual hierarchy and the Essene community of the Hebrew faith had already prepared the necessary channels for my birth as Jesus in the physical world. My parentage had been selected, my life blueprint was set in motion, and the events which later Christians would incorporate in their belief system began. . . .

> Yet, . . I beg you to understand that this was not an isolated event but rather one moment in the chronology of teachings brought to planet earth by many high or angelic teachers. . . . For later in this epoch ahead of us, called the Aquarian or Golden Age, the highest teachings will be brought forward even as I introduce the theme of it to you presently.[13]

## Old Lies in the Past—The 19th Century

We now make a leap of about 1700 years to the 19th century. Again we see the old lies of Satan very much present in popular thought. However, before we move fully into the 19th century, mention needs to be made of the contributions to mysticism and metaphysical thought by Emanuel Swedenborg and Franz Mesmer. Emanuel Swedenborg was born in 1688, the son of a Swedish Lutheran, who later became a bishop. Upon completing his higher education, Swedenborg took up a career in science in his native Sweden. By 1736, however, he began to take note of unusual dreams and bodily states that eventually became a major preoccupation for him. In 1747 he resigned his position with Sweden's Bureau of Mines and devoted the remainder of his life to exploring and developing his psychic contacts. "At this point, Swedenborg became what today would be called a medium, one who has contact with disincarnate spirit entities. He claimed that, in his vision, he traveled to spirit realms and from spirit entities gained revelatory knowledge of the nature of life, life after death, and God."[14]

Swedenborg believed that there were two realms of existence, the physical and the spiritual, with an exact correspondence between the two. As a psychic/medium, he claimed to be able to discern these correspondences. He especially focused on the nature of life after death, claiming to have gained knowledge about the subject from his numerous travels (astral or out-of-body travel) to the spirit world. He eventually taught the immortality of mankind while denying the resurrection of the body. Instead, depending on the age of the individual at the time of death, human souls continue either to progress or regress toward the point of the prime of adult life.[15]

It was not until after Swedenborg's death in 1772 that his writings and teachings began to be accepted and promoted largely through the efforts of a small group of men in England who formed the New Jerusalem Church in 1787. Their efforts helped establish Swedenborg's ideas and practices in an occult worldview.

> In the face of growing materialism, he championed the primacy of the spiritual, invisible world. He suggested that the world he explored in his dream-like states had greater metaphysical reality than the visible world more properly explored by science, which he considered an inferior, shadow-like realm. . . . This world was the product of divine influx, the ultimate origin of power and life.[16]

The next step in the development of what has become modern New Age ideas and practices can be traced to Franz Anton Mesmer, born in 1733 in Switzerland. There were others whose ideas also contributed to this development, but it was Mesmer who proposed the concept of a universal fluid (energy in the modern New Age philosophy) that he called animal magnetism. Mesmer (whose ideas gave us the term *mesmerism*) believed that the human body was a microcosm of the universe and that the universal magnetic fluid tied all things together. As a practicing physician, he supposedly achieved cures by passing magnets over the patient's body to manipulate the magnetic fluid. After a meeting with a Swabian priest, John Joseph Gassner, who drove out illness-causing evil spirits by passing his hands over the body, Mesmer began to believe that the power for healing resided in the human body itself rather than in instruments such as magnets.[17] "Mesmer's articulation of a scientific-like model in which to restate old claims about a magical power or a healing power or a sacred spiritual energy ... became known as animal magnetism, astral light, odic force, and psychic energy. Possessed states became mesmeric sleep and then hypnotism and the mediumistic trance."[18]

## Transcendentalism

Another part of the eclectic blend to which the NAM can trace its roots is *transcendentalism*. The leading lights of this movement in 19th century America were Ralph Waldo Emerson and Henry David Thoreau. Both were strongly influenced by the literature of Eastern mysticism, particularly the sacred writings associated with Hinduism. Emerson developed the concept of the "Over-Soul" as a mystic force in all nature including the human personality. Like the modern New Age, the transcendentalists were eclectic, blending ideas as diverse as Eastern mysticism and the Quaker concept of the Inner Light with the American emphasis on independence and individual autonomy. "In that important sense, they were the prototype of those who now form the New Age movement."[19]

The importance of the transcendentalists should not be underestimated in relation to the development of the NAM. In an essay prepared for the Wisconsin State Teachers convention of the Wisconsin Evangelical Lutheran Church at Milwaukee on October 25,

1991, Professor Marcus Manthey of the Michigan Lutheran Seminary at Saginaw wrote,

> It would be difficult to overestimate the importance of the transcendentalists in preparing America for the New Age ideas that are surfacing today. It was their thought, and even more the power of their art, that brought the first significant step in turning the average American's image of himself from a Christian to a mystic ideal.[20]

## Spiritualism

In the middle of the 19th century another trend began that essentially was a synthesis of the various strands of Swedenborgianism, mesmerism, and transcendentalism. "Spiritualism accepted the task of speaking in an acceptable scientific manner about cosmology and healing. But further, it proposed that, quite apart from traditional religious faith, Spiritualism could scientifically demonstrate the survival of individual humans after death."[21]

"Spiritualism is the Science, Philosophy and Religion of a continuous life, based upon the demonstrable fact of communication by means of mediumship, with those who live in the Spirit World."[22] Many people of historical fame became supporters of the claims of spiritualists. The list would include such notables as William Cullen Bryant, Sir Arthur Conan Doyle (creator of Sherlock Holmes), Mary Baker Eddy (Christian Science), Carl Jung, Abraham Lincoln, and Daniel Webster.

> To all of them, Spiritualism brought the message that "death" is only a transition to another level of spiritual growth and that the living can communicate with those who are no longer on the earth plane. Through the instrumentality of the medium in a church service or private circle, developed spirits are able to advise the living about personal problems and about how to live in harmony with divine and natural law.[23]

For orthodox Christianity Spiritualism posed a two-pronged threat. First of all, since Spiritualist theology claimed that all things operate in obedience to the laws of nature, it denied the possibility of miracles. It thereby denied some of the central teachings of the Christian faith—the virgin birth of Christ, his bodily resurrection, the miracles of Scripture that demonstrate that Jesus is who he claimed to be (John 10:37–38). Secondly, Spiritualist practice violated God's prohibition in Scripture (Lev. 20:27; Deut. 18:11) of trafficking with spirits.

That Spiritualism's emphasis on contact with spirits of the dead was a forerunner of the NAM can be seen in the NAM's emphasis on the channeling of spirit beings and the gaining of secret knowledge or wisdom from spirit entities that have evolved to higher planes of existence.

## Theosophy

Almost all who write on the subject of the New Age trace its most immediate roots to Theosophy, for which Spiritualism and Eastern mysticism provided the two-sided cradle. The *New Age Encyclopedia* begins its four-page chronology of the NAM with the year 1875 and the notation, "Theosophical Society is formed in New York City by Helena Petrovna Blavatsky, Henry Steel Olcott, and William Quan Judge."[24] Ron Rhodes writes, "[T]racing the historical development of the New Age view of Christ is a difficult task. For the sake of clarity, we will anchor on an important school of thought known as Theosophy."[25] Norman Geisler in his insightful article in *Bibliotheca Sacra* states, "The Russian mystic, occultist, and cofounder of theosophy Helena Petrova [sic] Blavatsky is the grandmother of the New Age movement."[26] Walter Martin writes, "For all practical purposes, the New Age Cult can be equated with the transplantation of Hindu philosophy through the Theosophical Society founded by Helena Blavatsky in the latter part of the nineteenth century in the United States."[27]

Blavatsky and Olcott traveled to India to sit at the feet of several gurus. When they returned in 1879, they incorporated their version of Hindu teachings into those of the Theosophical Society. As a result, through theosophical literature and centers, the religious ideas of both Buddhism and Hinduism began to make their way into Western thought and society.

Gnostic concepts also found their way into Theosophical Society teachings, particularly the idea that a series of emanations from God separate the Absolute from direct contact with the human race. Rather than the emanations of Gnosticism, theosophy posited the existence of seven planes through which the human soul evolves as it seeks to be reunited with God. Since evolving through seven planes would take a long time, the westernized version of the Hindu doctrine of reincarnation played an important role in the overall scheme of theosophical thought and has become a major doctrine of the NAM. That the New Age promotion of reincarnation through such celebrities as Jeanne Dixon and Shirley MacLaine has taken root in our society is demonstrated by recent polls and surveys that put acceptance of or belief in reincarnation at a level of "roughly one-fourth of all Americans."[28]

Along with the teachings of Eastern mysticism, the theosophists promoted the concept of Ascended Masters, "a group of formerly historical persons who have finished their earthly evolutions and, as they themselves are continuing to evolve toward the godhead, voluntarily help lesser-evolved human beings to reach their present level."[29] Tal Brooke contends that these turn-of-the-century fore-runners of the New Age got their ideas not only from Indian gurus but also through the "masters" by whom they channeled "higher" revelations.[30]

One of these higher revelations was received by Annie Besant, who took over the leadership of the Theosophical Society after Blavatsky's death in 1891. Together with C. W. Leadbeater, Besant formed the Order of the Star in 1911 to promote the idea that the "Lord Maitreya," the avatar or the savior for the dawning new era, was to possess the body of a young Indian, Jiddu Krishnamurti. "In 1929, however, Krishnamurti repudiated his messianic status and denounced the movement. The Order of the Star dissolved, and Annie Besant's Theosophical Society was never again the same."[31]

## Other Strands of the Old Lie

Under the leadership of Annie Besant, dissension broke out in the Theosophical Society. Three major offshoots developed. In 1912 Rudolph Steiner, the head of the German branch of the Theosophical Society, broke away to form the Anthroposophical Society. Steiner's distinction was his focus on what the Christ was able to accomplish through his incarnation in the human Jesus.

In 1923 Alice Bailey, supposedly the channel or medium of an Ascended Master known as The Tibetan, left the Theosophical Society to begin the Arcane school, "taking with her the Lucifer Publishing Company of the theosophists, which she renamed the Lucis Trust. The main remnant of her organization is now headquartered at United Nations Plaza."[32] However, she continued many of the same teachings of her former associates. One distinguishing feature of Bailey's teaching was

> ... that the second coming referred to the Christ coming in a single Avatar, not in all humanity. (An Avatar is one who descends into human form from above, never having gone through reincarnation. Such a one is considered a manifestation of divinity and seeks to reveal divine truths especially important to a particular age.) Bailey explained that "the advent of Christ, or His 'second coming,' is anxiously anticipated by many orthodox Christians.... Others, more orientally minded, await the appearance of an Avatar who will transmit from God the needed world message or new type of energy. Prophecy and astrology indicate a Coming One and their many differing opinions seem to converge on Him."[33]

Yet a third branch from the Theosophical Society was the "I AM" movement of the 1930's led by Guy and Edna Ballard. Guy Ballard claimed that an Ascended Master, Saint Germain, appeared to him and informed him that he, his wife, and their son were the only commissioned spokespersons for the Ascended Masters. Saint Germain also taught Guy about the "Great Creative Word" and that a person could attune to the I AM presence by chanting I AM decrees.[34] A modern descendant of the I AM movement is the Church Universal and Triumphant under the leadership of Mark and Elizabeth Clare Prophet. This group has created quite a stir in recent years because of their activities near the northern boundary of Yellowstone National Park. Shirley MacLaine's affirmations of "I am" are nothing new. This blasphemy of the name by which God revealed himself to Moses has been around for a long time.

Other strands of the multiple roots of the New Age can be found in the New Thought movement, the origins of which many would trace to the mental healing practice of Phineas Parkhurst Quimby in the mid-19th century. The developed theology of the New Thought movement "proclaimed that God was wholly good, evil was only error, ultimate reality was the mind, and one's life and one's world were predicated on one's thought."[35] Parallels to modern New Age philosophy are obvious. Some individuals and the organizations they founded that came out of the general New Thought movement are Mary Baker Eddy, Christian Science; Charles and Myrtle Fillmore, Unity School of Christianity; and Ernest Holmes, United Church of Religious Science. In the mid-1980s Terry Cole-Whittaker was a proponent of the Religious Science philosophy of Ernest Holmes. The parallels between New Thought and the New Age are perhaps best demonstrated in two quotes from Mary Baker Eddy's *Science and Health with Key to the Scriptures*:

> The divinity of Christ was made manifest in the humanity of Jesus.

> There is no life, truth, intelligence, nor substance in matter. All is infinite Mind and its infinite manifestation, for God is All-in-all. Spirit is immortal Truth; matter is mortal error. Spirit is the real and eternal; matter is unreal and temporal. Spirit is God, and man is His image and likeness. Therefore man is not material; he is spiritual.[36]

Before leaving the various strands of theology and philosophy that came out of the 19th century and contributed to the foundation of the NAM, it may be useful to summarize the diabolical nature of the source of this influence. On page 175 of *When the World Will Be as One,* Tal Brooke includes the following quotations from the writings of Helena Blavatsky that clearly indicate how forcefully the Great Deceiver is at work promoting his old lies in the New Age.

> The appellation Sa'tan, in Hebrew Satan, and Adversary . . . belongs by right to the first and cruelest "Adversary" of all other Gods— Jehovah; not to the serpent which spoke only words of sympathy and wisdom.[37]

> Once the key to Genesis is in our hands, the scientific and symbolical Kabbala unveils the secret. The Great Serpent of the Garden of Eden and the "Lord God" are identical.[38]

> Satan, the Serpent of Genesis is the real creator and benefactor, the Father of Spiritual mankind. For it is he . . . who opened the eyes of the automaton (Adam) created by Jehovah, as alleged. And he who was the first to whisper, "in the day ye eat thereof, ye shall be as Elohim, knowing good and evil," can only be regarded in the light of a savior. An adversary to Jehovah, . . he still remains in Esoteric Truth the ever loving messenger . . . who conferred on us spiritual instead of physical immortality.[39]

## Old Lies in Other Religions

The scope of this book does not permit a detailed presentation of the complex theology of the Eastern religions that have contributed so much to the New Age worldview. However, as one writer has put it, "Behind and underneath NAM are multi-roots: Hindu-Buddhistic pantheism and mysticism, Taoistic naturalism, Confucian humanism, and Shamanistic occultism. Without a grasp of these complicated phenomena, one can hardly comprehend NAM."[40] A brief review of some of the major tenets of several Eastern religions follows.

## Hinduism

Hinduism itself has no organized formal belief structure nor key doctrines summarized in creedal statements as is the case with Christianity. It has no single founder as do Buddhism, Islam, and Christianity. Generally it is a kind of "wisdom religion" that is very tolerant of a wide variety of religious beliefs as long as those beliefs are tolerant of it. While it has no single book as a source of doctrine, modern Hinduism has attached itself to the *Bhagavad-Gita* as its primary scripture. Hinduism is "a man-centered religion, a product of man's search to discover the reality and meaning of life and the universe."[41]

Dr. Philip Lochhaas in *How to Respond to the Eastern Religions* describes the fundamental teachings of Hinduism:

> Hinduism teaches that the universe exists from eternity, but has no material existence. It consists of pure energy. What appears to be material existence is merely an illusion, the *seeming* transformation of energy to form. God is the universe. As a dream exists for the sleeper, the universe exists for God. God is the one soul, the world-soul (*Mahatman*) and each "individual" soul (*Atman*) is but a reflection of the world-soul that pervades all.[42]

Karma, the law of cause and effect, is at the heart of Hinduism. Since evil originates in man, man is therefore responsible to suffer the consequences of the evil he produces. Karma's corresponding doctrine of reincarnation allows man to return to this world again and again to atone through his suffering for the evil of previous lifetimes. Salvation centers in enlightenment that can be achieved through the practice of the spiritual discipline of various kinds of Yoga. "For the Hindu, then, religion means 'faith in the divine in man,' and salvation consists of discovering 'the divine' through a self-imposed spiritual discipline."[43] Do you hear the message of the New Age coming through?

# Buddhism

Buddhism developed out of Hinduism. Its founder, Siddhartha Gautama, taught that all existence is suffering and that desire makes a person cling to existence and so experience suffering. Only by removing all desire from oneself can suffering be overcome. The *Eightfold Path* to removal of desire, and hence suffering, consists of right belief, right aspirations, right speech, right conduct, right livelihood, right effort, right memory, and right contemplation. "Everything in Buddhism, its rituals and techniques, its philosophy and art, has as its goal the destruction of the illusion that man exists."[44]

Buddhism brought with it from its parent religion, Hinduism, the concept of reincarnation. "Among the teachings of Buddhism, the doctrines of metempsychosis (reincarnation, transmigration) and nirvana play an important role. Breaking out of the constant cycle of birth-death-rebirth (transmigration)—the real cause of unhappiness, pain and suffering—is the only way to eliminate attachment to worldly cravings."[45] Two modern expressions of Buddhism in America are Zen Buddhism, with its discipline of meditation, and Nichiren Shoshu, with its teaching that chanting the formula *Nam Myoho Renge Kyo* will produce material as well as spiritual benefits.

# Taoism

While the religions of Hinduism and Buddhism are probably better known, Taoism as a philosophy has had just as much influence on the NAM. Originally Taoism was more a philosophy than a religion. It was a worldview, a way of life, to be lived. The *Tao* is *the Way* that is eternal and all-pervasive. "Taoism teaches that when events and things are allowed to exist in natural harmony with the macrocosmic forces, peace will result. The wise man is supposed to order his life according to the Tao, living passively in tune with the universe."[46]

The most important principle of Taoism in relation to the NAM is the dualism of *yin* and *yang*. These two opposite but complementary forces exist in all things. Yin is the positive force found in good, light, life, and masculinity. Yang is the negative force found in evil, darkness, death, and femininity. When the yin and yang of life are maintained in proper harmonious balance, life will flow smoothly and man will be able to pass through life peacefully.

The yin and yang principle of Taoism has taken a central place for many New Agers. "Books and university courses based on the 'Tao of physics' suggest that the principles of Taoism are scientifically verifiable."[47] A leading New Age thinker, Fritjof Capra, in *The Tao of Physics* suggests that in subatomic physics there is a duality that is a microcosm of the yin/yang principle that applies to all life.

Western materialism has called the human race to focus on greedy consumerism. In doing so, it has created a lifestyle full of stress and anxiety. The modern church with its drift toward liberal theology has questioned almost every aspect of the supernatural. Many churches have abandoned God's moral imperatives, turning the Ten Commandments into ten suggestions. Science and technology have not provided answers to the nagging problems of human existence. As a result many people are searching for answers to life's questions—who am I, why am I here, where is life going? The NAM is all too ready with the answers that can be traced through its multiple-root system to the Garden of Eden—you are god, you are here to become enlightened to your godhood through the secret knowledge of the ages, your life is moving toward a final and complete reunion with the Absolute. Follow the Tao, affirm your "I AM," practice your meditative discipline, listen to your spirit guides, use your mind power to visualize and create your own reality, and may the Force be with you.

The Christian faith has a different answer: You are the creation of a loving and personal God who is deeply concerned about your present and future life (Ps. 8:3–8; John 3:16). He has forgiven your past with its sin—which is not just ignorance or mental error (Ps. 103:12; 1 John 1:9). He did this by sending the Messiah (John 1:41) who is God from eternity (John 1:1, 14) and who was the Christ at birth (Luke 2:11). This Messiah, Jesus Christ, who will come again not to save but to usher his own into heaven and to judge the ungodly (Acts 1:11; 2 Cor. 5:10), has *already* reconciled you to God

(2 Cor. 5:18–19) by becoming the atoning sacrifice for the sin of the whole world (1 John 2:2). Your purpose in life is now to live for him who died for you (2 Cor. 5:15).

3

# New Age Occultism

**Item:** "The August 4 *Los Angeles Times* reports that Sedona, Arizona, has become very popular among New Agers because of the reputed 'vortex zones' in the area. (A vortex zone is allegedly a place in which the 'veil' between this world and the next [i.e., the spiritual world] is very thin.) According to the article, 'psychics say that Sedona rivals Stonehenge and the Bermuda Triangle as the world's top 'power' spot, radiating an unseen mystical energy reputed to enhance consciousness, make it easier to recall past lives, even communicate with space beings.' One Sedona resident calls the area a 'metaphysical Disneyland.' "[1]

**Item:** A catalog entitled "Pyramid Books and the New-Age Collection" provides these descriptions of items that can be purchased from the catalog: "Crystal-Clear Metaphysical Angel with gold-leaf wings, halo and ruffles around the hem of her gown. With hands folded in prayer, her ethereal angelic presence reminds you where you came from and who you truly are." "Chakra Wand Pendant is glowing in goldplate. Blown glass wand is encrusted with seven chakra stones and has a large amethyst gem at one end. The point is natural quartz crystal. Beautiful for wearing—promotes healing and balancing." "Healing Shaman Mask accompanies you on your travels! Feathered clay mask is an authentic miniature replica of ones used by Native Americans to embody and identify with the supernatural! Gorgeous, potent talisman to hang in your vehicle." "Singing Crystal Bowls. Thrilling new sounds in the tradition of Himalayan Bells. The singing of these crystal bowls vibrates the entire body, opening energy centers—shifting the brain/mind into altered states of consciousness."[2]

**Item:** "A New Age group wants to dig up a historic church graveyard in hopes of finding a vault it says contains writings that can save the world and prove that Sir Francis Bacon wrote the plays of Shakespeare. The Ministry for the Children, based in Santa Fe,

N.M., contends that if the writings thought to be buried at Bruton Parish Church aren't found by the year 2,000, world order will collapse. . . . The New Age group—*Christians* who espouse such things as clairvoyance and reincarnation—. . . says the writings outline Bacon's plan for a perfect society, a world united and at peace" (emphasis added).[3]

**Item:** At a meeting of the Society for the Scientific Study of Religion and the Religious Research Association, Michael Donahue of the Search Institute of Minneapolis released "results of a study showing that nearly one-third of some 20,000 members of denominations traditionally regarded as 'mainline' support 'humanistic' teachings." Respondents in the survey indicated their agreement with statements such as "Through meditation and self-discipline I come to know that all spiritual truth and wisdom is within me."[4]

**Item:** The Associated Press reported on a 1991 religious survey taken by the Barna Research Group. The survey found that "traditional Christian beliefs are eroding" while the idea of self-sufficiency is increasing. "82 percent of adults think that 'every person has the power to determine his or her own destiny in life.' This is 'one of the guiding principles of the New Age movement,' the report notes, adding that many Christians have 'unwittingly embraced' perspectives of popularized non-Christian religions."[5]

The above items demonstrate the two prongs of the fork with which the New Age is penetrating our society. There is the occult prong with its psychics, chakra points, quartz crystals for healing, energy balancing, and clairvoyance. There is also the humanistic prong with its emphasis on self-improvement and self-sufficiency, using mind-power to create one's own reality. Sometimes the occult or humanistic practices remain distinct. At other times the two prongs of the New Age fork are twisted into a confusing blend. Philip Lochhaas comments,

> The New Age Movement will appear to be a mass of confusing and contradictory beliefs and practices unless it is clearly understood that there are two distinct expressions of the movement, the occult and the humanistic. There is an *occult* expression— involved in reincarnation, crystal power, channeling, spirit guides, UFOs, extraterrestrials, and worship of self. And there is a *humanistic* expression—intent on developing unlimited human po-

tential and an ethical system centered in responsibility only to one's self.[6]

While the emphases in the occult and in the humanistic expressions of the New Age are obviously very distinct, one thing the two have in common is the "worship of self, . . . responsibility only to one's self." Two characteristics of the NAM mentioned in the definition in chapter 1 were *eclectic* and *man-centered*. Both are clearly demonstrated in the occult and humanistic expressions of the NAM.

Because of the eclectic nature of the New Age, one cannot always neatly categorize a New Age teaching or practice as being attached solely to the occult or humanistic prong. This chapter and the two that follow will focus primarily on the occult New Age. Chapters 6 through 10 will focus on the humanistic New Age. However, before examining the occult aspects, two other points need to be made.

## New Age Terminology

New Age terminology has moved into our general American vocabulary and is often used in various situations that have no connection with the NAM. One example may be sufficient to illustrate the point.

A common buzz word associated with the NAM is *networking*. Networking can be defined as linking together in web-like fashion people and organizations who have similar concerns and interests so that—through the sharing of information, skills, and abilities— they may work toward achieving common goals. Networking can be accomplished in various ways—through computer systems, telephone conferencing, workshops, or newsletters. Marilyn Ferguson describes the various networks within the NAM as crucial for bringing about global transformation. Such networking

> . . . has mushroomed among New Agers since the mid-1970s as a way to mobilize their numbers and pool their resources. Whether protecting baby seals on Canadian shores, installing "global education" programs in Colorado schools, or delaying construction of a nuclear power plant in California, networks can achieve social clout on a grass-roots level without reliance on party politics.[7]

However, the term and the practice of networking can also properly be used by people and organizations that have no association with the NAM whatsoever. For example, The Lutheran Church—Missouri Synod has adopted this term to describe efforts at linking together the various districts and congregations of the church body in a way that will help promote its ministry of the Gospel. It should be obvious that the mere use of a term or phrase by an individual or organization does not automatically classify such users as participants in the NAM. Constance Cumbey in *The Hidden Dangers of the Rainbow* (1983) suggested that part of the evidence that identified the New Age as a highly organized satanic conspiracy was the peculiar vocabulary that was used by people within the movement. However, simply because former president George Bush spoke about the need for a New World Order does not, by itself, identify him as a New Ager. Merely because a grade school teacher talks with her class about the "global village" in which we live does not, by itself, make her classroom a New Age learning lab. "Single buzzwords or phrases are inadequate for determining worldview orientation; a wider interpretive context is required," Burrows notes.[8] Discernment is needed along with knowledge of other teachings and practices before individuals or organizations can be categorized as active participants in the New Age.

Most of the terms used by and associated with the NAM would be recognized as part of the everyday American vocabulary. Such terms include *networking, holistic, transformation, personal growth, human potential, consciousness raising, ecological concern, biofeedback, paradigm shift, meditation, visualization, transpersonal psychology, Yoga, karate,* and *quantum leap.* Not included in this sampling are the occult terms associated with the New Age, many of which were part of our American vocabulary long before the NAM came to the attention of the general American population in the 1980's. The repeated use of New Age words and phrases in a person's speech or writing should cause us to listen more closely to what is being said and to read more carefully what has been written, while also paying close attention to basic themes and concepts that are being discussed.

## Not All New Age Emphases Are Bad

As indicated, many of the terms associated with the NAM are also used in non-New Age contexts. Moreover, some New Age emphases are not necessarily bad in themselves. As Robert Burrows points out, "Marx and Jesus were both concerned with the poor. That does not make Marx a Christian or Jesus a Communist."[9]

Caryl Matrisciana in *Gods of the New Age* describes a recipe for the New Age. She compares New Age beliefs to a large pie crust. The fillings placed in the pie crust may vary, but the pie crust remains the same. She states that the advocates of the New Age have created many alluring combinations of fillings rich in flavor and subtle seasonings that can so distract the average person with the aroma of what is about to be consumed that the person doesn't notice the ingredients of the pie crust. Matrisciana adds that, as with foods, so it is with various practices of the New Age. Some foods, such as salt or sugar, consumed in extreme amounts can be harmful. Yet in moderation they can be beneficial. Matrisciana comments,

> Similarly, many of the practices applied in New Age programs cannot be dismissed as "all bad" because in themselves they may be beneficial. For instance, keeping physically fit (an aggressively promoted New Age dictum) is commendable. Understanding and developing a healthy emotional and spiritual life is essentially good too, but too much emphasis on self can consume a person.[10]

As an example, Matrisciana notes that many New Agers emphasize the importance of a strict vegetarian diet. She recognizes that good nutrition can contribute to good health and a corresponding improvement of one's outlook on life. Good common sense advises that a proper, well-balanced diet is important regardless of a person's worldview. "But to promise that through vegetarianism one can grow more spiritual is a lie. To say that by eating certain 'wholesome' foods one's spirit is benefited is deceptive and dangerous."[11] Certainly the Bible doesn't indicate that any particular diet is of spiritual benefit. "One man's faith allows him to eat everything, but another man, whose faith is weak, eats only vegetables. The man who eats everything must not look down on him who does not, and the man who does not eat everything must not condemn the man who does, for God has accepted him" (Rom. 14:2–3).

Other writers point out that being involved in environmental issues, having concern about nuclear disarmament, and working for world peace—all primary New Age concerns—are commendable and should be of concern to all. To be active in such issues does not automatically classify such involvement as promotion of the New Age philosophy. However, these commendable pursuits become potentially dangerous when they are built on the spiritual philosophy that is at the root of the NAM—the six New Age principles described in chapter 1.

## The Occult Aspects of the New Age

The occult teachings and activities associated with the NAM are also often the attention-getting part of the New Age. The various occult aspects are popularized in movies and on TV, in much of what can be found in bookstores under the section of New Age books, in the writings and activities of Shirley MacLaine and others, and in the popular topics of conversation at parties and gatherings. In a book devoted to describing the broad impact of the old lies of Satan as packaged by the NAM, only brief descriptions can be given of the multitude of occult themes of the New Age. For more detailed study note the references to books and articles in the endnotes and bibliography.

## Reincarnation/Karma

Kevin Ryerson, one of Shirley MacLaine's spirit-guide channelers, casually says in his first session with her, ". . . the Bible says nothing about reincarnation either and it's quite well known that the Council of Nicea voted to strike the teaching of reincarnation from the Bible."[12] Ever since her New Age conversion, in her books, on TV talk shows, and in her five-hour television mini-series, MacLaine has been an avid promoter of the New Age version of reincarnation. She has also promoted the notion that, by New Age interpretation, the Bible still teaches reincarnation in spite of efforts by the early church fathers to remove any traces of this teaching from the Bible.

Of course, Shirley MacLaine is by no means the originator of the New Age version of reincarnation. Its modern Westernized version can be traced to the transcendentalists and the Theosophical School of the 19th century. Alice Bailey represents this teaching as she writes about the Law of Rebirth as universally taught by the Christ.

This doctrine will be one of the keynotes of the new world religion, as well as the clarifying agent for a better understanding
of world affairs. When Christ was here, in person, before . . . He
told them to "Be ye therefore perfect even as your Father which
is in Heaven is perfect" (Matt. 5:48).

This time, He will teach men the method whereby this possibility
can become accomplished fact—through the constant return of
the incarnating soul to the school of life on Earth, there to undergo
the perfection process of which He was the outstanding example.
That is the meaning and teaching of reincarnation.[13]

As Dr. F. LaGard Smith points out in the book he wrote as a
rebuttal to MacLaine's misuse of the Bible, Christ, and Christianity
to support her ideas, she is not alone in her beliefs:

Thousands of people are turning to belief in reincarnation. . . . For
centuries, while two-thirds of the world's population has believed
in some form of reincarnation, it has not really touched Western
civilization. . . . Now, dressed up in Judeo-Christian terminology
and accented with the current fascination surrounding paranormal
phenomena, reincarnation is sweeping through Western society.[14]

Smith refers to a 12-page color supplement that appeared in
*The Los Angeles Times* in which the Hare Krishna organization
claimed that one in four Americans "believes in past and future
lives" and also referenced a Gallup poll showing that "over 30% of
people under 30 accept reincarnation as an explanation of life after
death."[15] Others use numbers and statistics that may vary some from
those quoted by Smith, but the fact remains that "Reincarnation is
gathering believers by the hundreds, if not thousands, each day.
Stories about hypnotic 'regressions' and spontaneous 'recalls of
former lives' are almost regular features in newspapers and
magazines."[16]

Reincarnation and karma, two fundamental teachings of Eastern
religious philosophy, have been adapted by the eclectic New Age
in support of one of Satan's original lies, "You will not surely die."
Reincarnation is the belief that the immortal soul, the true inner
self that shares the divine essence, passes from one material body
to another over a series of incarnated existences. Between incar-
nations the soul continues to exist in the spirit realm. Ideas vary as
to the length of stay in the spirit realm. Some say that the soul

reincarnates within hours or days, or at most a few years. Others allow for thousands of years.

Reincarnation is required because of its corresponding doctrine—the law of karma, the Hindu law of cause and effect. According to karma, good will produce good, and evil will result in evil. Reincarnation and karma form the foundation of New Age "salvation," that a person, through a series of lifetimes and by his own effort, must balance the scales and pay off his karmic debt. "One's good karma from former lives can build up credits toward paying off the karmic debt, but few, if any, people so far have reached that level of karmic perfection."[17]

Mark Albrecht has a good analogy to illustrate these companion teachings.

> Perhaps the best way of picturing karma and its relationship to rebirth [reincarnation] is something like this: Each person is a sort of electronic sensor or microphone with a wire hooked up to a great computer in the heavens; the computer is "God." Each thought, motive and act, as well as all the things that happen *to* us, are relayed back to the computer and filed away. Upon death the data bank in the computer is activated, and the "readout" of our next life, based on how we have balanced our karma in the preceding lives, is cranked out and handed to us. If our negative karma (deeds, thoughts, motives, circumstances, and so on) outweigh our positive karmic pattern, we are assigned a more miserable existence in the next round, and vice versa. We have nothing to say about it. There is no mercy, forgiveness, or court of appeals.[18]

It may take thousands of lifetimes to work out one's karma. The person who has accumulated much evil in a given incarnation will have to work it off with much suffering in the next reincarnation. In Hinduism, the karma of a human being may be so bad as to require reincarnation as a lower form of animal life. However, the NAM has westernized the teaching of reincarnation so that its application is limited to the return of the soul to another human life.

Unfortunately, the teachings of reincarnation and karma result in human suffering and misery as demonstrated by the perseverance of the caste system in India, as well as the extreme poverty and horrible living conditions of the mass of Indian people. Caryl Matrisciana grew up in India as a child and teenager. She offers a graphic description of the horrible living conditions that reincarnation, karma, and the caste system have imposed upon the people. She tells of walking along a road with her mother, noticing a woman pulling two dead rats on a string, and asking her mother why the lady was doing that. The mother's answer was that perhaps the dead rats were some sort of good luck charm. Further along the road they discovered a temple where rats were worshiped as gods because, according to a Hindu sacred story, a god returned as a rat in one of his reincarnations. Now, fresh milk—too expensive for the peasants to purchase regularly for themselves—is fed daily to the thousands of rats that infest the temple. The rats spread disease and, ultimately, death.[19]

F. Lagard Smith recounts a similar experience of human misery and suffering while visiting in India. He contrasts the tremendous affluence of Western society with the extreme poverty of India and sees in this an explanation for Westerners being so accepting of the teachings of reincarnation and karma. For Westerners, who don't know real suffering, the karmic wheel of suffering is really a wheel of fortune. However, Smith points out, "The Hindu culture, based in large part on the teachings of karma and reincarnation, is not a culture to be envied or admired. Its religious teachings do not lead to the New Age of enlightenment; they lead to oppression, suffering, and spiritual as well as physical death."[20]

Did the Bible teach reincarnation before the early church fathers attempted to remove all evidence of such teaching? Does the Bible still teach reincarnation in spite of those efforts? Albrecht, Martin, and Gudel, Bowman, and Schlessinger provide helpful insights and references. Walter Martin has an especially helpful discussion that provides a biblical response to the misinterpretation of several Bible passages by New Agers. A brief quote will suffice for now: "Not only did none of the church fathers embrace reincarnation—not even Origen, who did hold to the preexistence of souls—but they explicitly rejected the notion as wholly contrary to the Christian faith."[21]

Obviously, reincarnation contradicts the Christian doctrine of the resurrection. Man is not born into many lifetimes by which he works off the debt of karma. Man is born once, and it is appointed unto man to die once (Heb. 9:27). Then comes the judgment, preceded by the resurrection of the just and the unjust. Furthermore, the New Age teaching of reincarnation ultimately removes any concern for social justice and for the physical well-being of others. "People are perceived as merely 'working out their karma,' and many reincarnationists feel it is unwise to disturb the process. As a result, people who are suffering are left to their fate until their karma is exhausted."[22] After all, who would want to disturb the cycle of karma in a person's particular incarnation by helping that person overcome suffering he/she is expected to experience? Reincarnation and karma have no room for feeding the hungry, clothing the naked, or bringing comfort to the sick and imprisoned.

# Channeling

Channeling, as much as any other New Age practice, demonstrates the occult nature of the NAM. It makes clear what many do not want to admit—that Satan and his demons are alive and well on planet earth and have in the NAM a prime vehicle for entering people's lives.

The reluctance to attribute to demonism such New Age practices as channeling can be traced to a general skepticism regarding the supernatural. Prior to the relatively recent renewal of interest in things spiritual as in the NAM, the general public was strongly influenced by the "God is dead" idea of liberal theologians and the denial of a need for God by atheistic secular humanists. Such denial of God led to a denial of the supernatural. Demons, devils, and evil spirits were considered the creation of overactive imaginations.

The Bible, however, clearly states that Satan is real, a spirit, a fallen angel (2 Pet. 2:4), the father of lies (John 8:44), who is quite capable of disguising himself as an angel of light (2 Cor. 11:14). He is truly what his Hebrew name describes, an adversary of God and man, who roams the earth (Job 1:7) seeking to devour mankind (1 Pet. 5:8). He is crafty and powerful (Eph. 6:11–12) in his opposition to God's will (1 Thess. 2:18). Although conquered by the triumphant death and resurrection of the Lord Jesus Christ (1 John 3:18; Heb. 2:14), he continues to use every means at his disposal (including New Age channeling) to practice his deceptive tactics that lead to spiritual destruction (2 Thess. 2:9–10).

Merrill Unger's *Demons in the World Today* (1971) was written just as the NAM was in the final stages of developing into what it has become today. He thoroughly depicts the influence of demonic power. He devotes a chapter to demons and the demonic influences of false Eastern religions that have contributed much to the New Age worldview. He describes the connection between the demonic and a variety of occult practices such as spiritism (channeling in the New Age), divination, dreams and visions (creative visualization with the aid of spirit guides?), and magic. He concludes, "People who dabble in the occult and in magical arts are recklessly flirting with demonism. Ancient pagan practices find their counterpart in today's spiritistic activities and psychical research."[23]

Kurt Koch echoes the off-quoted words of C. S. Lewis' *Screwtape Letters* about two extreme reactions to Satan: "It is imperative to seek a sound balance between these two extremes of on the one hand denying the very existence of the demonic and on the other hand of demonising everything."[24] Having said that, Koch then devotes over 300 pages to evidence of occult bondage and demonic oppression and possession based on his extensive personal counseling experience. Like Unger, he does not use the New Age term channeling, but much of his work is given to describing what he terms "mediumistic gifts." After studying what Koch and others have written, there can be no doubt that New Age channelers, like the mediums of old, are letting themselves become instruments of a massive deception by the Great Deceiver.

A channel is the New Age version of what used to be called a medium. The *New Age Encyclopedia* notes that *channeling* came out of the UFO contactee movement to replace *mediumship* "possibly because of the charges of fakery so widely publicized in connection with American spiritualists, and perhaps because the sources contemporary channels typically contact claim to be more evolved than recently deceased relatives."[25] "Channelers—often simply called a channel—go into a trance state to establish contact with a spirit, ascended master, off-planet being, higher consciousness, or even an evolved animal entity. The channel then receives and repeats the messages and impressions from the 'other side.' "[26] In other words, a major difference between a channel and the old-fashioned medium is that the spirit guides which speak through a channel are not thought to be the spirits of the recently deceased such as speak through a medium, but rather are considered to be living spirit entities who have ascended to a higher plane of existence.

When speaking as the spirit guide, the voice of the channeler often becomes much different than the normal speaking voice. Sometimes the channeler becomes the author of written material produced by the spirit guide. In his book on the New Age Elliot Miller identifies several different types of channeling, ranging from the channel that remains in complete control of both body and mind to a type of deep-trance channeling where the channel reports the human spirit leaving the body so that the higher spirit entity can take over. While some would say that such deep-trance channeling is just a theatrical creation of the human channeler, "from the Christian perspective, there is no reason to deny the *possibility* that it is rather an advanced form of possession, suited to an acceleration of satanic deception in our time."[27]

While channeling/mediumship has been practiced in various forms throughout history, channeling associated with the NAM can be traced to the entity identified as Seth, who channeled through Jane Roberts. The sessions began in the 1960s following Roberts' experimentation with the Ouija Board. The first book recording the teachings of Seth was published in 1970. This book and other Seth material became best sellers and popularized the current channeling movement.

Reference has already been made to the spirit guide, Ramtha, who uses J. Z. Knight as the channel to convey his spoken and written messages. Kevin Ryerson, who introduced Shirley MacLaine to the phenomena, channels entities named John; Tom McPherson, whose "favorite incarnation was that on an Irish pickpocket a few hundred years ago"; Dr. Shangru; and Obidaya, "a Jamaican who understands modern-day racial problems."[28] Other entities and their human channels who have gained much media attention include Lazaris/ Jack Pursel, credited by actress Sharon Gless for her success; Mafu/ Penny Torres-Rubin; and Bashar/Darryl Anka. Channeling has become a major product of the New Age at great profit to the channelers. Already in 1987 people were paying J. Z. Knight $400 for the privilege of hearing the wisdom of Ramtha channeled at one of her seminars. A recent estimate places the number of channelers in Los Angeles alone at over 1,000.

Richard Bach, author of *Jonathan Livingston Seagull*, has said that his work was the result of a spirit guide speaking through him. A New Age work that has become accepted even in some Christian churches is *A Course in Miracles* channeled through Helen Schucman in the 1970s. In introductory material Schucman describes her personal experience in writing this three-volume work:

> That was my introduction to the Voice. It made no sound, but seemed to be giving me a kind of rapid, inner dictation which I took down in a shorthand notebook. The writing was never automatic. It could be interrupted at any time and later picked up again. It made me feel very uncomfortable, but it never seriously occurred to me to stop.[29]

A more critical evaluation of *A Course in Miracles* will be made in chapter 11.

Is channeling to be taken seriously? Those in the New Age think so.

> Spiritual channeling is the process of leaving ordinary, waking consciousness and becoming a conduit for a source of energy not normally in your awareness.... The Master Teachers who are willing to work with you have a single purpose: to teach you to see yourself as they see you—a being of love, light, and creative potential who is one with God.[30]

What is the teaching of the various spirit entities? It follows a remarkably similar pattern, all of it a contradiction of Christian teaching—mankind is divine, death is not real but is a creation of humanity, we create our own reality, we are our own saviors, improved self-love will result in improved unconditional love toward others.

> "Lazaris's" themes should be now seem quite familiar to us, since they closely echo what we have already found in "Seth," *Course in Miracles*, "Ramtha," and Ryerson material. It is basically a spiritual, united universe, "Lazaris" says, and we are essentially evolving, spiritual, immortal beings within and at one with it. Self-empowerment includes the causal, creative, intuitive ability to access what we need from our higher selves and from the universe as "God/Goddess/All That Is."[31]

Are the spirit entities real, disembodied beings? Brooks Alexander of the Spiritual Counterfeits Project addresses this question in an article for *Christianity Today*. "There seem to be four basic options: (1) the entities are real and are telling us the truth about themselves; (2) the entities are real and are lying to us; (3) the entities are a 'dissociative reaction,' a mental dysfunction unrec-

ognized as such; (4) the entities are a conscious fraud for the purpose of gain."

Because the message of the entities contradicts the truth of Scripture, option number one can be eliminated. "Thus the full answer
to our question could involve options (2), (3), and (4) at various
times and in various combinations. After all, deception and der-
angement are basically variations on the demonic theme. We should
not be surprised to see them turn up as items on the demonic
agenda."[32]

We have devoted considerable space to reincarnation, a fundamental doctrine of the occult New Age, and to channeling, a prime
attention-getting, money-making practice of the occult New Age. In
the remaining pages of this chapter, *brief* attention will be given to
other occult aspects of the New Age.

## Crystals

The use of quartz crystals is one of the better known occult
activities of the NAM. Crystals are odd-shaped rocks used by New
Agers for meditation and as a source of healing energy. Of course,
not all in the New Age appreciate the spiritual and physical benefits
that some attribute to crystals. David Spangler, a leading New Age
thinker, "feels these interests [channeling, crystals, etc.] tend to di-
vert people from the more central concerns of leading a creative,
empowering, and compassionate life."[33] However, while admittedly
just a fad for some, others in the New Age take crystal use seriously.

Frank Alper, a channeler who founded the Arizona Metaphysical
Center in 1976, was a major force in launching the focus on crystals
that has become a trademark of the NAM. Alper traces the power
and use of crystals back to the lost continent of Atlantis. J. Gordon
Melton in the *New Age Encyclopedia* writes,

> According to Alper, crystals actually absorb and store energy which
> may be used at a later time. They may be used to store electrical
> energy or, more importantly, universal energy, which is referred
> to by Alper as "our Father's light." It is this latter energy that is
> most at issue in the New Age use of crystals. Alper also makes the
> point that, while all crystals have their special uses, essentially the
> healing of particular diseased conditions, clear pure quartz crystals
> are the most efficient energy retainers.[34]

The basic use of crystals in the NAM is to transmit the spiritual energy flowing through the universe to individuals for their growth and healing. Given the New Age doctrine that All is One and God is All, it is understandable that many New Agers believe that the same energy force that flows through the universe and through the human body is also radiated by a hard, inanimate object such as a quartz crystal. Add to this that clear quartz crystal is the most abundant mineral on earth and New Agers have a seemingly unlimited supply of what some have called "rocks of ages" that can help a person "improve your love life, excel in your career, make more money, lose weight, and cure whatever ails you by simply holding a beautiful stone in the palm of your hand. . . ."[35]

A 1987 article in *Time* reported on the growing number of Americans who were jumping on the crystal bandwagon and subscribing to the "pseudoscientific belief that such natural gemstones as quartz crystal, citrine, tourmaline and amethyst have paranormal healing and restorative powers." Brett Bravo, who conducts weekly seminars on the programming of crystals, explains, "The way the stones heal is by man's electrical field combining with the crystal's electromagnetic field. This affects the cells of the body."[36]

The capacity of quartz crystals to transmit electrical energy is a fact of physics. Crystals have been used in radios, and the silicone chip is used to store and transmit electrical energy. However, there is no scientific evidence that crystals have the capacity to transmit spiritual energy or healing power. Why then do some make such claims? Bob Larson writes,

> Validation for such assertions rests solely on the questionable proof of personal testimony. It must be assumed, therefore, that the power of crystals is in the mind of the beholder. Anticipatory autosuggestion has a way of fulfilling self-made prophecies. If a person thinks a crystal will do a certain thing, in all likelihood such expectations will be satisfied, even if it means altering circumstances to produce "proof."[37]

## Creative Visualization

An occult New Age technique that is finding its way into the mainstream of American life is creative visualization. Shakti Gawain describes her experience at a Silva Mind Control workshop: "The most important technique I learned in that course was the basic technique of creative visualization—relaxing deeply and then picturing a desired goal in your mind exactly the way you want it to be. I . . . was powerfully affected by the idea that we all create our own reality."[38]

As with most New Age techniques, creative visualization is nothing new. Man's attempt to manipulate his thoughts and to use his mind to control his existence is of longstanding, particularly in the healing of diseases. For example, creative visualization parallels the teaching of the Mind Science religions, such as Christian Science, that disease is basically a product of the mind and that healing will take place when the body is visualized as being whole. According to the NAM, all material reality is merely an illusion, *maya*, that a person can learn to control and manipulate by the power of visualization that resides in the mind.

Creative visualization is also identified as "guided imagery" and "positive imaging." Some may question whether there is any difference between such a practice and positive thinking. Certainly a positive attitude toward a life situation, or the imaging by an athlete of the physical steps for accomplishing a particular athletic endeavor, or the visualization of a project by an architect before anything is committed to paper are all proper uses of the mind that contribute to a successful completion of one's goals. However, occult-oriented New Agers "see visualization as a powerful metaphysical force."[39] Bob Larson states that New Age visualization "is more than mind over matter. Visualization claims to produce an entirely new reality." He describes it thus:

> Creative visualization involves a mind-body synthesis, beginning with relaxation techniques, followed by breathing exercises. Self-hypnosis procedures may also be employed. First, the desired image is centered in the mind and enforced with repeated affirmation. Contradictory thoughts must be allowed to float only fleetingly through the mind. At this point, any doubts about the visualized goal must be suspended. No outside authority is allowed to intervene, not even a transcendent God. At this moment, the one visualizing is thought to be in touch with his Higher Self, a projection of God, and therefore no harmful or selfish visualization is possible.[40]

In the NAM, creative visualization continues to find new applications in American society, especially in education, business, and, as one might imagine, the holistic health movement. An example is identified by David Hunt and T. A. McMahon in *The Seduction of Christianity*, where a leading distributor of home-care products, Bunny Marks, explains the power of visualization on a motivational tape. She says,

> So the first thing we must do if we wish to achieve and live the life of success, the life of plenty and happiness, is first of all to visualize it. We actually create reality by what we visualize. . . . The picture you hold in your mind will develop the same way a film develops. . . . If you start visualizing what you desire, you shall have it![41]

The mind is God's creation, his gift to humans created in his image. To use the powers of the mind in creative ways to enrich the living of life in a God-pleasing manner is certainly proper. To use the mind in occult efforts to manipulate reality to serve selfish interests contradicts God's will that "whatever is true, whatever is noble, whatever is right, whatever is pure, whatever is lovely, whatever is admirable—if anything is excellent or praiseworthy—*think* about such things." (Phil. 4:8)

# Divination

"In every age man has sought to peer into the future with crystal balls, the throw of dice, oracles speaking through sacred smoke; and our so-called materialistic, mechanistic era is no exception."[42] As with other New Age practices, various divination tools and practices have been around for ages. Many in the NAM have simply adopted and adapted them as additional means of tuning one's psychic awareness and heightening one's cosmic consciousness. Some in the New Age have also adopted and adapted divination tools and practices because they have proven to turn a healthy profit for them.

Evidence for the ancient practices of divination as well as God's word about them are found in Deut. 18:9–13:

> When you enter the land the Lord your God is giving you, do not learn to imitate the detestable ways of the nations there. Let no

one be found among you who sacrifices his son or daughter in the fire, who practices divination or sorcery, interprets omens, engages in witchcraft, or casts spells, or who is a medium or spiritist or who consults the dead. Anyone who does these things is detestable to the Lord, and because of these detestable practices the Lord your God will drive out those nations before you. You must be blameless before the Lord your God.

However, for many people, God's word in the Bible doesn't count for much. Like the people of St. Paul's day, "they not only continue to do these very things but also approve of those who practice them" (Rom. 1:32). Such divination practices ultimately have the same demonic source. David Hoover, in his book on the occult, identifies four possible sources of supernatural phenomena—God, the demonic, psychological, artificial. Hoover then says,

> Fortune-telling, since it is forbidden many places in the Scriptures, is not divine. Rather, fortune-telling, or divination, is the offspring of idolatry. And since some people have the genuine ability to foretell the future (a supernatural ability), the power to do such phenomena is one of the last three possibilities of source. Our attention will be focused on the demonic; that is, that the supernatural ability to foretell the future is the power of the demonic bestowed upon a person with the aim that the person and others will eventually transfer their faith from the Creator to the created.[43]

Once again the old lies of Satan seek to lead the human race down the primrose path of secret wisdom to its own spiritual death.

Psychic practitioners continue to be popular and are increasingly accepted in society. "900" numbers are now available to call and receive psychic counseling for one's love-life, business ventures, or life in general. The numbers are advertised on late night TV programs, in popular magazines, and in many newspapers. Psychic fairs draw thousands, many of whom take the opportunity to have their fortune told, their tea leaves read, or their own psychic abilities tested. To be sure, many who claim to have psychic powers are frauds and charlatans, out to make a quick buck. However, Christians believe that Satan and his demons are real and operative and can certainly work through people whose psychic powers deceive and lead people away from a spiritually rewarding relationship with God.

# Astrology

Another ancient divination practice associated with the occult aspect of the NAM that continues to be popular today is astrology. "According to the Gallup polls, 50 million Americans believe their destinies are determined by the movements of celestial bodies."[44] A 1991 survey by the Princeton Religion Research Center produced the alarming statistic that "Six in 10 teenagers (59%) believe in astrology, more than twice the proportion found for adults (25%)." [45]

Astrology divines the future based on the placement of fixed stars as well as sun, moon, and planets. Astrology comes from two Greek words *astro* (star) and *logos* (word), meaning "words from the stars." Astrology has been practiced almost since the dawn of creation as man in his fallen state looked to a "word" from creation rather than *the Word* from the Creator for guidance and direction. It is a type of fortune telling trivialized by abundant use of horoscopes in newspapers (1,800 in the United States and Canada in 1985).[46] However, many New Agers as well as non-New Agers place great confidence in astrology. The arrangement of the planets at the time of one's birth are seen as conferring various strengths and weaknesses that will influence the outcome of that person's life. Most popular psychics, Jeanne Dixon for example, use astrology and the signs of the zodiac to make their prognostications.

The origins of astrology are difficult to trace. China, ancient Babylon, and Egypt are all given credit. It is certain that ancient astrology was based on the knowledge of only five planets observable by the naked eye. Furthermore, a slight shift of the earth's axis "has resulted in the shift of an entire astrological house. Modern astrologers have never updated their blueprint of the heavens to include this alteration."[47] Nor have they changed their charts to take in the discovery of Copernicus that the earth is not the center of the universe around which the sun, moon, planets, and stars revolve. All of which is to say that the wisdom and advice which astrologers claim to provide has no basis in physical science. Some astrologers are willing to admit this. Alan Oken, former Director of the Aquarian Association of Astrologers, in *As Above, So Below: A Primary Guide to Astrological Awareness* writes (p. 27), "Astrology is a metaphysical science, an occult science, not a natural or physical one."[48]

Certainly those engaged in traditional scientific methodology have no use for either the faddish or serious pursuit of the signs of the zodiac. Nathaniel Lande reports on a statement issued by scientists upset with the practice of astrology.

> In the fall of 1975, 186 prominent scientists, including 18 Nobel Prize winners, issued a statement challenging the "pretentious claims of astrological charlatans." Stating flatly that there is no scientific basis for astrology, they regret that "acceptance of astrology pervades modern society." The statement continues: "We are especially disturbed by the continued uncritical dissemination of astrological charts, forecasts and horoscopes by the media and by otherwise reputable newspapers, magazines and book publishers. This can only contribute to the growth of irrationalism and obscurantism."[49]

The connection between astrology and the New (Aquarian) Age can be seen in the theme song from the 1970s stage musical *Hair*, which speaks of the peace that will lead into the Age of Aquarius when the planets are properly aligned. On the other hand, astrology may not seem to relate directly to the NAM with its principles that all is one, all is God, and therefore humanity is God. Nevertheless, it is an expression of mankind's desire to determine the future, believing that there is a oneness to the entire universe that finds expression in astrological signs and charts. Astrology becomes a technique for getting a grasp on the future and for being transformed as a person moves in the direction of that oneness projected by the stars.

To be sure, God created the stars and the constellations into which they have been placed (Ps. 147:4; Job 9:9). The stars do declare God's glory (Ps. 19:1). Some may wish to find a symbolical Christian message in the ancient names for the stars and constellations.[50] However, efforts to find guidance in the stars for future actions or decisions ultimately are bound to fail. "Let your astrologers come forward, those stargazers who make predictions month by month, let them save you from what is coming upon you. Surely they are like stubble; the fire will burn them up. . . . Each of them goes on in his error; there is not one that can save you" (Is. 47:14–15).

## UFOs and Extraterrestrials

"Extraterrestrials and UFOs also play an important role in occult New Age thinking."[51] "Messages from outer space also seem to fall into a recognizable pattern. . . . Cosmic intelligences have come via UFOs to guide us into the New Age, teaching us to rise to higher levels of consciousness."[52]

> [Whitely] Strieber [who has written two books about his alleged abduction by aliens] was one of the leading drawing cards at the Whole Life Expo in New York City, October 6–8, 1989—the largest New Age festival ever held on the East Coast. But he was not the only workshop leader who spoke about space beings. A number of people representing UFO sects were manning their booths—spreading their messages of benevolent space brothers and furnishing instructions from outer space on how mere humans could usher in a new Golden Age.[53]

These quotations should indicate that yet another focus of the occult New Age is on Unidentified Flying Objects (UFOs) and Extraterrestrial Intelligence (ETIs). These interests are not peculiar to the New Age. Some in the scientific community seriously study the UFO phenomena. However, the eclectic New Age has seen in UFOs and ETIs support for the belief that there are beings of much higher intelligence than humans who are seeking to impart to us their great wisdom so that the human race may accomplish the worldwide transformation necessary for ushering in the New Age.

A major question arises about all of the personal testimonies that have been noted about "Close Encounters" of the first through sixth kind.[54] Are the "beings" that have been in touch with apparently thousands of human contactees interplanetary or interdimensional? The reported conduct of the aliens and the "wisdom" of their message is consistently in opposition to the Christian faith. This has led many in the Christian community to conclude that "space creatures" are another manifestation of the demonic.

The modern interest in UFOs can be traced to 1947. Kenneth Arnold, an Idaho businessman, was piloting his private plane near Mount Ranier in Washington when he observed what he described as silver disks moving at incredible speed, considering the technology known to humans at that time. He said they moved like "saucers skipping across water." Hence, the term "flying saucers." In the 45 years since then numerous sightings of mysterious, unidentified flying objects have been reported from all parts of the globe. Yet "there is little agreement among UFOlogists over almost anything. They have no idea of the UFOs' point of origin, their purpose, or the technology that empowers them into impossible (by earthly standards) maneuvers that sometimes include changing shape and vanishing like Cheshire cats."[55]

Various explanations have been given for UFOs and ETIs. Already in the late 1950s psychoanalyst Carl Jung published *Flying Saucers: A Modern Myth of Things Seen in the Skies*. It was Jung's view, built on an occult foundation, that UFOs were not spaceships of a material nature but rather "beliefs" of a psychic and metaphysical nature created by the mind. Brad Steiger, New Age/UFO author of over 100 books on psychic phenomena, is of the opinion that with UFOs we are dealing with an interdimensional paraphysical phenomenon that has the goal of guiding mankind to unification, peace, and harmony. Zecharia Sitchin has promoted the theory (in books of a scholarly nature that draw on archaeological "evidence") that the modern appearance of UFOs is testimony to the continuing presence of the super race that originally populated planet Earth. He equates this super race with the Nephilim of Gen. 6:1–4.[56]

Whitely Strieber has done as much as anyone to popularize UFOs. In his books *Communion* and *Transformation* Strieber recounts an abduction by space creatures in which he was subjected to horrifying experiences, some of a sexual nature. In the introduction to his first book, he writes,

> People who face the visitors report fierce little figures with eyes that seem to stare into the deepest core of being. And those eyes are asking for something, perhaps even demanding it.
>
> Whatever it is, it is more than simple information. The goal does not seem to be the sort of clear and open exchange that we might expect. Whatever may be surfacing, it wants far more than that. It seems to me that it seeks the very depth of the soul; it seeks communion.[57]

As careful studies are done in comparing the many encounters with UFOs and ETIs, what is becoming increasingly evident is both the demonic and anti-Christian character of these encounters. A typical UFO/ETI experience includes confrontation with a superior intelligence that has no physical mass. While it often has a bright and shining appearance, it can appear and disappear and even change shape. This higher intelligence is both secretive and deceptive as it attempts to change a person's worldview and promote global unification.[58]

William Alnor has reported on the antichristian messages of many UFO/ETI contacts. One in particular is the case of Eduard "Billy" Meier, who supposedly has been repeatedly visited by aliens from the Pleiades constellation. Part of the message Meier has been given by the aliens to convey to the human race is that Jesus was never called Jesus Christ, he never died on a cross, the virgin birth never occurred, and Jesus was not the Creator or the Son of God.[59]

Not all UFO encounters contain a message. C. S. Lewis was convinced that UFO phenomena could well be legitimate, nonthreatening, and consistent with the Christian faith. But one can be certain that UFOs combined with ETIs do not intend to honor the Creator of the universe and the Redeemer of all mankind. Rather, their message reinforces the old lies of Satan as it echoes the man-centered, evolutionary message of the New Age philosophy.

## Martial Arts

While it may seem strange to include something as ancient as the martial arts in a discussion of the NAM, the connection becomes more obvious when one realizes that the Eastern religious philosophies of Buddhism and Taoism strongly influence the conduct of the martial arts. While in Western schools of most martial arts the spiritual disciplines have been all but eliminated in exchange for an almost exclusive focus on physical exercise and training, Christians should be knowledgeable and discerning with regard to the spiritual philosophy that undergirds the various martial art disciplines. Perhaps quotes from three different non-Christian descriptions of the martial arts will underscore the spiritual connection.

The *New Age Encyclopedia* states that there is no necessary connection between the martial arts and a form of spirituality. However, it also points out that the Buddhist monks in China who developed the early forms of martial arts discovered that "the discipline of regular practice could assist them in developing the kind of one-pointedness of mind that is necessary for effective *meditation*. This discovery was so fruitful that it is presently difficult to find a traditional martial art that is not somehow associated with a religious vision of the world."[60]

*An Index of Possibilities: Energy and Power* was originally published in Great Britain as a companion volume to the American-published *Whole Earth Catalog*. Rather than a catalog of resources, however, the book became a collection of information from various sources dealing with subjects ranging from "entropy to Zen, metabolism to PSI." In a major section of the book simply titled "God," the editors included a two-page description of the martial arts that includes the following statements.

> The oriental martial arts are spiritual disciplines as well as fighting techniques. Their ideas are primarily Taoist, based on the concept of the harmony of the universe, and the eternal inflow and outflow of the divine, universal energy which suffuses all things and beings, including man.

> The numerous schools . . . [have in common] the idea of an energy flowing through the human body which man is able to harness. In Chinese this energy is known as *ch'i*, in Japanese *ki*.

> His [the martial artist's] true purpose is an inner, spiritual transformation. Invincibility in combat, and the ability to kill at a touch—these are merely fringe benefits resulting from his gradual harmonisation [sic] with the divine energies of the universe.[61]

*Mindstyles/Lifestyles* includes a section on the martial arts in the chapter on "Body Styles." Regarding the martial art T'ai Chi Ch'uan Nathaniel Lande writes, "Since *Chi* literally means 'intrinsic energy,' the exercises aim to master this energy and circulate it throughout the body as an extraordinary power and strength which regenerates and revitalizes the organs and vital systems, freeing them from disease." With regard to Kung Fu, Lande indicates that "the whole art cannot be perfected unless mental and spiritual discipline are present." He continues, "Serious students of Kung Fu soon learn that they are confronting not an attack technique but a commitment to higher consciousness . . . and the energy of concentrated motion."[62]

On the other hand, there is considerable difference between major branches of the martial arts as to the amount of Eastern spirituality connected with them. While Aikido, Ninjitsu, and Tai Chi are deeply steeped in Eastern mysticism and therefore "cannot be reconciled with Christianity," Judo, Jujitsu, Karate, and Tae Kwon Do have, in their Western practice, become almost totally physical disciplines.[63]

As martial arts developed in ancient China and Japan as a form of self-defense, they also became an expression of the meditation, mind-control, and self-discipline associated with awakening the inner self to a higher consciousness, eventually to achieve oneness with the universal energy flowing through all things. The source of power for the tremendous, almost mystical, feats accomplished by some masters of the martial arts is identified as Ki (Ch'i). Ki is known among the occult arts as the "life-energy-creative force of the universe."

Taoism (see chapter 2) is the religious philosophy behind the Chinese martial arts. In keeping with Taoist philosophy, the martial artist seeks to live in harmony with the Tao (the Way) by using the exercises and meditation of the martial art to keep his yin and yang in balance. When such balance is maintained the individual is able to harness the power of the universal energy to increase the power or force of the physical aspects of the martial art being practiced.

The Eastern philosophy behind the Japanese martial arts is primarily that of Zen Buddhism, which exhibits a strong Taoist influence. Zen Buddhism may be defined as concentration with an empty mind. Through intense meditation the individual empties his mind of all surrounding distractions, so that through extreme concentration he might experience the condition of knowing all reality is one. Such is the obvious New Age philosophy associated with the practice of the martial arts.

To be sure, there are many who participate in martial arts without intending to be involved in the NAM or adhering to an Eastern religion. They participate in martial arts to get good physical exercise and to learn some forms of self-defense. Nevertheless, the Eastern religious philosophies so deeply associated with the NAM underlie the practice of the martial arts. The participant may get more than he or she bargained for. "The Christian practitioner of the martial arts must ask himself whether or not any involvement in such physical disciplines implies an inherent approval of the religious principles behind them."[64]

The occult aspect of the New Age demonstrates clearly that the old lies of Satan are still at work deceiving man into believing that he controls his eternal destiny. He and his demons disguise themselves as perfected beings of great intelligence whose only interest is to lead the human race to a self-achieved state of perfection. Many New Age tools become his instruments of spiritual destruction. In the face of such an onslaught, what is the Christian's hope? "The reason the Son of God appeared was to destroy the devil's work" (1 John 3:8).

> "Put on the full armor of God so that you can take your stand against the devil's schemes.... Stand firm then, with the belt of truth buckled around your waist, with the breastplate of righteousness in place, and with your feet fitted with the readiness that comes from the gospel of peace. In addition to all this, take up the shield of faith, with which you can extinguish all the flaming arrows of the evil one. Take the helmet of salvation and the sword of the Spirit, which is the word of God." (Eph. 6:11, 14–17)

4

# New Age Entertainment

**Item:** A popular movie of several years ago has two sequels. All three movies glorify the martial arts as a means of enhancing self-esteem and confidence by developing the power resident in each individual. In the movie, *The Karate Kid,* an oriental handyman and martial-arts master helps transform a shy and submissive teenager into a karate champion. In doing so, he teaches the teenager and the entire movie audience, including many impressionable children, his Eastern religious philosophy: "what is within" is always right, and "the Buddha provides."

**Item:** " [T]he King Arthur legends have been rewritten for the Age of Aquarius. Marion Zimmer Bradley, in her widely-selling novel *The Mists of Avalon*, tells the legend of Camelot through the eyes of Morganna. . . . As a pagan priestess she is intelligent, strong-willed, mostly benevolent, clear of purpose, and sort of a fifth-century feminist. . . . It is an entertaining and engrossing novel, but also it is skillful propaganda for the New Age."[1]

**Item:** "I am proud of you, my sons. Tonight you have learned the final and greatest truth of all . . . that ultimate mastery comes not of the body but of the mind. Together, there is nothing that your four minds can not accomplish." (Words of Master Splinter to the four Teenage Mutant Ninja Turtles)[2]

**Item:** Actor Dennis Weaver of *Gunsmoke* and *McCloud* fame has been a longtime follower of Swami Paramahansa Yogananda. As such he meditates on a regular basis. Weaver says, "The Bible tells us that in the beginning of creation, Spirit moved. That Spirit is beyond vibratory creation. When *It* (emphasis added) decided to create this dreamlike reality of matter, this finite world, It vibrated. . . . The sound of the original vibration coming out of Spirit is *AUM*, which can't be heard with physical ears . . . but it can be heard in meditation."[3]

**Item:** A newspaper reports that the military has made connections with a California-based organization called the Institute of

HeartMath. The institute makes use of a musical tape, *Heart Zones*, to reduce stress. The recording, which debuted in July 1992, quickly climbed to the top 20 on the New Age music chart. While some might classify the music on the tape as easy listening elevator music, the liner notes state, "The music activates a neuro-electrical connection between the left and right hemispheres of the brain and activates high-end beta frequencies. At the same time it stimulates and engages the feeling world in different rhythmic patterns which involves wider frequencies of the human energy system."[4]

From movies to television, from books to music, from entertainment personalities to children's cartoon heroes the influence of the NAM, particularly its occult aspects, has been increasingly felt. The concern is serious, for it is obvious the influence these entertainment areas have on the minds of people, particularly on impressionable teens and children, as well as undiscerning Christians. "Movies and the media, in the hands of the few, become irresistible propaganda tools over the minds of the many—the simple masses— and can create likes and dislikes by turning an image or innuendo."[5]

The scope of this book does not include the "Christian bashing" so prominent in the entertainment media by both New Age and non-New Age sympathizers. Mocking Christ and the Christian faith, ridiculing Christian morality, and depicting Christians in an unfavorable light in movies, TV programs, and books is common fare and could be the subject of an entire book. Our purpose here is to show that New Age philosophy has entered those areas that provide much of the entertainment for Americans.

## Movies

Numerous movies in the 1980s and 1990s show the NAM's pervasive presence. Reference has already been made to the Karate Kid trilogy. Perhaps the *Star Wars* saga uses New Age themes and teachings most blatantly, implanting them in the minds of millions of viewers. If asked, the vast majority of these millions of viewers would not identify themselves as New Agers. Yet for many their concept of God has been identified with "the Force."

In his book on the New Age, Dr. John Eidsmoe asks, "What contemporary theologian has influenced people's ideas about God more than any other?"[6] His own answer to that question is George

Lucas, the producer of the *Star Wars* trilogy. Eidsmoe points out that the "theology" of George Lucas has reached millions of people who never attend church. However, millions of people who do attend church have also been reached by the pantheistic, Taoist theology of George Lucas and have been exposed subtly but entertainingly to Satan's old lie that man has the fullness of divinity (the Force) within himself. "Vision and values taught in movies are not accountable to truth and reality. They are accepted, not on the basis of reason but because they excite the emotions, challenge the imagination, entice human nature, and manipulate minds."[7]

The God of New Age theology is (chapter 1) an impersonal force or energy. George Lucas wrote, "When you are born, you have an energy field around you. . . . When you die, your energy field joins all other energy fields in the universe, and while you're still living, that larger energy field is sympathetic to your own energy field."[8] This concept of an impersonal "energy field" empowering all life is introduced to movie audiences by the Jedi Knights, who had mastered the Force that animates the cosmos and dwells within each person. Obi-wan Kenobi says, "The Force is what gives the Jedi his power, Luke. It is an energy field created by all living things. It surrounds us and penetrates us; it binds the galaxy together."[9]

Furthermore, the Force is neither good nor evil per se. Rather the Taoistic dual aspects of this universal energy field find expression in the lives of individuals. Darth Vadar expresses the dark side of the Force, while Luke Skywalker expresses the good or light side of the Force. In *The Empire Strikes Back*, Yoda sits in his meditative yoga position, employing the good side of the Force to raise Luke Skywalker's spaceship out of the swamp and thereby demonstrate that a person can use mind power to create reality and accomplish anything one wants.

The children's movie, *The Dark Crystal*, was written, directed, and produced by Jim Henson, the mind behind the Muppets. "It is essentially a fairy tale of monism."[10] Two groups of creatures, the Mystics and the Skecsees, represent the two rival factions in the land. The Mystics are lovable and good; the Skecsees are evil and depraved. The problem emerges because a chard has been split off from the planet's magic crystal. When Jen, the hero, "overcomes all obstacles with the help of astrology, mystical chanting, telepathy, clairvoyance, and other psychic tricks",[11] a major transformation takes place. It is not that good overcomes evil. Rather good and evil are transcended and blended into a cosmic unity. All is one, with ultimate reality in the end transcending good and evil.

The movie *Willow* is filled with a mixture of biblical allusions and occult wonders, another effort by George Lucas to fill the minds of children with the message: the Force is with you. Instead of space age creatures, "the cosmic force shines through ugly trolls, pretty pixies, good as well as evil witches, and a courageous dwarf called Willow."[12] Berit Kjos notes that the story line of *Willow* blends veiled biblical references with occult symbolism, weakening the Christian message but providing the counterfeit message with credibility.

The November/December 1990 issue of the New Age magazine *Body, Mind & Spirit* in an article on the movie *Ghost* stated, "*Ghost* has made it big because it reawakens us powerfully and passionately to who we really are as multidimensional beings. Its depiction of death and the astral world breathes magic back into our daily lives." When asked the source of his inspiration for writing the screenplay, Bruce Rubin replied,

> From my own spiritual life.... I want to give people a sense that there is a larger universe than their conscious minds allow them to perceive. The sensory realities around us are limited realities, and that, if we can expand our consciousness, we can begin to see that there is infinitely more going on in the universe we inhabit. I want to make movies about that.[13]

The *Indiana Jones* trilogy also demonstrates the presence of New Age philosophy in movies. "The search for the Holy Grail is the search for the divine in all of us."[14] George Lucas, that influential "contemporary theologian" and producer of *Star Wars*, also produced the saga of *Indiana Jones*. In a *Rolling Stone* magazine article, Lucas is quoted, "*Raiders* will be the most action-oriented of the Indiana Jones movies—the others should deal more with the occult."[15] In *Raiders of the Lost Ark*, the ark of the covenant is treated as an occult talisman whose power the Nazis are seeking in order to bring the world under the rule of Hitler.

In the first sequel, *Indiana Jones and the Temple of Doom*, the focus shifts to Hindu magic and the Sankara stones given by the Hindu god Shiva to ward off evil. A "left hand" Tantric sect is intent on bringing all the Sankara stones together and by their combined magical and occult power bringing the world under the power of the sect's high priest. The Tantras are a set of Hindu scriptures that focus with a heavy sexual emphasis on the deification of the life force. While the Tantra philosophy asserts that all reality is one, it also recognizes the duality of male and female, light and dark. In keeping with this duality, those who practice Tantra are designated as "left hand" or "right hand," depending on whether they interpret the teachings as being literal or figurative. In *Temple of Doom* the hero fights against the left hand Tantric sect in order to gain possession of the Sankara stones and save the world.

What of the second sequel? Is our hero, Indiana Jones, indeed the savior of the world as he searches for and finds the Holy Grail? The *Watchman Expositor* reported the following information published in *Circle of Light: Community Magazine of Emerging Ideas*:

> "The Holy Grail is a symbol of the *magic of Christ*, that *potential within us* which we may unleash by purification and clear intention to serve the Father's Will.

> "It has been sought through the ages as the one object which would contain unlimited Divine Energy. As the cosmic symbol of love, joy, and overwhelming blessings, it represents the ultimate container, the *receptive human soul which can hold so much of Divine Energy*.

> "At the highest level, the Chalice represents the Christ becoming the vessel of the living grail holding the *Christ Spirit and consciousness*. The Chalice is the symbol of the *new covenant of a oneness* and a spirit of all life in the new age" (April 1984, p. 2).

> Just add a chase scene and this could be the script for the movie *Indiana Jones and the Last Crusade*.[16]

## Television

Most Americans have television sets and video cassette recorders in their homes. They don't have to pay five dollars for a movie to have the New Age philosophy planted in their minds. They watch the same movies free of charge on network programming, rent a video for three dollars or less, or receive an almost unlimited supply of movies in exchange for a monthly cable fee. Through television the occult mysticism of the NAM readily accesses the minds of almost everyone in the nation.

In addition to movies, television has produced its own share of broadcasts with New Age ideas. Among the better known television programs that obviously promote the New Age are Shirley MacLaine's five-hour miniseries, *Out on a Limb*, and the special hosted by Bill Moyers with Joseph Campbell, *The Power of Myth*. The Shirley MacLaine special was broadcast in 1987 on the ABC network. It offered viewers a slick and entertaining account of how she came to accept the New Age philosophy, including channeling and spirit guides, a belief in reincarnation, and the climax of New Age thought: "I *know* that I exist, therefore I AM. I *know* that the God-source exists. Therefore *IT IS*. Since I am part of that force, then *I AM* that *I AM*."[17]

The special with Joseph Campbell was first broadcast on public television in 1988. Interestingly, this six-part series was filmed at Skywalker Ranch, the movie compound of *Star Wars* producer George Lucas for whom Campbell had become a kind of guru who helped shape much of Lucas' New Age philosophy. Joseph Campbell was a professor of literature for many years at Sarah Lawrence College. He also was a prolific writer on mythology and literature. Tal Brooke states that Campbell's erudite and persuasive arguments on *Bill Moyers Special* and in the corresponding book are very compelling in support of a common global creed.

> Mythology, Campbell taught, is the key of mystery that opens the massive gateway for the unity of all religions, faiths, and paths. Campbell's insight appears to be exactly what the world has been waiting for in its desire to get over local religious squabbles among the various faiths. During this critical period, when the world is crying out for a workable unity, Campbell seems to supply the key to make it all work. All we need to do is let go of our culturally-conditioned preferences for certain metaphors. Once we get over that "hang-up," we will see that a deeper message has been trying to emerge from all the world faiths[18] [see the material in chapter 1—"All religions are one and lead to cosmic unity"].

Like others who think and write on mythology, Campbell attempts to mythologize Jesus and the Bible in New Age terms. Douglas Groothuis points out that in discussing the idea that "God was in Christ,"

. . . Campbell affirms that "the basic Gnostic and Buddhist idea is that it is true of you and me as well." Jesus was an enlightened example who "realized in himself that he and what he called the Father were one, and he lived out of that knowledge of the Christhood of his nature." According to Campbell, anyone can live out his or her Christ nature. Campbell noted that a priest who heard him make this point in a lecture called it "blasphemy."[19]

Other television programming subtly implants New Age thinking. One evening after the late news, as I was switching channels, I came upon one of the *Star Trek: The Next Generation* programs. In this program the crew of the starship Enterprise encountered yet another alien life form known as the Borgs—robot-like creatures with human body and facial shapes but composed of both living and inanimate matter. It was discovered that the individual creatures were apparently mentally plugged into a collective mind whose power was equal to the power of the individual Borg minds combined. The collective mind controlled the operation of the Borg space ship even to the point of being able to regenerate spontaneously those portions of the spaceship destroyed by the weapons of the Enterprise. In other words, I found myself exposed to the idea of a Universal Mind or Energy that presumably flows through all things in the universe, animate and inanimate, and that heals and restores the person who is plugged into this Life Force.

Concerning television, Berit Kjos writes,

With television, mass programming has become a chilling reality. Media spokesmen wield power to censor facts, select information, ridicule vital principles, build illusive expectations, and direct America's thinking. Today's information glut has produced an audience ill-equipped to argue with the "experts."[20]

Kjos and others have pointed to the occult themes that are found even in children's cartoons such as the Smurfs (Papa Smurf uses good magic to conquer evil) and the Care Bears (who transform their world with loving vibrations). He-Man and She-Ra use their occult and magic powers to be the Masters of the Universe. Such cartoons and toys "use occult symbolism and concepts to draw children into their world of error."[21]

# Personalities

Entertainment personalities greatly influence millions of Americans whose lives often revolve around entertainment pursuits. People often remark that they adore a certain entertainer. Or they comment that they can't wait until their favorite TV show comes on. Many seem to assume, "If something is good enough for my favorite entertainer, it's good enough for me."

The lifestyle of popular entertainers strongly influences our thinking. That is why organizations such as the Church of Scientology and the Mormon church use entertainment and well-known athletic and political figures in attractive advertisements urging people to join their organization. It is amazing that people will believe entertainers such as Shirley MacLaine when they make extravagant claims, but they can readily recognize the same claims of the average person on the street as fake.

When popular entertainers promote New Age teachings and when their lifestyle follows New Age goals, Satan has yet another avenue to plant his old lies into the hearts and minds of undiscerning people.

Shirley MacLaine, by deliberately promoting her own personal experiences, has become the leading spokesperson for the NAM among entertainment personalities. More articles have been written and interviews published about her New Age spiritistic encounters than about any other person of stage, screen, or television. Her picture appeared on the cover of *Time* in 1987 when its lead article dealt with the NAM. A TV special about her New Age conversion caught the attention of millions of viewers. Her books have made the best-seller lists. Those who have at least a passing familiarity with the NAM would probably name Shirley MacLaine as the first New Age celebrity who comes to mind.

Especially in 1987 following the television mini-series *Out on a Limb*, articles about MacLaine were in great abundance in newspapers and in magazines—from *The Christian Century* to *Money* and the *National Enquirer*. In recent years, interest in her New Age views has waned, and MacLaine herself has backed off some in her strong promotion of the NAM. On the other hand, she has already made her fortune from books, TV series, and lecture tour/seminars. Her lecture tour consisted of two-day seminars at a cost of $300 per participant. The profits were to be used for building New Age spiritual centers. The seminars included the typical New Age mix, emphasizing getting in contact with one's Higher Self. The general message is predictable. "MacLaine, ... proceeded to deliver a lengthy version of the New Age message of narrow self-interest—that understanding of self and fulfillment of self lead to a better life. The central belief is that each person is his or her own god. As such, everybody determines his own destiny. There is no such thing as luck or misfortune."[22]

There is no doubt that Shirley MacLaine has contributed greatly to the acceptance of new Age ideas, particularly the occult variety, on the part of many people. At her New York seminar, one individual who said he came from a Yoga background lauded her contributions to the NAM. "Just her sense of humor about it made me realize she's the perfect one to bring this to people who wouldn't otherwise hear of it. She's well-loved already. Some of these middle-class Americans might never become involved if it weren't for Shirley MacLaine."[23]

To be sure MacLaine is not alone in her search for spiritual meaning and identity in her life. Recent surveys indicate that the Baby Boomers are increasingly more spiritual (but not necessarily more Christian) than their parents. Why? Because of life's problems, complexities, and uncertainties. "Conditions are indeed favorable for mediums and wizards; one can bank on people's anxieties, and many have. MacLaine and her band of psychics, clairvoyants and trance channelers are neither the first nor the last to go out on a limb to propose remedies for perplexity or antidotes for anxiety."[24]

Other entertainment personalities may not have had the publicity Shirley MacLaine has received but are just as committed to the New Age. John Denver (the "Pied Piper of environmentalism") actively pursues environmental causes through the Windstar Foundation which he founded in 1976. However, his concern is with more than what is happening to natural resources. "The environment is more than just whales. We each have our own personal environment—the emotional, the physical, the spiritual environment."[25] Along with Shirley MacLaine and thousands of other New Agers, Denver participated in the August 16–17, 1987 Harmonic Convergence promoted by Jose Arguelles. Drawing from "a body of occult lore, UFO contactee theology, and fringe archaeology" the Harmonic Convergence was to be "an occurrence characterized by a collective shift in humankind's mental orientation."[26] John Denver's mental and spiritual orientation had already shifted to the New Age philosophy. In a 1986 magazine article he was quoted, "Every time I sing, I meditate. Every time I sing, I experience God in me."[27]

Other entertainment personalities who have displayed interest in and support for the New Age include Linda Evans, Lindsay Wagner, Dick Gregory, Dirk Benedict, Cloris Leachman, Richard Gere, and Oprah Winfrey. What a powerful pulpit for Satan's man-centered, self-deifying old lies for a New Age!

# Books

In an age of television, VCRs, and computer games, the reading of books may not seem like entertainment. Yet the number of books devoted to the NAM has mushroomed in the last five years. Sales show that millions find these books informative, educational, and entertaining. Once again Shirley MacLaine and her 1987 TV special have played a major role. Her series "caused a run on the occult sections of major bookstores. B. Dalton Bookseller, a nationwide chain owned by BDB Inc., says sales in its occult and astrology sections jumped 90% in the week after the mini-series."[28] Russell Chandler reports that in that same year MacLaine's books sold eight million copies. Based on information in the January 1988 *American Bookseller* magazine, Chandler also writes, "[A]t least 2,500 book-stores specialize in New Age books (twice the 1982 number); and 25,000 titles are in print, accounting for more than a billion dollars in sales in 1987 (up 30% over 1986), according to industry figures."[29]

However, not only the New Age bookstores but the major book-store chains such as B. Dalton and Waldenbooks have extensive sections clearly labeled New Age. To the dismay of some serious New Age promoters, the New Age category has become so broad as to almost defy definition. It includes an almost endless list of books about channeling, native American shamanism, astrology, *The Tao of Pooh* for children, female spirituality, neopagan religions, divination through the use of tarot cards, and many others. Many New Age books that were published long before the New Age be-came a household term now appear with a New Age label on the cover. Placing a book in the New Age category can have its advan-tages. Physicist David Peat, while somewhat apprehensive about having his book on the origin of the universe included on Bantam Book's New Age list, said, "If being on the New Age list means more people will read it, and it's in a good position in the bookstore, then fine."[30]

Even public libraries are feeling the pressure of demands for New Age titles. Martha Powers, an energetic librarian of the Tigard, Oregon public library compiled a guide for New Age resources. Because New Age is so broad, she identified 29 categories where New Age books might be found, ranging from acupuncture and astral projection to reincarnation and yoga—three double-columned pages of "a sampling of classics, most-asked-for titles, intriguing diversions, and some of our personal favorites."[31] The authors constitute a virtual Who's Who in the New Age —Lynn Andrews, Richard Bach, Joseph Campbell, Fritjof Capra, Deepak Chopra, Matthew Fox, Shakti Gawain, Shirley MacLaine, Ramtha, the Enlightened One, Bernie Siegel, David Spangler, Starhawk, Gary Zukav. The library reference resources included the *National New Age Yellow Pages* and *New Age Marketing Opportunities; A Comprehensive Directory*.[32] "Of making many books there is no end" (Eccl. 12:12). The making of books has become yet another means for Satan to promote his old lies.

## New Age Music

A remaining category of New Age entertainment is the music. Some have called the New Age music *audio Valium* or *Yuppie muzak*. Others think of it as *elevator music,* the soft, dreamy, instrumental music intended to relax and relieve stress. Most New Age music is instrumental, with no verbal message that "preaches" New Age philosophy. How can we know whether "easy listening" music has the potential of leading us into New Age thought or practices? Again it is a question of spiritual discernment, as well as, in this instance, the motivation or purpose for listening to New Age music.

As with other music genres, the New Age variety is variously expressed depending on the composer and performer. Some of it has an "Eastern" quality. Others is a fusion of jazz and rock. Various stringed and keyboard instruments are used with a seeming preference for the synthesizer. At the one end of the spectrum, "hardcore" New Age music creates an inner harmony with the universal energy force and is intended for meditation and healing sessions. At the other end are the jazz-folk-rock combinations that seem to concentrate on artistic expression and financial gain, the type that is played on many New Age radio stations. "The common thread that unites these otherwise diverse forms of New Age music is supposed to be *feeling*—listening to them generates a peaceful and uplifting mood."[33]

As with most of what has been termed New Age, the surge of interest in New Age music has come in about the last five years. Like much of the New Age, its music also has had its commercial side. *The Wall Street Journal* reported that on Valentine's Day, 1987, a major Los Angeles radio station "switched full time to New Age and other music it calls, 'light, hypnotic, uplifting.' No longer KMET, the station is now KTWV—'The WAVE.' "[34] Since then numerous stations, especially in metropolitan areas, have followed suit. The playing of New Age music by such radio stations has increased the commercial potential for this music. More people in this stressed-filled society are being attracted by its mellow sounds. New Age labels such as Windham Hill and American Gramaphone have grown into multimillion dollar record companies.

Is New Age music for the most part rather innocent? Here is where motivation and intent on the part of composer, performer, and listener become important. "Some New Age music is intended not just to soothe the soul but to trigger a meditative change in consciousness. This could be called meditative or mystical New Age music."[35] Douglas Groothuis, referring especially to Steven Halpern, an innovator of New Age music, says that Halpern's "Spectrum Suite" is "designed to enable listeners to focus on each of the seven chakras (energy centers) in their body, which he thinks correspond to seven separate colors and sounds."[36] As another example of music that is obviously intended to have a mystical or consciousness raising effect, Groothuis refers to the tape *The Eternal One*:

> The OM is all sound and silence throughout time. . . . It invokes the ALL that is otherwise inexpressible, and it is the highest spiritual sound on the earth. And now, using the latest in electronic technology, we have synthesized various pitches from human voices, and all intoning the OM together at the prescribed vibrations. In the background is an almost subliminal sounding choir.[37]

The above type of music is termed "inner harmony" New Age music. The more mellow, easy listening type of music is sometimes labeled "progressive." Some place the soundtrack from the movie *Chariots of Fire* in this category. Much New Age music, both *inner harmony* and *progressive,* is characterized by repetitious sounds and harmonic progressions that never seem to lead anywhere and never come to resolution. This has led F. LaGard Smith to comment,

> What I find interesting about most New Age music is the way in which it reflects the aimlessness and purposelessness of the New Age message. Largely unstructured and circular in form, it resembles the *lawlessness* of New Age philosophy and the *reincarnational* theme of never-ending, repetitious life forms. Not surprisingly, then, New Age music often lacks resolution. And just as the line between right and wrong, good and evil, is blurred, so too we find a blurring of tones.[38]

Will listening to New Age music, whether intentional or non-intentional, place a Christian in a spiritually dangerous environment? Bob Larson says it well: "Music is music. There is nothing inherently evil in its components of harmony, rhythm, and melody. But for those who seek the assistance of music to leave their bodies and alter their consciousness, the music could indeed be dangerous."[39] The key is in purpose, intent, and discernment. As stated, some New Age music is produced to help create altered states of consciousness, others primarily to relax a person. The alert Christian listening to New Age music will be seeking only an environment of sound that is pleasing and relaxing. "It would seem to me that if the discerning Christian remains alert to the possibility of undesirable influences occasionally coming through, he or she could listen to the progressive varieties of New Age music, in moderation, without ill effect."[40]

As I was writing this chapter, a copy of Terry Mattingly's weekly column for the Scripps Howard News Service came to my attention. Mattingly addressed yet another expression of the "Star Trek" worldview that is rooted in Eastern mysticism. He quoted Vishal Mangalwadi of India, a Christian theologian at the Himalayan L'Abri Resource Center who watched the premier episode of *Star Trek: Deep Space Nine* while on a lecture tour of the United States. Mangalwadi said, "I felt overwhelmed. . . . It would almost be easier to talk about the parts of the show that were not rooted in an Eastern worldview. . . . There would be less to talk about." He continued, "Now it seems like the gurus are making films." In the *Deep Space Nine* premier, the spaceship commander is instructed in the truth revealed by god-like prophets: "Look for solutions from within."[41]

Unfortunately, Shirley MacLaine and several of her fellow entertainers encourage looking inside oneself as the remedy for anxiety and the perplexities of life. But this is not in harmony with the reality God describes. According to Scripture, when a man looks inside himself, all he will find is "that nothing good lives in me, that is, in my sinful nature" (Rom. 7:18). However, when a person looks deep within himself and sees his sinfulness (1 John 1:8–10) and acknowledges his own helplessness (Rom. 5:6), he will be open to the power and grace of God to work in his life. Then he will know that "[God's] grace is sufficient for you, for [his] power is made perfect in weakness" (2 Cor. 12:9). Then, by God's power and grace through Jesus Christ, the image of God in a person will be renewed (Eph. 4:22–24). Such a person will experience a radical transformation, not through meditation, listening to New Age music, or other occult means, but "in view of God"s mercy" will "be transformed by the renewing of [his/her] mind" (Rom. 12:1–2). Renewed and transformed by God's power and grace, a person will then be able to "deny himself and take up his cross daily and follow" the I AM who is the "light of the world" (Luke 9:23; John 8:12).

5

# New Age Neo-Paganism

**Item:** "An entire subdivision of New Age music exists that is devoted to women's music and to the *Neo-Pagan* religious movement, with which it overlaps."[1]

**Item:** An article in the October 1992 issue of the *Rocky Mountain News* from Denver, Colorado, about Judith M. Brownlee, who teaches a course in witchcraft, states, "The course includes the history of paganism, magic, meditation, healing and past lives." Brownlee is quoted, "The neo-pagan renaissance is a real thing. When I first started teaching classes like this, maybe a dozen people would attend. The third one in the summer of '88, I had 42 people. This time, who knows? Paganism is an umbrella word. Modern witchcraft is an attempt to recreate how ancient Celts and other tribal peoples worshipped before the advent of Christianity."[2]

**Item:** On May 1, 1987, fifteen men and women dance around a maypole to celebrate Beltane, the fertility festival of the ancient Celts. This coven's dance is in Inwood Hill Park at the northern tip of Manhattan Island. The celebrants "call themselves followers of the Craft or the Old Religion or Wicca. They have nothing to do with either black magic or Christianity or, for that matter, with any monotheistic religion, as they are Neo-Pagans. . . . Whatever their understanding of the deities, these witches seek harmony with nature and to enhance their spiritual life."[3]

**Item:** On December 21, 1992, about 30 people gathered at the Midtown Art and Ornament Gallery in Kansas City, Missouri, to celebrate Yule, a pagan holiday. The celebration was organized by the Heartland Spiritual Alliance, a group organized in 1988 "to educate people about alternative religions such as paganism and Wicca, the pagan-based religion of witches." At this celebration the "high priestess, dressed in white, traced a circle around the celebrants with a ceremonial sword. The high priest, dressed in dark robes, followed her with burning incense. During Yule, pagans celebrate the birthday of the Sun King who brings light and hope into the world."[4]

**Item:** A New Age catalog lists a variety of audio tapes that will provide instruction in subjects ranging from astrology to healing your body with your mind to the practice of Zen Buddhism. One tape entitled "Our Hearts and the Heart of the Earth Are One" is described as follows:

> Introduces you to ancient meditation rites based on Cherokee religious tradition. The Venerable Dhyani Ywahoo is Clan Chieftaness of the Etowah Cherokee Nation. She is your instructor in the art of Sunray Meditation—which centers on attunement with the pure vibration that is the essence of all life and matter. You are guided in chants that stress breath control as your most basic connection with the life force within, and in visualizations that draw from sacred Indian mythology. Through spiritual devotion to Sunray Meditation we create a vision of beauty and wholeness in our lives and in the universe.[5]

**Item:** The Joy Lake Mountain Seminar Center, a New Age retreat about a 45-minute drive from Lake Tahoe, serves "gourmet vegetarian meals." From late April to the end of September, the center provides more than 60 seminars and workshops on planetary herbology, Tibetan healing, reincarnation, sacred psychology, opening oneself as a creative healing channel, and others. A catalog describes the workshop "The Path of Power" with Sun Bear as the presenter:

> Sun Bear, founder of the Bear Tribe, author of *The Path of Power*, . . . will teach about seeking medicine, working with the Thunder Beings and the natural forces, understanding Native healing ways and the sweat lodge ceremony, understanding ancient prophecies, preparing for the world of tomorrow, finding power spots, learning to live with nature, communicating with natural powers, getting in touch with the life force within each person and blending it with all of nature.[6]

A chapter on Neo-Paganism may not seem appropriate for a book on the NAM. To be sure there are differences in beliefs and practices between the strict adherents of Neo-Paganism and "dyed-in-the-wool" New Agers. "The Neo-Pagan movement in America and other English-speaking nations parallels the New Age Movement in some ways, differs sharply from it in others, and overlaps it in some minor ways."[7] Yet, as this quote from the *New Age Encyclopedia*[r] indicates, enough parallels warrant including this burgeoning movement in the broad picture of New Age spirituality. As for the magick (the letter "k" is added to the usual spelling of "magic" to distinguish occult magick from stage magic) employed by many Neo-Pagans, Russell Chandler identifies the most serious parallel between Neo-Paganism and the New Age: "The New Age magick is, in fact, the Edenic longing for godhood through a certain and secret wisdom that disperses limitations and suffering with the wave of a wand."[8]

## Definition and History

What is Neo-Paganism? Simply put, it is a renewing (neo) of ancient pagan spirituality and practices. More specifically, Neo-Paganism is a renewal of interest in nature religions that seek either to follow ancient traditions or to create new forms of pagan ritual. Margot Adler, priestess of a coven of witches and author of a definitive study on the subject of Neo-Paganism, provides this definition:

> By *pagan* they [the pagans] usually mean the pre-Christian nature religions of the West, and their own attempts to revive them or to recreate them in new forms. The modern Pagan resurgence includes the new feminist goddess-worshipping groups, certain new religions based on the visions of science fiction writers, attempts to revive ancient European religions—Norse, Greek, Roman—and the surviving tribal religions.[9]

As can be seen, the Neo-Pagan branch of the eclectic New Age is itself very eclectic and includes a variety of expressions of nature-based religions, of which the most predominant expression is Wicca (witchcraft). Other Neo-Pagan groups include Druid organizations, Norse pagans, at least one based on ancient Egyptian religions, the women's spirituality movement, and the revival of various Native American religious practices. Because of the nature-based character of Neo-Paganism, there will be some close parallels between this chapter and the one on New Age Environmentalism that follows.

We note here that Neo-Paganists are not Satanists, at least not in the sense that the term is normally used. Neo-Pagans are quick to assert that Satan or the devil as a malevolent spirit is a creation of the Christian religion. Neo-Paganism, they contend, does not practice Satan worship, does not engage in mocking Christian ritual (the

Black Mass), and does not sacrifice animal or human life as part of its religious rituals. (This is not to say that such Satanist groups do not exist.) Neo-Pagans insist that those who discover they have a witch or a Neo-Pagan for a neighbor have nothing to fear, for the basic creed of Wiccans which could apply to all Neo-Pagans is, "If it harm none, do as you will." However, from the Christian perspective, Neo-Pagan practices are but another form of worshipping the creature rather than the Creator. They must ultimately be viewed as Satanic in origin. Such practices lead the participants away from the worship of the true God who has loved them and given his Son to be their Savior.

Some would claim that Neo-Pagan practices simply revive ancient nature religions that Christianity attempted to suppress but which really never completely died out. "Modern day witches ... want to feel that they are part of a tradition, rooted in the ancient and the true. But in order to do that, they have to invent their history and mythologize their origins."[10] Most Neo-Pagans acknowledge that the only connection between modern and ancient pagan practices is the emphasis on nature, occult magick, and the use of ancient names for gods and goddesses. The forms of ritual and practice of contemporary Neo-Paganism are actually and almost exclusively of modern invention. The one exception is Native American rituals, which also, in some instances, struggle to identify genuine traditional native spirituality.

Most who have studied the Neo-Paganism phenomenon trace its modern origins to the 1930s following the publication in 1921 of Margaret Murray's *The Witch-Cult in Western Europe*.[11] Murray developed her theory that "witchcraft could be traced back to pre-Christian times" and that "it was once the ancient pagan religion of Western Europe."[12] Although others have demonstrated that Murray's writings are based on poor scholarship and filled with unwarranted conclusions, nevertheless her work "was an important preparation for the later rise of neo-paganism. Her theories set off a wave of enthusiasm for things ancient, native, and pagan that is still with us and gaining strength."[13]

Gerald Gardner (1884–1964) is generally credited with contributing the most to developing Neo-Paganism, particularly as expressed in witchcraft. As with Murray, Gardner's scholarship with regard to the relationship between ancient paganism and Neo-Paganism is questioned, yet his importance for the development of modern witchcraft is unquestioned. Concerning his first book Margot Adler writes, "There's a whole lot of questionable scholarship, but if it wasn't for Gardner, *Drawing Down the Moon* would never have been written, and most of us Wiccans would not be around."[14] In his lifetime Gardner was deeply involved in various occult practices and organizations. Upon retirement from the British civil service, he allegedly contacted witches. One such witch, Dorothy Clutterbuck, supposedly initiated him into witchcraft.

Gardner wrote *Witchcraft Today* in 1954 and *The Meaning of Witchcraft* in 1959. He claimed that his initiation into witchcraft was a continuation of the "Old Religion" that predated Christianity. However, it is more likely that Gardner picked up on Margaret Murray's theory and developed his own religion. Craig Hawkins writes,

> In his writings Gardner drew upon his occultic experiences, travels, the writings of Murray, the help of [occultist] Aleister Crowley, and his knowledge of Freemasonry, Rosicruciansim, Theosophy, Western ritual/sex magic, magical texts (e.g., the *Greater Key of Solomon*), and various native Asian and near Eastern religions and their occultic paraphernalia. Borrowing from these and other sources, Gardner invented his own religion—founding it upon the Mother Goddess. To this witches' brew he added the doctrine of reincarnation. Thus, rather than merely revealing and reviving an ancient Goddess religion as he claimed, the resourceful Gardner actually *created* modern witchcraft.[15]

Hawkins points out that as a result of Gardner's efforts modern witchcraft developed as people became familiar with Gardner's concepts and were initiated into this "new" paganism.

While not all Neo-Pagan groups are direct expressions of witchcraft, the Neo-Pagan movement gets its primary thrust from a growing popularity and openness in the practice of the Wiccan religion. In fact, in the broad spectrum of the NAM, books on witchcraft are beginning to outnumber just about any other aspect of the eclectic New Age. A quick survey of the ten-shelf New Age section at a B. Dalton Bookstore revealed that approximately 20 percent of the shelf space was devoted to witchcraft. Since the revival of witchcraft dominates Neo-Paganism, we will use witchcraft in identifying Neo-Paganism's place in relation to the NAM.

Wiccan Neo-Paganism is in many ways similar to basic New Age thinking and in some respects an exact duplication. Among the beliefs of witchcraft, foremost is an emphasis on the *experience* of being one (monism) with all life. Neo-Pagans are basically animistic. They believe that all things, animate and inanimate, share in the vital energy, the Life Force. Hence they emphasize living in harmony with nature and are correspondingly concerned about the environment. (More on this in the next chapter.) From here it is a short step to *pantheism*. Not only do all things share in the Life Force, but the entire world is divine. The earth itself is a Goddess to be revered, and all things are sacred. "The same life force that animates the gods, the wind, the sun, and the sea animates us. We in the West, neopagans say, need to attune ourselves to it, direct it, and use it. . . . This is the spark of divinity that is in every man."[16]

Margot Adler summarizes the monistic, animistic, pantheistic, sacredness-of-nature, man-is-divine Neo-Pagan beliefs that are comparable with similar New Age beliefs. She says the following are basic beliefs shared by those she writes about in her book.

> The world is holy. Nature is holy. The body is holy. Sexuality is holy. The mind is holy. The imagination is holy. You are holy. A spiritual path that is not stagnant ultimately leads one to the understanding of one's own divine nature. Thou art Goddess. Thou art God. Divinity is imminent in all Nature. It is as much within you as without. . . .

> [W]omen (and men too) will never understand their own creative strength and divine nature until they embrace the creative feminine, the source of inspiration, the Goddess within.[17]

As with the New Age in general, Neo-Pagans pride themselves in being tolerant of a wide range of spiritual beliefs and practices. "If it harm none, do as you will." There are no absolutes in terms of right or wrong, good or evil. All is relative to an individual's perception. All of which sounds very much like, "You create your own reality." Because reality is diverse and multiple and dependent upon one's own perception, there is no particular codification of beliefs to which all Neo-Pagans subscribe. Nor is there a set of beliefs or rules of conduct the transgression of which can be called sin and can produce guilt. " . . . [T]here is no such thing as sin . . . and guilt is never very useful."[18] This "basic belief" of Neo-Paganism sounds very much like the teaching of *A Course in Miracles*, a leading New

Age work that is finding support in some Christian churches.

Since all things are relative, including spiritual paths to achieving oneness with the divine, Neo-Paganism, like the rest of the NAM, is very syncretistic. In their highly valued concept of tolerance, Neo-Pagans accept as valid any religious expression that meets a person's individual needs. However, they have a problem with monotheistic religions such as Christianity.

> According to the neopagans, the exclusivistic religions—Christianity, Islam, and Judaism—are unnecessarily dogmatic in their insistence on one way, one truth, one God. Neopagans make much of this point. They are bothered by what they perceive as intolerance and a tendency to persecute dissenters.[19]

As a result of such perceived intolerance, the Council of American Witches has included the following in its "Principles of Wiccan Belief": "Our only animosity toward Christianity, or towards any other religion or philosophy-of-life, is to the extent that its institutions have claimed to be 'the only way' and have sought to deny freedom to others and to suppress other ways of religious practice and belief."[20]

As mentioned, there are also noticeable differences between those who would identify themselves as Neo-Pagans and those who call themselves New Agers. New Agers would avoid the use of terms like magic and witchcraft. In New Age bookstores, books on Neo-Paganism are usually shelved with books on women's studies. On the other hand, while there is some networking, and attempts have been made to provide some organization and structure to the Neo-Pagan movement, most Neo-Pagans are anti-authoritarian and would shy away from accepting the authority of any guru, spirit guide, or authoritarian structure. In agreement with New Agers, most Neo-Pagans believe in reincarnation and karma. However, they "reject the dualism of the Eastern traditions and consider the guarantee of rebirth to be the goal of their spiritual practices. . . . Focused on the pagan religions of the past, they are not particularly interested in a New Age in the future."[21]

## Wiccan Rituals

Most witches invoke or worship the female Mother Goddess and her male partner, the Horned God. The Mother Goddess is sometimes referred to as the triple Goddess because of her three primary roles as mother, maiden, and crone. Modern witchcraft has revived a variety of ancient names for the Mother Goddess and the Horned God. The Mother Goddess, who is believed to be eternal, is addressed as Aphrodite, Artemis, Astaroth, Diana, Gaia, Luna, Venus, and many more. The male consort, the Horned God, who is associated with the sun and is believed to die and be reborn every year, is invoked by such names as Apollo, Baphomet, Eros, Lucifer, Odin, Pan, and others. A person who has searched the Scriptures will recognize many of these as names of idols in both the Old and New Testament periods. "Different witchcraft traditions and solitary practitioners diverge in the importance they attach to the Mother Goddess and the Horned God. Some emphasize the Goddess, some the Horned God, while many seek a balance between the two."[22]

While not having any particular organization or structure for the entire movement, most witchcraft practitioners form small groups called covens. The High Priestess and her High Priest are responsible for the conduct of coven activities and for the instruction of initiates. Wiccans have special times for assembly.

> The four great festivals are seasonal: (1) Spring *Equinox*, March 21; (2) Summer *Solstice* or Midsummer, June 22; (3) Autumn *Equinox*, September 21; and (4) Yule or Winter *Solstice*, December 22. These are joined by four cross festivals related to the agricultural and herd-raising year: (1) Candlemas, February 2; (2) May Eve or Beltane, April 30; (3) Lammas, July 31; and (4) Halloween, October 31. Besides these eight, most Wicca groups meet either weekly or bi-weekly (on the full and new moon). Major holidays are termed sabbats, and weekly or bi-weekly meeting [sic] are esbats.[23]

Out of their reverence for nature, Neo-Pagans attempt to gather outdoors whenever possible. For obvious reasons, a secluded area is preferred. In an article for *Christianity Today*, David Bass describes a "typical" gathering as including,

> 1. Creation of a sacred space, the circle. This is seen as a place between this world and the other where the worshiper communes with the gods. Those within it are also protected from the forces released in the ceremony. This step is called "closing the circle."
>
> 2. Invocation of gods and spirits. Worshipers invite them into the

circle, and thereby into fellowship with the participants. This is called "drawing down the moon."

3. Evocation of "magical" forces. These the worshiper intends to master and use for some willed purpose. The energy or force is often "sent" where change of any kind is desired. [This is sometimes referred to as "raising the cone of power."]

4. Opening of the circle. Here the circle becomes simple space again. Farewells are often taken with a "Merry meet, merry part, and blessed be."[24]

## The Feminist Connection

It should be quite apparent that a religion that elevates the Mother Goddess to the highest position would have great appeal to many women with a militant feminist viewpoint. "Of course, not all neopagans are feminists, and not all feminists are neopagans. Nonetheless, neopaganism has a magnetic pull on many feminists."[25] In her book Adler points out that already in the mid-1980s exclusive feminist covens were developing in which overt efforts were made to connect women's spirituality with political activism. In such covens an almost monotheistic form of devotion to the Goddess takes place. "The various Goddesses of ancient culture serve as symbols of liberation from spiritual inferiority and personal and political powerlessness. Goddess enthusiasts usually advocate either the superiority of women or some kind of androgenous [sic] ideal."[26]

In one sense, the feminist connection with Neo-Paganism has separated the Neo-Pagan movement from the New Age fascination with the mysticism of the East. After an interview with new religions expert Robert Ellwood, Russell Chandler wrote, "[W]omen—exhilarated over the discovery of a religion that exalts the female role—now realize that many of the Eastern religions 'have been repressive in many ways. They [those religions] don't have the appeal they did in the 1960s.' "[27] Chandler says that Neo-Paganism, particularly the Wiccan variety, has great appeal to ecofeminists. Ecofeminism will be discussed in the next chapter.

## Native American Spirituality

A full chapter could be devoted to the renewed interest in Native American ceremonies and rituals. Two of the interest items at the beginning of this chapter refer to Native Americans and practices of Native American spirituality that have close correspondence with New Age beliefs and practices. "Counter culture spirituality has often depended for inspiration on Native American religious traditions. The high visibility of shamanism and the increasing practice of American Indian-type ceremonies within the New Age Movement have, in relatively recent years, evoked responses from certain segments of the Native American community."[28]

That response has not always been positive. In fact, at times it has been hostile. Members of the American Indian Movement condemn the commercialization by non-natives of the sacred symbols and religions traditions of Native American peoples. Some have even labeled as "cultural imperialism" the New Age appropriation of Native American spirituality, comparing the original stealing of the land from the Indians by the first white settlers with the modern stealing of native religious traditions. One can certainly sympathize with such a view when looking at the ads in New Age magazines that promote sacred pipes, the revival of the medicine wheel, sweat lodges, and courses in shamanism.[29]

On the other hand, many Native Americans as well as non-natives see a direct connection between New Age monistic pantheism and the oneness with nature and the Great Spirit that is at the heart of much Native American spirituality. An interest item at the beginning of this chapter referred to a seminar hosted by Sun Bear at the Joy Lake Mountain Seminar Center. Sun Bear is a Chippewa Indian teacher and medicine man (an example of a *shaman*) who, together with three non-Native American women, founded the Bear Tribe in Reno, Nevada, in 1966. After several moves, the Bear Tribe finally settled in 1974 near Klamath Falls, Oregon. "Sun Bear credits Hopi Indian prophecies with the idea that medicine people should teach the medicine ways to all who sincerely ask to learn the ancient knowledge." After moving to the Klamath Falls, Oregon area "the idea for the Medicine Wheel gatherings began to form, and the Medicine Wheel would enter the New Age movement in America as one of its principal ceremonies."[30]

The use (sometimes misuse) of medicine wheels in Arizona and at the Medicine Wheel National Historic Landmark in Wyoming caused considerable difficulties for the U. S. Forest Service in 1992. Russell Chandler describes his experience attending a 1987 Medicine Wheel assembly sponsored by Bear Tribe. The purpose of this particular assembly was to bring together medicine people and shamans from a variety of spiritual traditions to share their beliefs and ceremonies. With regard to the Medicine Wheel ceremony, Chandler quotes Sun Bear: "You begin to realize your interconnectedness with the Earth and with all other life." After two paragraphs describing the ceremony that includes "placing a buffalo skull in the center of the wheel to represent the Creator," Chandler says, "Sun Bear is one of an increasing number of modern-day medicine men and women—*shamans*—who combine reverence for the circle of life and traditional native healing methods with New Age technologies and assumptions."[31]

The word *shaman* is becoming so widely used that its meaning is often no longer clear. In some cultures the shaman is one who fulfills a variety of roles that in modern terms would be described as healer, priest, and counselor. The shaman is the mediator between his people and the spirit world, particularly as the spirits supposedly find expression in animals and in nature. A feeling of oneness with nature and an interest in the spirit world are the links in the chain that connect Native American spirituality, shamanistic practices, and Wiccan rituals with New Age interest in the broad spectrum of Neo-Paganism. Margot Adler notes that the word *shaman* has varied applications:

> A shaman is someone who enters an altered state of consciousness and goes on a journey in order to gather knowledge from a different reality. The knowledge depends on a deep connection with the forces of nature—with the spirits of plants and animals. The methods used to enter this altered state depend on the culture.

> In the last five years, Pagans have begun exploring some of these pathways [to altered consciousness]. The most common, and a feature of many recent Pagan festivals, is ecstatic dancing, drumming, and chanting, often lasting for hours. There has been an increased interest in fasting, vision quests, and sweat lodges, and there is also more interest in working with nature spirits and earth energies.[32]

Douglas Groothuis summarizes the book and seminars of Michael Harner on shamanism. He writes, "His seminars on shamanism focus on the interrelationship of the human, animal and spiritual realms. The approach is a blend of animism (spirit contact) and pantheism: by becoming a kind of shaman one may harmonize the spiritual and natural worlds within oneself. Psychic abilities may be cultivated and utilized."[33]

A blending of Native American spirituality and shamanistic practices has been made popular through the marketing of many books. Sun Bear has published several. Michael Harner, to whom both Adler and Groothuis refer, is the author of *The Way of the Shaman: A Guide to Prayer and Healing* in which he provides instruction and guidance for those who want to become shamans. Carlos Castaneda and Lynn Andrews have written popular books on shamanistic and Native American lifestyles.

*Values & Visions*, a bi-monthly magazine devoted to the spiritual dimensions of life in books, films, and other cultural resources "for those who have embarked on a spiritual journey," discusses a variety of spiritual traditions. A recent issue has information on the following books: *Buffalo Woman Comes Singing* by Brooke Medicine Eagle "presents a fine blend of Native American and New Age spirituality." *The Sacred Hoop: Recovering the Feminine in American Indian Traditions* by Paula Gunn Allen "examines the religions and mythic concepts at the heart of Native American culture with a focus on the often ignored female tradition." *Secret Native American Pathways: A Guide to Inner Peace* by Thomas E. Mails "outlines spiritual practices of the Hopi, the Cherokee, the Apache, and the Sioux along with ideas on how these ancient power sources can be adapted into contemporary rituals."[34] As mentioned earlier, many Native Americans are quite upset by the monetary profit many are making from books, tapes, and seminars on such subjects. However, many in the eclectic Neo-Paganism of the New Age are genuinely concerned to spread the wisdom of the ancients and the spirit world, convinced that such wisdom provides the answers in one's spiritual search to find life's meaning and purpose.

## The Size of the Neo-Pagan Movement

How widespread are the practices that come under the broad heading of Neo-Paganism? How many are involved in some way in this branch of the NAM? The answers are not easily determined. Membership statistics on Wiccan covens, witchcraft organizations,

Native American spiritual organizations, and the like are generally not available. J. Gordon Melton's *Encyclopedia of American Religions* includes a subheading for "Witchcraft and Neo-Paganism." More than 25 active groups are identified along with many defunct groups. In almost all cases membership is not reported.[35] Furthermore, there are no major central organizations supervising the branches of Neo-Paganism as is the case with Christian denominations. Neo-Paganism, especially among its active witchcraft practitioners, emphasizes autonomy.

Numbers of Neo-Paganism adherents are also difficult to determine because many practice witchcraft rituals privately due to the stigma attached to admitting that one is a witch. Hence membership estimates vary widely. Margot Adler, who has much knowledge about and contact with the Neo-Pagan movement, writes, "Since the Craft is so decentralized, since each coven is autonomous, there is no way to compile accurate statistics." She notes the spontaneous creation of new covens by those who do nothing more than read a book or two and then gather together a few friends of similar persuasion to begin a coven that has no contact with other covens or witchcraft publications and therefore remains statistically uncounted. "Probably no more than ten thousand people in the United States identify with the broad Neo-Pagan phenomenon, its journals and newsletters, its covens, groves, and groups. But many other groups and individuals may exist without such links."[36]

Though Adler's numbers are revised in the second edition of her book, they are based on mid-1980s information. Furthermore, her reference is exclusively to the Wiccan branch of Neo-Paganism. The list should include the Norse, Druid, and Egyptian religion-based groups, women's spirituality organizations that are not necessarily oriented toward practicing witchcraft, and the revival of interest in Native American rituals. Again without reference to the latter two categories the *New Age Encyclopedia*, published in 1990, uses the circulation of national periodicals, sales of specialized books, and attendance at national festivals to arrive at numbers "between 1000 and 5000 covens, whose members (numbering in the tens of thousands) serve as clergy for the overall movement which has perhaps several hundred thousand members."[37]

Ultimately, the current number of participants is not of major importance. What is of concern is that "witchcraft [also other branches of Neo-Paganism] is growing at a steady pace, and unless something drastic happens to reverse the spiritual climate in America and the trend toward occultism, the witchcraft community will become an even more significant minority—a sobering possibility the church cannot afford to ignore."[38]

Perhaps an even greater concern than mere numbers is the growing proportion of individuals with a Christian background who are leaving biblical teachings in order to celebrate nature and the religion of the Goddess. Margot Adler stresses that few are "converts" to Neo-Paganism in the traditional sense of active recruitment or proselytizing on the part of Neo-Pagan groups. She describes how she personally became a witch after having been "brought up in a family of agnostics and atheists." However, she also recounts how Allison Harlow, on a Christmas Eve following the celebration of the midnight mass, climbed a hill behind the church to look at the full moon. In this environment she experienced a "presence" that seemed "very ancient and wise and definitely female." After that "experience" Harlow knew she had to find out more about this "presence" and has now become a priestess in her own self-created Wiccan tradition.[39]

Unfortunately, while Neo-Pagan groups may not actively recruit, many people are following the path of Allison Harlow. They offer a variety of excuses—Christian dogma is too stuffy, the church is too limiting of human freedom, it preaches too much about sin and guilt, its teaching that man is to have dominion over the earth has promoted the "rape" of the earth. They leave the church to practice the Goddess religion and rituals. My office files contain numerous articles about people who were raised in the Christian faith, some in "conservative Christian homes," but who are now practicing some form of Neo-Paganism.

Others are rejecting the Christian faith without seriously considering its teachings and in their spiritual search have opted for Neo-Pagan practices. Margot Adler summarizes in six categories the reasons that Pagans and Witches have given for their choice of religion. One category is freedom: "Many people said that they had become Pagans because they could be themselves and act as they chose, without what they felt were medieval notions of sin and guilt. Others wanted to participate in rituals rather than observe them."[40]

To be sure, Christians have failed to communicate the real essence of Christianity as they should. Modern churches have shown a lack of spirituality, a loss of the mystery of God, and a dead formalism that not only leaves a bad impression on non-Christians but may even suggest that Christians do not mean what they say. But this is clearly nothing more than an excuse. We have here simply the age-old problem of the creature not wanting to submit to the Creator. Ever since Eden mankind has wanted a religion without demands (Gen. 4:9), that allows the individual to create God (or gods and goddesses) in man's image (Ex. 32:4; Rom. 1:23), and that permits the individual to define truth (reality) in his or her own terms rather than on the basis of God's revealed word (Rom. 1:18, 25). As a result, instead of knowing true freedom in Jesus Christ (John 8:31–32) and freedom from the condemnation of the law "because through Christ Jesus the law of the Spirit of life set me free from the law of sin and death," (Rom. 8:1–2), practitioners of Neo-Paganism remain enslaved to a false freedom: "if it harm none, do as you will." Blinded by the father of lies, the Neo-Pagan lives in a self-created, imaginary world without sin. This is self-deception and contrary to God's revealed truth (1 John 1:8).

Obviously, since Neo-Pagans do not accept biblical teachings, their beliefs and practices are incompatible with the Bible. The occult practices associated with Neo-Paganism are clearly condemned in the Scriptures (Deut. 18:10–12; 2 Kings 21:1–6; Acts 13:6–10). The Bible explicitly condemns the worship of gods and goddesses (Judges 2:10–14; 1 Sam. 7:3–4) while also making clear that there is only one true God who is to be worshipped and served (Deut. 6:4, 13; Mark 12:29–31). Craig Hawkins writes,

> Some witches have actually tried to reconcile the above passages and others with their own practices. Nonetheless, the Bible—particularly in the original languages—renders any such maneuvering futile. We therefore ask that witches at least acknowledge that the Bible in no sense condones their practices, but rather expressly condemns them.[41]

The church needs to reach out in love to the growing number involved in some aspect of Neo-Paganism so that they may come to know "the Truth" that makes them free, a concern that we will address in chapter 12.

6

# New Age Environmentalism

**Item:** Ed McGaa, Eagle Man, is the author of *Mother Earth Spirituality: Native American Paths to Healing Ourselves and Our World.* The book explains "seven Mother Earth ceremonies including the peace pipe ceremony, the sweat lodge ceremony, the giveaway, and the vision quest, pointing out their lessons for Indians and non-Indians alike. McGaa hopes that Native American spirituality will encourage new warriors in the environmental movement to heal the planet."[1]

**Item:** A flyer from a New Age bookstore in Sedona, Arizona, promotes the services of Rev. Seana Featheringill, a Universalist minister, and Bruce Kellogg, an "empathic spiritual healer." The flyer describes their work as follows: "We have pioneered the earth healing and the volunteer healing meetings, working together, in a circle of love, united, with a pillar of light, channeling life force from spirit, to critical and terminal cases, including long distance projections and healing for our earth mother."

**Item:** The July 20, 1992, issue of *Christianity Today* reported on the Earth Summit held in Rio de Janeiro. At the Global Forum, the nongovernmental portion of the Summit, some evangelicals presented a Christian view of environmental issues. Generally, however, the Christian presence was overwhelmed by numerous feminist, universalist and monist groups. These groups argued that the old paradigm that had been shaped by patriarchy, capitalism, theism, and Christianity must be replaced by a new religious paradigm. In fact many blamed the "old paradigm" for the environment's destruction.[2]

**Item:** In the Sierra Club Environmental Health Sourcebook, *Well Body, Well Earth* by Mike Samuels and Hal Zina Bennett, emphasis is placed on individuals developing a sense of spiritual connectedness with the earth. The practice of visualization is emphasized as a means of doing so. Reference is made to ancient Greece where "[When] people wanted help in solving difficult problems, they consulted the Oracle at Delphi. [There] the priests acknowledged a spirit of the living Earth for which the Greek name was Gaea." The priestesses of Gaea were trained in the art of visualization and utilized the technique of visualizing a consultation with Gaea to provide an answer. Samuels and Bennett later wrote, "The visualization exercises we describe here are intended to help people focus on the concept of the living Earth . . . . to help us get in touch with our planet . . . ."[3]

**Item:** The *Watchman Expositor* reported on 1992 Earth Day observance plans as recorded in an article in the January/February, 1992, issue of *New Age Journal*. According to the article, Earth Day International hoped to use Earth Day to demonstrate that "saving the planet is a burning issue." The 1992 Earth Day observance was to include the lighting of traditional sacred fires in six Celtic regions. The plan to do this was the idea of Sorcha McEwan, director of Indigenous Programs at Earth Day International, who hoped that the first fire would be lit "at Kildare in Ireland at a site where a sacred fire to the Earth Mother burned for thousands of years before being extinguished by Christian church authorities."[4]

Personifying the Earth and viewing her as "the Earth Mother" or as a goddess whose name is Gaia has become a popular New Age theme. In 1981 in their *Wellness Workbook*, Regina Ryan and John Travis wrote, "The recent upsurge of volcanic action, earthquakes and unusual weather patterns may well be messages from Gaia, calling us to pay attention to her needs. If we continue to ignore her communications, there may be even harsher outbursts as Gaia is forced to take more drastic action to regain balance."[5]

Fueling the ecological theme within the NAM is the increasing Neo-Pagan/New Age connection discussed in chapter 5. The revival of both witchcraft and Native American spirituality has contributed greatly to the New Age focus on the environment. In her book Margot Adler gives an account of a 1976 interview with a modern witch, Sharon Devlin, who responds to a question about the relationship of paganism and witchcraft to the ecology movement by saying, "Paganism is the spirituality of the ecological movement."[6]

However, involvement in the concerns of the environmental

movement is not limited to individuals and groups associated with Neo-Paganism and the New Age. Humanists and both liberal and conservative Christians, along with many others of no particular religious persuasion, are demonstrating concern over the destruction of the environment. That the destruction of the environment has become a serious problem is not debatable. What is debated is the root cause for such destruction and the proper approach for correcting it.

The growing concern about the environment is sometimes referred to as the Green Movement, a network of groups and individuals who share a desire to correct environmental abuse. Three broad categories in the Green Movement can be identified. One category includes groups such as The Audubon Society and the National Wildlife Federation that focus on what has been traditionally known as conservation. Many Christians are active members of such organizations. A second category includes the more socially and politically active organizations such as Greenpeace and Earth First. The third category includes those who have added a deep spiritual dimension to ecological concerns. For them the earth is a self-sustaining organism who alone has power within herself to overcome environmental pollution. Built upon the Gaia hypothesis, those who subscribe to a spiritual environmentalism are called deep ecologists.

There is no precise dividing line between these three categories. Some conservationists see a need for political action. Some who are politically active are becoming more accepting of the spiritual themes of deep ecology. As a result, an organization like the National Wildlife Federation has formed a partnership with John Denver's Windstar Foundation to train teachers in both New Age philosophy and practical ecology.[7]

## Christianity Is Blamed

While those in the Green Movement may differ as to how to heal mother earth, most agree that the Judeo-Christian tradition that man is to have dominion over the earth is the primary cause for the environmental crisis. This is the view especially of those who are spiritually involved, particularly Neo-Pagans. "From Druid Witchcraft to Tibetan Shamanism, a religious pluralism rides the great hydra of modern environmentalism. This is the spiritual side of the ecology movement, and it is increasingly shrill about the bad stewardship of 'Christian' civilization."[8]

Many trace the impetus for the modern environmental movement to the publication of Rachel Carson's *Silent Spring* in 1962, which highlights environmental pollution and the dangers of nuclear fallout. However, the accusation that Christian theology is the chief culprit can be traced to a paper by historian Lynn White, Jr., presented to the American Association for the Advancement of Science, "The Historic Roots of Our Ecological Crisis," published in *Science* magazine in March, 1967. White contended that "Christianity is the most anthropocentric religion the world has ever seen" and that Christianity "also insisted that it is God's will that man exploit nature for his proper ends."[9]

John B. Cobb, Jr., feels that White's intent was not so much accusatory as it was a call "for a profound reform within Western Christianity, appealing to other resources within its rich and complex tradition."[10] He points out that White does not even consider the command to have dominion in Genesis 1:28. Instead, as the above quotation from White's paper indicates, he names the anthropocentrism of the Bible that has historically shaped Western Christianity's view of creation as having the sole purpose to serve the needs of man. However, Cobb would agree with Loren Wilkinson who writes, "Lynn White's case against Christendom (valid or not) has become conventional wisdom in the environmental movement, and Christians continue to discover—and try to refute—its argument."[11]

## Confronting the Reality of the Problem

In spite of conflicting reports and opinions of environmental experts, enough hard evidence shows that environmental pollution has become a serious threat to life on earth. The atmospheric concentration of carbon dioxide has increased 25 percent during the past century. Acid rain continues to destroy forests and lakes. Dozens of plant and animal species become extinct every month. The world's oceans, a major link in the chain of the world's food supply, are becoming contaminated with fertilizers, pesticides and industrial wastes. Serious environmental problems do exist. We dare not bury our heads in the sand in the hope that the problems will disappear.

Yet it is also important to distinguish between genuine ecological concerns and those created by politicians, the media, and those who have a particular social agenda. In 1992 the Spiritual Counterfeits Project organization devoted an entire issue of its *SCP Journal* to the environment. In a very insightful article Tal Brooke refers to the Club of Rome's 1972 publication *Limits to Growth*. The doomsday scenario of this publication was based on the computer models of MIT professor and Club of Rome member, Jay Forrester. This report predicted that by the 1980s and 1990s the earth would be depleted of its minerals and ores and that overpopulation would threaten the very existence of life. Pointing out that none of Forrester's predictions have materialized, Brooke writes, "We face the challenge of dividing *actual* environmental crises from *contrived* crises (formulated to alarm the public?)."[12] He further suggests that, given the elimination of the cold war as a tool to motivate a unifying of peoples and nations against a common enemy, *genuine* ecological concerns are being magnified out of all proportion to reality in order to manipulate people into surrendering their freedoms in the common cause of combating the new enemy, the life-destroying pollution of the earth.

The ultimate goal of such manipulation of the ecological crisis, says Brooke, is very possibly the desire on the part of the movers and shakers of the world to introduce a whole new social order. What is needed is a collective villain, such as "the Christian world view in league with Western Civilization and Capitalism," upon whom to place the blame for earth crimes. Brooke writes,

> The advantage of a guilty *collective* villain is that its accusers can recommend broad scale remedies to end the problem, such as, societal restructuring and social reform. Once they have won this mandate, then history books, textbooks, newspaper reports, television shows, documentaries, movies, and historical novels, will have the sanction to openly declare who has caused the problem. The past can now be reinterpreted. [Is this why the media concentrates on some eco-criminals and downplays others?][13]

Brooke readily acknowledges the serious pollution problems and that the entire human race, including Christians, "since leaving

Eden" shares the collective blame for the earth's ecological woes. However, he also writes,

> If pollution is evil enough in itself, an even greater evil would be to use this legitimate problem to barter a program of social change that would not solve the problem of pollution after all but would instead enforce an anti-Christian program which would further erase God while polluting the souls of the collective.[14]

## The Earth Summit

Because of the recognized seriousness of environmental concerns, the Earth Summit (the United Nations Conference on Environment and Development) was held in Rio de Janeiro in the summer of 1992. The stated purpose was for representatives of the world's nations to reach agreement on the implementation of policies to reduce environmental pollution. In the judgment of many observers, the results of the Earth Summit were not very favorable. If anything, it was an exercise in futility, demonstrating the truly selfish nature of men and nations. In the *Christianity Today* article about the Earth Summit and its Global Forum for nongovernmental entities, Loren Wilkinson writes, "The Earth Summit in Rio de Janeiro may or may not go down in history as a turning point in humankind's treatment of planet Earth. But it quite likely will stand as the first celebration of a new synthesis of world religions." Concerning the Global Forum Wilkinson says,

> The majority of the talk there, however, sounded more like vague pantheism than Christianity. An all-night vigil held there on June 4 opened with "invocations of the sacred" by some 30 religions, and concluded with an address by the Dali Lama and a Hare Krishna mantra. On another occasion, a large contingent from the United Church of Christ joined with members of several other religions in a demonstration, which opened with the singing of the hymn "Were You There When They Crucified My Lord?"— substituting the word *Earth* for *Lord*.[15]

A "synthesis of world religions"; "vague pantheism"; "crucified my Earth"? With its religious syncretism and pantheistic themes, the Earth Summit successfully promoted devotion to the Earth as the mother goddess of the New Age.

# Earth in the Balance

Present at the Earth Summit as the head of the U. S. Senate delegation was Vice-President Albert Gore, at that time still a senator. He asserted his Christian commitment and his personal belief that the earth was God's creation which God had entrusted to human care. However, in his book *Earth in the Balance*, Vice-President Gore displays an affinity for New Age terminology. He speaks about the human race having lost its "feeling of connectedness to the rest of nature." He joins deep ecologists in identifying the human problem as viewing the resources of the earth "having an intrinsic value no larger than their usefulness at the moment."[16] Of course, using New Age phraseology does not automatically place one in the category of a New Ager.

In the issue of the *SCP Journal* that is devoted entirely to the subject of ecology, Douglas Groothuis provides an enlightening critique of *Earth in the Balance*. Space here does not permit an extensive review of Groothuis' critique, but several interesting observations can be noted. While admitting that Vice-President Gore correctly highlights ecological problems that should be addressed, Groothuis also points out that Gore offers little scholarly evidence to support his claims about certain environmental concerns that need emergency governmental action. However, the main focus of the critique is on the relationship between the Vice-President's professed Christianity and his statements and proposals regarding solutions to healing the earth. While frequently speaking about God as the creator, Gore's book also contains many statements indicating that he "accepts macro-evolutionary theory without batting a skeptical eyelash and posits global climactic changes as essential to human evolution. . . . So it seems that Gore is a theistic evolutionist: God created the raw materials which evolved through natural processes over eons of time."[17] Man's evolving nature is a key component of New Age thinking. Perhaps Gore picked up this concept from books by New Ager Fritjof Capra and atheist scientist/astronomer Carl Sagan listed in the bibliography of Gore's book, *Earth in the Balance*.

Groothuis identifies other New Age leanings in *Earth in the Balance*. On two occasions Gore uses the New Age pedagogical device—the hologram—to extend the image of God from mankind in particular to creation in general. By extending the image of God to all creation, Gore's holographic theology devalues humanity as the crown of God's creation while falsely exalting the nonhuman creation.

Yet one other concern with Vice-President Gore's book touches directly upon the New Age themes found in the environmental movement. Groothuis notes that Gore's theology finds ecological principles in all the world's religions to which even a Christian can supposedly subscribe. In a chapter titled "Environmentalism of the Spirit," Gore writes,

> The richness and diversity of our religious tradition throughout history is a spiritual resource long ignored by people of faith, who are often afraid to open their minds to teachings *first offered outside their own system of belief*. But the emergence of a civilization in which knowledge moves freely ... has spurred a renewed investigation of the *wisdom distilled by all faiths. This panreligious perspective* may prove especially important where our responsibility for the earth is concerned [emphasis added].[18]

Gore continues by pointing out the earth-honoring "wisdom" in American Indian spirituality, Hinduism, Buddhism, Islam, and the Baha'i faith. He gives credence to anthropological studies which strive to show that in prehistoric Europe the prevailing spirituality centered around the worship of a "single earth goddess" in a religion whose basic tenet was a reverence for the sacredness of the earth. It was Christianity, says Gore, that in the 15th century eliminated the last vestiges of organized goddess worship. Regarding this ancient religious practice Gore writes, "[I]t seems obvious that a better understanding of a religious heritage preceding our own could offer us new insights into the nature of the human experience."[19]

Regarding this syncretistic New Age tendency Douglas Groothuis correctly observes,

> It is one thing to recognize some truth outside of one's religion if that truth agrees with the central tenets of one's religion. It is something else entirely to recognize truths that conflict with one's own tradition; in that case one has betrayed the faith. ... Gore cannot simultaneously appreciate a pantheistic goddess religion and also conserve the Christian view of a personal God who is transcendent over the creation. By accepting the primeval goddess

theories, Gore cuts his own theological throat—that is, if he adheres to classical Christian theism.[20]

## The Gaia Hypothesis

Many New Age themes regarding solutions to environmental problems come together in the Gaia hypothesis, the belief that all life on planet Earth and the earth itself constitutes a living organism. While humanity is viewed as the nervous system of the planet, nevertheless all life is of equal value. The Gaia hypothesis, named after the earth goddess of the ancient Greeks, has become an influential scientific theory and for many a spiritual idea. Tod Connor writes,

> Gaia is the New Age darling of spiritual feminists, neo-pagans, political environmentalists, and animal-rights activists. Yet in the past three years, more that 100 *scientific* and *technical* articles have been written on the Gaia theory. Gaia, the Greek earth goddess, has scientists hotly debating the reality of her existence.[21]

James Lovelock, an atmospheric biochemist, is most responsible for developing the Gaia hypothesis. In a 1972 article, "Gaia as Seen Through the Atmosphere," and in a second article, "A Quest for Gaia," Lovelock brought the Gaia hypothesis to the attention of the scientific community. His 1979 book, *Gaia: A New Look at Life on Earth*, further promoted the hypothesis: "[T]he entire range of living matter on Earth, from whales to viruses, and from oaks to algae, may be regarded as constituting a single living entity, capable of manipulating the Earth's atmosphere to suit its overall needs and endowed with faculties and powers far beyond its constituent parts."[22] The Gaia hypothesis proposes that the earth itself shapes the environment to suit its own needs. (Whether intentional or not, Vice-President Gore uses Gaia language when writing about "the global process by which the earth regulates the amount of ultraviolet radiation from the sun that is allowed through the atmosphere to the surface."[23])

Central to Lovelock's original hypothesis is the idea of a Gaian mind, the intelligence and consciousness that controls the Earth's geophysical and biological processes. His theory emphasizes the unlikelihood of the Earth evolving by random and purposeless processes. However, in order to find acceptance in the scientific community, Lovelock had to revise his theory so as to remove any implied purpose or intelligence behind the development of life on planet Earth. A second book, *The Ages of Gaia*, substituted mathematical formulas and computer simulated models for the guiding intelligence of the Gaian mind.

While Lovelock's revised theory has been accepted by many in the scientific community, the spiritual implications of the original hypothesis have been overwhelmingly accepted by those who endorse the New Age philosophy. In his article in a 1991 *SCP Journal,* Stuart Chevre writes,

> The New Age Movement is quickly incorporating Gaia worship into its system of spiritual beliefs and practices. The feminist and ecologically based spiritualities (witchcraft, goddess worship, ecofeminism, paganism and other earth worship groups) have become strong supporters of the mystical quasi-religious Gaia. Earth spirituality, in particular, is quickly becoming equated with Gaia worship, to the applause of most New Age leaders.[24]

Although his second book revised the hypothesis in order to find greater acceptance by the scientific community, Lovelock devoted the final chapter of that book to the spiritual inferences of the Gaia hypothesis. He was convinced (and most New Agers would concur) that the Judeo-Christian worldview destroyed the goddess oriented culture of pre-Christian Europe and is responsible for our present ecological woes. He believed that we need to return to ancient forms of goddess and nature spirituality.

## Deep Ecology

Another theme of the environmental movement that clearly expresses the monistic/pantheistic themes of the New Age is "deep ecology." In one of his books, *The Turning Point*, New Ager Fritjof Capra advocates deep ecology which, he says, is to be based on the mystical religious philosophy of Taoism. Capra claims that the best expression of the spirituality of deep ecology is in the goddess worship of radical feminism. Ecofeminism will be discussed later. Now we turn our attention to gaining a better understanding of deep ecology, one of the most extreme of the Gaia-based ideologies.

The phrase *deep ecology* can be traced to the early 1970s and the Norwegian philosopher Arne Naess who coined the terms *shallow* and *deep* ecology. Shallow ecology is described as a narrowly focused, anthropocentric, short-term approach to ecological problems. Deep ecology is focused on the big picture, ecocentric, and long-range in its approach. In these distinctions, the primary focus is on anthropocentric versus ecocentric. Deep ecologists view the shallow, anthropocentric approach as the old paradigm that seeks solutions to environmental problems in order to serve primarily the needs of the human race. Included in this old paradigm is the resource management approach, which tries to control nature so as to attain an optimum human lifestyle. Environmental (Christian) stewardship, which closely resembles resource management, adds the idea that humans have the authority given by God to control nature in order to serve a higher purpose. What is needed, deep ecologists say, is a new paradigm, one that will serve all life forms equally.[25]

Deep ecologists also distinguish between instrumental and intrinsic value theories. The instrumental value theory is that only humans have value in and of themselves. The nonhuman world has value only as an instrument to serve human needs. The intrinsic value theory is that all life forms on earth have inherent worth and value apart from any necessity of serving human need. Some have described Warwick Fox's *Toward a Transpersonal Ecology: Developing New Foundations for Environmentalism* as the best introduction to deep ecology. Fox identifies five applications of the intrinsic value theory. Two of these, ecosystem ethics and ecosphere ethics, maintain that local ecosystems and the planetary ecosphere (which some call "Gaia") are living systems that have intrinsic value.[26]

Concerning deep ecology, Fox is quoted elsewhere as saying, "It is the idea that we can make no firm ontological divide in the field of existence: That there is no bifurcation in reality between the human and the non-human realms."[27]According to deep ecology, therefore, mankind is not unique and is certainly not in the image of God any more than is the rest of creation. It also means that all distinctions are unreal and that there is a great oneness of being that encompasses everything from God to humans to plants to animals. This great insight of deep ecology sounds much like the monistic/pantheistic "oneness" of the New Age.

In 1984 Arne Naess and George Sessions published eight "basic principles" of deep ecology. These include the following:

> The well-being and flourishing of human and nonhuman Life on Earth have value in themselves. . . . Richness and diversity of life forms contribute to the realization of these values and are also values in themselves. Humans have no right to reduce this richness and diversity except to satisfy *vital* needs. . . . Present human interference with the nonhuman world is excessive, and the situation is rapidly worsening. Policies must therefore be changed.[28]

These principles have led the more vocal zealots of deep ecology to develop militant forms of eco-activism such as the *animal rights* movement and the Earth First organization. Earth First threatened to blow up Arizona's Glen Canyon Dam in order to restore a free-flowing Colorado River. In 1991, Dave Foreman, cofounder of Earth First was charged along with four others with conspiracy to sabotage power lines to nuclear plants. Earth First's credo is, "No compromise in the defense of Mother Earth."

Deep ecologists are highly critical of Christian stewardship, which they mistakenly believe teaches that humans are the measure of all things, the source of all value. Surprisingly, they are also very critical of the New Age version of resource management. Nevertheless, deep ecology shares with the New Age its monistic/pantheistic worldview that leads ultimately to making "Mother Earth" the measure of all things, the goddess who demands our devotion.

## Ecofeminism

An earlier quotation in this chapter referred to feminist and ecological spiritualities such as witchcraft, goddess worship, ecofeminism and paganism. Ecofeminism is our last subject area for consideration concerning the mother goddess of New Age environmentalism. In chapter five we pointed out that while New Agers, Wiccans, and Neo-Pagans differ in some of their beliefs and practices, there are often many similarities between them, particularly in the monistic/pantheistic worldview of the New Age and in the emphasis on a return to goddess worship. Margot Adler writes,

> Most Neo-Pagans sense an aliveness and "presence" in nature. They are usually polytheists, or animists, or pantheists, or two or

three of these things at once. . . . This religious movement of people who call themselves Pagans, Neo-Pagans, and witches is only partly an "occult" phenomenon. Often it is interwoven with the visionary and artistic tradition, the ecology movement, the feminist movement, and the libertarian tradition.[29]

*Women of Power*, a journal devoted to politics, feminism, and spirituality, provides a "Statement of Philosophy" that summarizes the concepts of the women's spirituality movement and ecofeminism. It includes the following statements:

WOMEN'S SPIRITUALITY is a world-wide awakening of woman-power whose vision is the transformation of our selves and our societies. The ancient spiritual voice of woman now speaks its long-hidden wisdom and becomes an active force for the conscious evolution of our world.

This emerging voice speaks of . . .

• the recognition of the interconnectedness of all life

• the awareness that everything has consciousness and is sacred

• the remembering of our selves as sacred beings, . . .

• the creation of world peace, social justice, and environmental harmony

• the honoring of woman's divinity

• reverence for the earth, and the celebration of her seasons and cycles, and those of our lives.[30]

It is obvious that the women's spirituality movement, particularly as it is expressed in ecofeminist activities, is very much in tune with the monistic/pantheistic themes that honor planet Earth as the mother goddess of the New Age.

## Biblical Stewardship of the Earth

In an article for the March 1, 1992, issue of *Parade Magazine*, Carl Sagan wrote,

True, there is nothing in the Judeo-Christian-Muslim tradition that approaches the cherishing of nature in the Hindu-Buddhist-Jain tradition or among Native Americans. Indeed, both Western religion and Western science have gone out of their way to assert

113

that nature is just the setting and not the story, that nature should not be viewed as sacred.[31]

Certainly nature should not be viewed as sacred in the sense that all things are inherently divine and therefore deserving of our worship. The creature ever remains creature and does not share the divinity of the Creator. While God is the Creator of all that exists, he does not indwell His creation. However, neither is God the God of the Deists, a God who created this world and then totally removed himself from any involvement in it. God is both transcendent and imminent. He is a personal being who entered into his creation in the person of His Son to deal with the problem of sin that alienates the creature and all creation from their Creator (Col. 1:19–20). Yet God as Creator remains transcendent in His essential nature, majesty and power (Ps. 99:1–3; Is. 42:8).

What is needed to solve the environmental problems of our time is an implementation of biblical truth. Human beings, made in the image of God, the crown of God's creation, are separate and distinct from the rest of creation, yet we are also united to it because both mankind and the rest of nature are created by God. In this sense there is a oneness within all creation, not because it is divine in itself but because all creation shares the same source of existence, the creating power of God.

Francis Schaeffer in *Pollution and the Death of Man—the Christian View of Ecology* says it well:

> Both man and other creatures have been created by God to fit a common environment. . . . I am not overwhelmed or threatened, because I know I am made in the image of God. . . . Nature begins to look different. I am separated from it, yet related to it. . . . We should realize, and train people in our churches to realize, that on the side of creation and on the side of God's infinity and our finiteness—we really *are* one with the tree. . . . We should treat each thing with integrity because this is the way God has made it. . . . The Christian is a man who has a reason for dealing with each created thing on a high level of respect.[32]

This is the biblical truth for dealing with problems of the environment. It needs to be instilled in the people of God and imparted to all the world. To exercise dominion over God's creation in order to serve man's selfish ends is to despise the Creator who made it.

Dominion does not equal exploitation. We treat each created thing—vegetation, animals, natural resources—with a high level of respect, not because they are inherently divine, but because, together with us, they have been created by God.

If the field for solving environmental problems is not to be left to devotees of the goddess of the New Age, those who profess Christ to be Savior and Lord must step forth to provide solutions in harmony with the truth revealed in God's Word. Proposals for solving environmental problems should not be disdained simply because some who endorse such solutions do so on the basis of faulty theological suppositions. Instead, Christians need to take the lead in developing a proper relationship between the crown and the rest of God's creation that will direct people away from devotion to the Earth as the mother goddess of the New Age and to the worship of the Creator and Redeemer of all creation. What is needed is not only the teaching, but also the living of the biblical stewardship of creation. Christian preachers and teachers must clearly proclaim that God is the Owner of all creation and has simply entrusted to people the wise stewardship of all life. God's people must clearly demonstrate care and compassion for all that God has created. God-given dominion calls for care and protection so that all creation, including the earth and all stars, might join in singing to the Lord a new song (cf. Ps. 19:1–6; 96:1).

Tod Connor's article says it well: "Christians should not abandon environmental concerns because of the taint of Gaia-inspired pseudoscience. Rather, the emergence of the spiritual side of environmentalism provides us with the opportunity to offer life-giving truth to an increasingly fearful humanity."[33]

# 7

# New Age Politics/ Globalism

**Item:** A newspaper advertisement announced a citizen's forum co-sponsored by Indiana University-Purdue University at Fort Wayne, Indiana, and *The Journal-Gazette* of Fort Wayne. The title for this November 10, 1990, forum was "America's Role in the New World Order." Attached to a copy of the newspaper ad received in the mail was the following: "Fort Wayne New Agers have a recorded message hotline!!! Keep this phone number next to your telephone and call periodically for updated messages as the world approaches the New Age Millennium."

**Item:** Captain Planet, TV mogul Ted Turner's latest entry into the world of television cartoons, is a superhero assisted by a hand-picked group of young people called Planeteers. Together their goal is to save the earth from the ravages of pollution. An Earth spirit named Gaia gives each Planeteer a power ring to assist them and Captain Planet in accomplishing their earth-saving work. There is also a political agenda behind Captain Planet. At the end of a cartoon children are given an action plan to follow, often including writing to their congressman or taking some other political/social action.

**Item:** The *Religion Watch* newsletter reported a survey of editorials in the religious press following the election of Bill Clinton and concluded that "those on the liberal end of the spectrum—from New Age to mainline Protestant—tended to view the Clinton presidency as providing a second spring for exerting their influence on such concerns as environmentalism, civil liberties, feminism, gay rights, and poverty and health."[1]

**Item:** It is debatable how much the Earth Summit (see Chapter 6) will accomplish in the long term. However, some feel that one achievement that could have lasting effect was the creation of the United Nations Commission on Sustainable Development. "This body will oversee follow-through on the promises made in Rio, shining the spotlight on countries that renege and pushing through stronger commitments as necessary." The commission is to include "high-level" government representatives with decision-making power. Further, nongovernmental watchdog agencies such as Greenpeace can pursue their political agendas by alerting the commission to violations of agreements reached at Rio.[2]

Committed New Agers would be the first to admit that theirs is not a highly organized political base with the same clout as the two major political parties. Yet the combined influence of those who have identified with beliefs and social concerns of the NAM is considerable. Already several years ago Russell Chandler addressed the subject of a New Age political agenda: "Its influence on the overall political climate of the nation has so far been modest, and its aims are diverse and diffuse. But there are clear signs of growing power and consolidation as the decade of the eighties moves to a close."[3]

## The Humanistic New Age

Chapter 3 referred to the two-pronged aspect of the NAM—the occult and the humanistic. While the eclectic blends of the New Age do not always neatly fit into one or the other of these two categories, concerns such as New Age environmentalism and New Age politics are of a more humanistic bent. Perhaps we first need to clarify some of the distinguishing marks of New Age humanism before discussing the main subject of this chapter.

Two documents, *A Humanist Manifesto* (1933) and *Humanist Manifesto II* (1973), summarize the philosophy of secular humanism and show that there are many similarities but also some differences between it and New Age humanism.[4] Both believe that life today is the result of a long period of evolution. "Humanism believes that man . . . has emerged as the result of a continuous process."[5] Both elevate the self-sufficiency of mankind to godlike status. The New Age ascribes innate deity to all things including the human race. Secular humanism says, "While there is much that we do not know, humans are responsible for what we are or will become. No deity will save us; we must save ourselves."[6] Personal transformation is a foundational principle of the NAM. The humanistic New Age carries this principle to the extreme claiming that human potential is un-

117

limited. Here secular humanism is somewhat more conservative, merely urging the maximum development of human potential: "[H]umanism considers the complete realization of human personality to be the end of man's life."[7]

Perhaps in promoting a world transformation and a global community the New Age and secular humanism are most closely parallel. A global transformation that results in the peaceful coexistence of all life is the ultimate goal of the NAM. The globalism of secular humanism is expressed in these words:

> The world cannot wait for reconciliation of competing political or economic systems to solve its problems. . . . We urge that parochial loyalties and inflexible moral and religious ideologies be transcended. We urge recognition of the common humanity of all people. . . . At the present juncture of history, commitment to all humankind is the highest commitment of which we are capable. . . . What more daring a goal for humankind than for each person to become, in ideal as well as practice, a citizen of a world community.[8]

New Age humanism has many avenues for infiltrating society. The pathways of public education and holistic medicine will be considered in later chapters. In the remainder of this chapter we will consider the humanistic globalism that is at the heart of New Age politics.

## Emerging New Age Politics

In the latter half of the 1970s an increasing awareness spread among New Agers that they could be a force for social and political consciousness. In 1978 the New Age theorist Mark Satin published *New Age Politics: Healing Self and Society*. The same year marked the forming of California's New Age Caucus. Their founders wrote,

> Ten years ago or so, only the most perceptive prophet could have foreseen New Age thought leaving the incense-filled, esoteric chambers of its origin to expand dramatically all over the American scene. Ten years ago a New Age political movement would have drawn amused chuckles from established politicians. Today, however, such a movement would draw the politicians' anxious attention and respect. . . . There is an expectant feeling in the air.

New Age people are sensing that the time is super-ripe for a fresh, original, nonpartisan New Age movement.[9]

That statement was made more than 15 years ago. The NAM is still not visible as an organized political movement, but its influence is felt from the United Nations down to local grassroots environmental organizations. At the heart of New Age politics is *monism,* the One as both source and goal of all life and secondly, necessity of *transformation.* "The whole society must be brought into harmony with the One as the New Consciousness produces the New Age."[10]

The foundational principle—all is one—is balanced by the affirmation that the diversity that exists in the world enriches the ultimate unity of all things. A worldwide political system that strives to accomplish global harmony and unity in all things, while also acknowledging the interdependence of the diversity that exists at the local level, is the ideal expression of New Age politics.

How this works out in a practical way can be seen in Vice-President Al Gore's approach to the ecology issue. In the previous chapter reference was made to Tal Brooke's suggestion that, since the nonexistent cold war no longer provides a common enemy, genuine ecological concerns are being magnified out of proportion to reality in order to motivate people and nations to *unify* against a new common enemy—the pollution of the environment. In his book Vice-President Gore asserts that "we must make the rescue of the environment the central organizing principle for civilization [the global community]." He continues, "The emphasis on the rights of the individual [diversity at the local level] must be accompanied by a deeper understanding of the responsibilities to the community [unity at the global level] that every individual must accept if the community is to have an organizing principle at all."[11]

A second key principle of New Age politics is this: "The political system needs to be *transformed*, not *reformed*. We need something else, not just something more."[12] The transformation begins with the individual self achieving higher consciousness of the divinity shared with all things. Personal transformation will eventually produce social transformation. "Just as personal transformation empowers the individual by revealing an inner authority, social transformation follows a chain reaction of personal change."[13] The awareness of innate divinity gives power, and it is personal power, says Ferguson, that defines our politics. The result of social transformation will be the development of new political paradigms that will allow for a new approach to government described as *Radical Center*. Radical Center politics will not adopt an either/or position on issues but will take a holistic approach that is at the same time visionary as well as pragmatic. Ferguson writes,

> In the long run, it is the evolving Radical-Center constituency that will engender increasing numbers of candidates and elect some of them to office. This new constituency will support those who seem likely to create and conserve. It will admire them for refusing to make simplistic choices. . . . [T]he followers will help transform the leaders—those leaders who sense the shift to higher needs.[14]

According to Mark Satin, the New Age political order would root itself in radical feminism, environmentalism, Eastern philosophy, and Western psychology. It would be energized by "life-oriented" people with New Age virtues who would lead the nation into a loose confederacy of small communal villages and ultimately into planetary consciousness. "All of this would have to begin, however, with *personal* transformation. This would become, in time, a worldwide transformation once a 'critical mass' saw the New Age light."[15] Although Satin's views have moderated somewhat, personal and societal transformation remain at the heart of his and all New Age politics.

## New Age Networking

Since New Agers are not formally organized into a political party and do not have an otherwise structured political power base, how can they bring their influence to bear in any significant manner? There are several avenues open to them. Ferguson states that personal power defines our politics. Individuals combining their personal power through the forming of networks gives the NAM its basic political power base. Organized structure is not important but rather the sharing of a common ideology—the New Age worldview. "But people *can* coalesce into self-organizing groups to powerful effect. And they are devising ways to govern themselves without determining a boss or establishing a clear agenda. Such self-organizing groups are the fabric of the Aquarian Conspiracy."[16]

Ferguson cites an example of a self-organizing group that developed into a networking of ideas and shared values. A December 1978 meeting included a congressman, heads of various foundations, the head of an Ivy League college, the owner of a major league baseball team, an artist, a publisher, and several federal policymakers. A letter inviting them to this meeting indicated what these otherwise diverse people had in common.

> We tend to share a conviction that this nation, and industrialized society in general, is experiencing profound transformation. . . . We agree that at the heart of this transformation is a change in the basic social paradigm, including fundamental beliefs and values underlying the present form of the industrial economy. In our own positions in government, business, education, or professional life, we sense a deep need for the society to find its spiritual moorings, its sense of destiny, of right direction.[17]

Ferguson indicates that as a result of this meeting linkages were formed and joint projects planned. Several participants set up an international foundation for peace and presented seminars on the new consciousness for generals at the U. S. Army War College. Those who lived within convenient distance of each other began to share their connections and enlarge their networks. "The congressman enlisted the aid of the participants in his effort to obtain testimony and funding for research into altered states of consciousness."[18]

This example of a self-organizing group and network illustrates the basic operating method of the NAM. It also demonstrates the central importance of social transformation in the New Age ideology along with its spiritual and occult roots—"society to find its spiritual moorings . . . research into altered states of consciousness." Without using the term "networking" Elliot Miller sums up how the networking pattern develops in terms of New Age politics.

> Basic New Age *presuppositions* and *spiritual experience* give rise to a particular set of *shared values*, which engender corresponding *social concerns*. Depending on temperament and interests, individual New Agers identify with one or two of many possible causes consistent with their values. This motivates them to commit to *social and political action* in their areas of concern, which eventually necessitates forming *alliances* for greater political clout with others in different but compatible fields. As a result these

121

assorted causes coalesce into a single political *platform* and *agenda*.[19]

Networking also allows for a balancing of both local diversity and global unity as key principles of New Age politics. Networks can maintain local independence while fostering an ever growing sense of global interdependence. "You don't have to choose between involvement on a community or global scale; you can have both. Networks are the strategy by which small groups can transform an entire society."[20]

## Green Politics

For some, Green Politics is synonymous with New Age Politics. As noted above, the specturm of New Age politics is much broader than merely environmental concerns, but the Green Movement has been a major focus of New Age political activism. As previously stated, Vice-President Gore wants to make the saving of the environment the central organizing principle of civilization. Organizations such as Greenpeace strive to arouse national concern about the environment.

On March 6, 1983, the new Green Party in West Germany surprised the world by winning two million votes in the national elections and gaining 27 seats in the West German parliament. Built on a platform of peace, social justice, and ecological responsibility, the party emphasized ecological, feminist, antinuclear, and peace issues—an agenda that obviously includes far more than ecology. "Other political fallout from New Age ecology includes advocacy of zero population growth, sexual freedom, abortion, and the use of solar, rather than fossil, fuels."[21]

The Green Movement is hindered by its New Age insistence on harmony and almost unanimous consensus before any substantive action is taken and by introducing New Age spirituality, which has caused division in both the European and American expressions of the movement. Some atheist Greens feel that religion has no place in the movement. Yet, a nationwide meeting of American Greens adopted a spirituality plank by a 78 percent vote. "The draft of the spirituality plank was drawn up by a United Methodist minister, a Catholic, a Quaker, an atheist, a Pagan, a Buddhist, a Hindu and a Native American."[22]

122

In 1984, Fritjof Capra and Charlene Spretnak co-authored *Green Politics: The Global Promise*. They analyzed the Green political movement and pleaded for the development of the Green movement in this country, insisting that the Green movement here needed to develop from "a deep understanding of the essential oneness of all beings."[23] Capra and Spretnak also wrote "Who Are the Greens?" for the April 1984, issue of *New Age* magazine. In it they wrote, "The emphasis on relations and interconnections—in Gregory Bateson's words, 'the pattern which connects the crab to the lobster and the orchid to the primrose and all four of them to me'—is the foundation of Green thought and being."[24] Perhaps Capra and Spretnak will see their vision come true. The September 6, 1992, edition of the *St. Louis Post-Dispatch*, reporting on the large number of candidates that would be on the Missouri ballot in November, commented that two were Green Party candidates, one running for the Missouri House and one for Congress.

## New Age Political Action Groups

New Agers have formed a variety of networking organizations to promote their political goals. Organizations, such as Planetary Citizens, World Goodwill, Lucis Trust, and Beyond War, have an agenda similar to that of the Green Movement with a focus on human rights, population control, nuclear disarmament, and ecology.

Planetary Citizens was founded in 1972 by Donald Keys, former consultant to the United Nations. Membership has included New Agers such as David Spangler, William Irwin Thompson, former astronaut Edgar Mitchell, and Michael Murphy of the Esalen Institute. Keys feels that humanity is on the verge of evolving toward a new consciousness that will lead the way to planetization with the United Nations in the forefront of such an achievement.

In 1982 Planetary Citizens and several other like-minded organizations promoted a consciousness-raising gathering called Planetary Initiative for the World We Choose. This in turn led to a June 1983 Planetary Congress. "Nearly five hundred people, including New Age notables Barbara Marx Hubbard and Ram Dass, met with people from twenty countries during the four-day event." The gathering produced a document that "reveals its New Age orientation on ecology, economics, politics, and other topics. It also affirms the pivotal need to achieve 'the individual human potential and . . . the essential spiritual identity of each person, giving rise to a oneness with all life.' "[25]

Another New Age political organization, World Goodwill, is headquartered on United Nations Plaza as was Planetary Citizens before its relocation to California several years ago. World Goodwill is sponsored by the Lucis Trust, an occult organization that developed when Alice Bailey broke away from the Theosophical Society (chapter 2). World Goodwill is committed to work "the Plan" for a new world government and religion as outlined in the teachings of Bailey, who said the concept of the plan was telepathically received from Djwhal Khul, a Tibetan master. The plan would be fulfilled when "the Christ" reappeared. This Christ is not the Jesus of Scripture but a highly evolved ascended master.

New Agers like Donald Keys, Alice Bailey, and Benjamin Creme (who has announced the coming of Bailey's Christ figure, the Maitreya)—all support the idea of a world leader who will establish a one-world government. In this they differ substantially from people like Mark Satin, Marilyn Ferguson, and Barbara Marx Hubbard, who promote a unified world order while also calling for decentralized government. Yet all would agree that a major transformation of society built upon the enlightened transformation of individuals is needed if the human race is to save itself and the planet.

Beyond War is another New Age oriented organization that has made the establishment of peace a major part of its agenda. It claims about 10,000 members. It does not outline specific steps for achieving world peace. "Beyond War explains that details matter less than conviction, and that once 20 percent of any group believes in something, such as peace, the idea is 'unstoppable.' "[26]

In addition to politically active organizations, the New Age finds support in the liberal elements of traditional American politics. Douglas Groothuis refers to former California governor Jerry Brown as having New Age leanings and provides the reminder that in 1984 Barbara Marx Hubbard campaigned for the vice-presidency. He also refers to the Congressional Clearinghouse on the Future as having a heavy New Age influence. This congressional caucus keeps politicians informed about futures research and also "organizes lectures and dialogs with such New Age activists as Fritjof Capra, Hasel Henderson, Marilyn Ferguson, Jeremy Rifkin and John Naisbett, thus providing a governmentally sponsored forum for New Age approaches."[27]

Marilyn Ferguson also identifies New Age influence among more traditional politicians and government agencies. In 1976 a coalition of California state legislators, Congressmen, and citizens formed an organization called Self Determination. An invitation to join stated, "Self Determination proposes a practical and powerful alternative to cynicism: changing both ourselves and society by transforming the most basic myth by which we live—our assumptions about our nature and potential."[28] Ferguson describes the work of California state assemblyman John Vasconcellos, who was instrumental in developing legislation to humanize education and medicine. She quotes a public statement by Vasconcellos: "We need to see to it that our institutions, including government, become peopled by those who share our struggle, our vision about this human transformation."[29]

Ferguson writes about an "Aquarian Conspirator" at the cabinet level of United States government who set up human development seminars for government staff. She also states that various research projects in such New Age areas as meditation, biofeedback, psychic phenomena, and alternative medical approaches have been funded by the Department of Defense. "Political aikido, the power that comes from turning a potential opponent's energy to one's own advantage, can include the use of government funds, even defense grants, for humanistically oriented research and pilot projects."[30]

## The Role of the United Nations

Networking, Green politics, New Age political action groups, politicians, and government agencies are some of the diverse means by which the New Age political philosophy is influencing society. But what about the global level? For many New Agers the United Nations is the organization to coordinate a world transformation leading to global unity. This is especially true of New Agers who, like Donald Keys, place their hopes in a one world central government.

While Vice-President Gore expresses some New Age leanings in his book and calls for a "Global Marshall Plan," he acknowledges that a world government or some other supranational authority is both a political and a practical impossibility. Although skeptical about how much the United Nations can do, he feels that it has a role to play, at least concerning environmental matters. "Specifically, to help monitor the evolution of a global agreement, the United Nations might consider the idea of establishing a Stewardship Council to deal with matters relating to the global environment. . . . Such a forum could be increasingly useful and even necessary as the full extent of the environmental crisis unfolds."[31]

As indicated, some in the NAM view the United Nations as a world savior. Robert Muller, a retired United Nations Assistant Secretary General, believes that the UN will be an important catalyst for global transformation. Not only does he wish to see the globalism of a one-world government develop, but he strongly supports both global spirituality and global education. More will be mentioned in chapter 8 about his "World Core Curriculum" now being used in many public school classrooms across the country. With regard to the United Nations, Muller "recommends that it become the planet's central statistical office and data bank and be strengthened regionally, bringing each continent to bear its full contribution and role in the total world order."[32]

## Globalism and Planetization

What makes the United Nations so attractive to many New Agers is that it was founded on the principles of globalism. In turn, globalism is founded upon planetary consciousness or planetization. Planetary consciousness "is a worldview that emphasizes loyalty to the community of humanity rather than local loyalties to nation, tribe, or other social groupings."[33] National boundaries are to be eclipsed in concern for the good of the "global village" of mankind. Leaders of nations who want to retain power and control obviously would resist such a worldview. For planetization to be accepted, popular support must be garnered. The NAM is actively working toward that goal of personal transformation.

Globalism is not just a cause of New Agers. Secular humanists also strongly support it. Already in 1973, committed humanists stated,

We deplore the division of humankind on nationalistic grounds.

We have reached a turning point in human history where the best option is to *transcend the limits of national sovereignty* and move toward the building of a world community in which all sectors of the human family can participate [emphasis in original].[34]

## The Implications of New Age Politics for Christianity

The central doctrine of monism coupled with the need for personal and social transformation provides a foundation upon which New Agers can build their networks for globalization—a world unity (a one world government in the minds of some) in which peace and harmony will reign.

Christians certainly can support some ideas of New Age politics—environmental concerns, world peace, improving the lot of the impoverished, nuclear arms control, and others. But Christians are concerned about the spiritual roots of New Age politics as well as the effect of planetary consciousness on the freedom of religion.

When the drafters of a spirituality plank for a social and political movement (American Greens) include individuals who practice the philosophies of Eastern mysticism and Neo-Paganism, the result cannot be one that will honor a transcendent Creator and imminent Redeemer of all life. The planetary-consciousness worldview is open to learning from other historic pre-existing cultures and worldviews. Yet David Spangler indicates that "adherents to this worldview acknowledge that no single human path can contain all of God's possibilities and truths."[35] Precisely at this point Christianity's claim to the exclusive and full truth of God first becomes a "stone of stumbling"—concerning the nature of God and of man, the present purpose and future end of man, how man is to live in relation to the rest of creation, the morality by which man is to live, and the full revelation of God in Jesus the Christ—and second, becomes a "stone of stumbling" and sets it in opposition to a New Age, one-world order that includes a global spirituality.

Tal Brooke points out that the 36th General Assembly of the United Nations in 1981 adopted a resolution, "The Declaration on the Elimination of All Forms of Intolerance and of Discrimination Based on Religion or Belief." It said that no one is to be subject to coercion (read *evangelism*) which would restrict freedom of choice when it comes to religious beliefs. Section 3 of Article 1 states, "Freedom to manifest one's religion or belief may be subject only to such limitations as are prescribed by law and are necessary to protect public safety, order, health, or morals or the fundamental rights and freedoms of others."[36]

Under such guidelines, presumably, Christianity could be freely practiced. However, the New Age world order tolerates only those religious beliefs that make no exclusive claim to the truth. Intolerance toward the Christian faith and its moral values is already obvious in the media and among the liberal elements of society, and is increasingly felt in various parts of the world. Tal Brooke describes a goal of the New Age concerning religion:

> If Western countries are going to initiate globalism, they need to set the precedent for a new unitive generic religion, since religion itself is an enormous factor in creating lines of demarcation and thus preventing transnational unity from happening. Therefore, a new type of spirituality is needed: one that disavows the old order, one that can synthesize the beliefs of both East and West.[37]

Christians daily strive to live their faith. We live responsibly concerning the environment; we minister to the poor and needy; we seek to promote peace in our local community, in our nation, and in our world. But Christianity cannot be synthesized with other religions. The Christian faith confesses the One "who loves us and has freed us from our sins by his blood and has made us to be a kingdom of priests to serve his God and Father." It is to him that we give "glory and power for ever and ever" (Rev. 1:5–6). We do not give our ultimate loyalty and allegiance to a nation or to a concept of the unity of all mankind. Our primary devotion is given to the Lamb who was slain who is worthy "to receive power and wealth and wisdom and strength and honor and glory and praise!" (Rev. 5:12). Our ultimate allegiance is not to a one world government or ruler but to the "King of Kings and Lord of Lords" (Rev. 19:16).

8

# New Age Education

**Item:** Marilyn Ferguson devotes one 42-page chapter in her 1980 book to "Flying and Seeing: New Ways to Learn." She states, "The deliberate use of consciousness-expanding techniques in education, only recently well under way, is new in mass schooling." She writes about the innovative curriculum and programs being used in classrooms. "Altered states of consciousness are taken seriously: 'centering' exercises, meditation, relaxation, and fantasy are used to keep the intuitive pathways open and the whole brain learning. . . . There are techniques to encourage body awareness: breathing, relaxation, yoga, movement, biofeedback."[1]

**Item:** Russell Chandler writes about New Age curriculums being offered in various institutions of higher learning. The Citrus Community College in Azusa, CA, gives credit for parapsychology courses that teach students how to see and interpret auras and how to recognize out-of-body experiences. As one of several alternative-style universities in the San Francisco Bay area, the John F. Kennedy University promotes itself as "the graduate school for the study of human consciousness." Chandler quotes educator Gay Luce, a consultant to the President's Scientific Advisory Committee. Luce "fully expects meditation techniques involving 'the body's energy chakras' to be taught in kindergarten soon."[2]

**Item:** For more than two years the Watchman Fellowship organization has been running in its *Watchman Expositor* newspaper a series of articles regarding the influence of New Age occultism and humanism in the public schools. It reports, for example, on a kindergarten-level program in the Science Research Associates reading program series. Lesson 10 in Listening Skill Builders is titled "The Witches' Ride." Kindergarteners are introduced to a young boy called "the bobo" who observes witches being able to fly on a broomstick when they speak the magic words, "Fly me faster than a fairy—Without God—without Saint Mary!" The bobo attempts to follow the witches' example and initially is successful, but then he misspeaks the magic words saying, "Fly me faster than a fairy—Fly with God and good Saint Mary." As soon as the misspoken words are out of his mouth, the bobo begins to fall to the ground. The *Watchman Expositor* comments, "As long as the bobo was flying *without* God, he was having a very enjoyable time. But the poor bobo, terrible things happened when he tried to fly *with* God."[3]

**Item:** An article in the January/February 1993 *New Age Journal* reported that New Age concepts and techniques associated with human potential seminars are finding their way to inner cities and schools in the form of self-esteem curriculum and violence and drug abuse prevention programs. California state assemblyman John Vasconcellos introduced the self-esteem emphasis into the public schools in the mid-1980s. Since then it has "gained powerful currency as a social vaccine: a new organizing principle for reframing the way America solves problems. Today, three-fourths of California schools have some self-esteem component."

The *New Age Journal* article gives other examples of self-esteem programs—the Alianza Dominicana, a center for immigrants from the Dominican Republic in New York City, combines self-esteem programs with Dominican folk versions of aromatherapy and acupressure to heal addiction; a community center for street youths in Saratoga Springs, NY, offers such activities as shamanic drumming and Vipassana meditation. A leader at the center said, "Underneath their resistance, they're really hungry for forms they can accept. The Native American and pagan traditions meet that need; church doesn't."[4]

**Item:** In an award winning essay, New Ager John Dunphy stated,

> The battle for humankind's future must be waged and won in the public school classroom by teachers who correctly perceive their role as the proselytizers of a new faith: a religion of humanity that recognizes and respects the spark of what theologians call divinity in every human being.... The classroom must and will become an arena of conflict between the old and the new—the rotting corpse of Christianity, ... and the new faith of humanism.[5]

Stories with occult themes in textbooks, New Age visualization techniques and meditation practices, affective learning methodology with an aversion to moral absolutes that promotes the values-neutral philosophy of secular humanism—such man-centered, self-deifying, occult-based, evolution-promoting themes and practices are increasingly found in the public school systems of our country. "In the ideological contest for cultural supremacy, public education is *the* prime target; it influences the most people in the most pervasive way at the most impressionable age. No other social institution has anything close to the same potential for mass indoctrination."[6] Unfortunately, fallout from the New Age in public education is also found in some course material and self-esteem programs used in Christian schools.

## A Counterfeit Anti-Christian Spirituality

In the opening chapter of *Your Child and the New Age*, Berit Kjos writes about a fifth-grade teacher in Lakewood, CO, who had made a large variety of books available to his students for their daily reading times. A parent complained that two of the books were based on the Bible. As a result, the principal ordered the teacher to remove the two books from the classroom, and a judge upheld the principal's order. Kjos writes, "In school the children could legally read books on Buddhism, Indian religions, and Greek mythology—but not on Christianity."[7]

There seems to be an appalling double standard spreading throughout the nation in matters related to religion and spirituality. A double standard is found in the entertainment media, in liberal politics, and especially in the public schools. It is a double standard which says that it is permissible to read about, to study, or to otherwise promote in the public arena any religious belief or philosophy that in some way speaks to the spiritual nature of the human race unless that religious philosophy happens to be the teachings of the Christian faith. In that case, Christian history, beliefs, and practices are either ridiculed or totally excluded. This, of course, is to be expected in the NAM's goal of a syncretistic, one-world religion. Other religions can be blended in an eclectic mix, but the exclusive claims of Christianity require that its "rotting corpse" (Dunphy's phrase) be shunned.

It is shunned in school textbooks. Both Douglas Groothuis and Berit Kjos refer to a 1985 federally funded study of public school textbooks conducted by Paul Vitz. The results were reported in his

131

book, *Censorship: Evidence of Bias in Our Children's Textbooks.* According to Groothuis, Vitz concluded that all levels from first grade through high school "America's substantial Christian heritage is overwhelmingly edited out. . . . Although other cultures' religious concerns are not avoided, Christianity in America is rendered invisible."[8] Kjos reported that Vitz's study revealed that out of 670 stories from third- and sixth- grade readers not one included any Christian or Jewish religious motivation while one story did feature a white girl who practiced Native American religion. Vitz also found that a sixth-grade reader had adapted an original story by Isaac Bashevis Singer in which "the main character prayed 'to God' and later remarked 'Thank God.' In the story as presented in the sixth-grade reader, the words 'to God' were taken out and the expression 'Thank God' was changed to 'Thank goodness.' "[9] Some may consider such a minor change to be insignificant. However, excluding references to God is typical of a growing counterfeit spirituality while at the same time repressing the Christian faith.

## The New Age Classroom Agenda

The New Age agenda in public schools embraces all grade levels, in almost every subject area, and in program components ranging from global education to value clarification to self-esteem programs to occult activities. John Eidsmoe writes, "New Age ideas can be taught as part of almost any subject, but some of those to especially watch for are death education, values clarification, health, home economics, sociology, literature, and psychology."[10]

Evidence supporting Eidsmoe's statement abounds. Eight-year-olds are taken on a field trip to a cemetery where they must think about death. Upon return to the classroom they are asked to decide which three family members are to be admitted to a bomb shelter in the face of a nuclear attack and which family members are to be left out because there is no additional room. Ninth graders are shown a film with graphic pictures of the destruction of the environment and then asked to complete an exercise called "Who Shall Populate the Planet?" Three people are to be chosen from a list that includes a priest, a football player, a black minister, a microbiologist, a pregnant woman and a teacher. "Another life or death decision. One senses that the two Christians are the most expendible [sic] in making way for a new world."[11] More examples of the New Age influence in schools will be noted below.

## Teacher Transformation

Personal transformation that leads to global transformation has been identified as a key principle of the New Age. If the public schools and the children who attend them are to be transformed to the point of accepting the New Age philosophy, that transformation must begin with the personal transformation of educators engaged in curriculum planning, classroom teaching, and school administration.

Transformed educators will be open to using a new paradigm of teaching and learning called *transpersonal education.* The concept of transpersonal education is to move students beyond what they would ordinarily learn to know about themselves and the world around them through the old education paradigm and to lead them to an awareness of the Inner Self, to an integration of body and mind, so that by achieving a higher consciousness the students may transcend what, under the old paradigm, was believed to be the limits of human potential. Marilyn Ferguson further describes transpersonal education.

> The name derives from a branch of psychology that focuses on the transcendent capacities of human beings. In transpersonal education, the learner is encouraged to be awake and autonomous, to question, to explore all the corners and crevices of conscious experience, to seek meaning, to test outer limits, to check out frontiers and depths of the self. . . . Transpersonal experience aims for a new kind of learner and a new kind of society. Beyond self-acceptance, it promotes self-transcendence.[12]

Except for Ferguson's last statement, one may not have much difficulty accepting her concept of transpersonal education. Certainly there is room for improvement in the educational system of this country. A concept of education that encourages the learner to be awake, to ask questions, to seek meaning in what is being learned is a concept to be applauded. Unfortunately, the means and methodology of the transpersonal education paradigm are steeped in God-denying humanistic and occult New Age techniques and practices such as man-centered, self-esteem programs, values clarification, self-hypnotism, guided imagery, and talking with spirit guides. Unfortunately, many educators are already engaged in personal transformation and implementing transpersonal education. Pointing out that it is not what happens in school classrooms that is the first arena for necessary change, but rather that educators themselves need to be changed, Ferguson writes,

> Subtle forces are at work, factors you are not likely to see in banner headlines. For example, tens of thousands of classroom teachers, educational consultants and psychologists, counselors, administrators, researchers, and faculty members in colleges of education have been among the millions engaged in *personal transformation*. . . . They are eager to share their discoveries with those colleagues ready to listen.

> And many *are* ready, veterans of earlier, partially successful movements to humanize schools. . . . Teachers, administrators, and sympathetic schoolboard members are working together rather than confronting one another.[13]

Keep in mind that Ferguson's book was published in 1980. If her statement was true then, it is even more true now. Berit Kjos points out that educational reformer John Dewey, a 1933 signer of *Humanist Manifesto I*, was intent on eliminating Christian absolutes from the educational system and substituting "truths" consistent with a changing culture. Kjos then calls attention to the support given to Dewey's ideas by the leadership of the National Education Association "who doggedly followed Dewey's plan to provide a 'purified environment for the child.' Historical facts that clashed with 'progressive education' were distorted or erased."[14] The trend toward humanistic/New Age educational methodologies seems to continue unabated.

## Humanistic and New Age Educational Methodologies

Eric Buehrer says that a major theme of transpersonal education focuses upon whole-brain learning. The old educational paradigm centered too much learning through the analytical (left) side of the brain and too little on the affective (the intuitive and creative right) side of the brain. New Agers in education make much of the need "to join the two aspects of the brain and have holistic education that teaches the whole brain."[15]

Recent research in brain functioning has demonstrated the distinctiveness as well as the interrelationship between the left and right sides of the brain. The accuracy of these findings is not being questioned. What is of concern is the emphasis New Age educators place upon the affective right side of the brain and how they aim to achieve whole brain learning. Ferguson says that while the left brain can logically organize new information it cannot creatively generate new ideas. Therefore, increased use of the right brain is essential if the human race is to make the evolutionary leap and transform society. "Without intuition, we would still be in the cave. . . . Is it any wonder that our educational approach, with its linear, left-brain processes, has failed to keep pace with the times?"[16]

But after centuries of time in which the use of the left brain has dominated the use of the right brain, what can be done to use both brain hemispheres equally so that whole brain learning can take place? Ferguson writes,

Meditation, chanting, and similar techniques increase the coherence and harmony in the brainwave patterns; they bring about great synchrony between the hemispheres, which suggests that higher order is achieved. . . . Language releases the unknown from limbo, expressing it in a way that the whole brain can know it. Incantations, mantras, poetry, and secret sacred words are all bridges that join the two brains.[17]

What is the ultimate goal of harnessing as much brain power as possible, especially in the realm of education, while using such techniques as chanting mantras or meditating on secret sacred words? Ferguson has an answer to that question for us. "[W]hat counts is that *something* in us is wiser and better informed than our ordinary consciousness. With such an ally within our selves, why should we go it alone [emphasis in original]?"[18] In other words, the goal is to be in regular contact with our higher consciousness in which all knowledge resides. For in Ferguson's words, "We only learn what we always knew."[19] Elliot Miller writes about what some have termed the "unborn Self." He says,

It is the teacher's responsibility to "unbury" or awaken within each child this sleeping Self (variously called "God within," "Inner" or "Higher Self," "Inner Wisdom," "Infinite Potential," and so forth). This goal is the *cornerstone* of all transpersonal education. It is believed that each student *already has* all knowledge and wisdom. He or she needs only to be taught (through meditation, guided imagery, and so forth) how to tap it.[20]

Affective learning is the teacher's primary method for awakening the Inner Self within each child. *Affective* is defined as that which is caused by or expresses emotion or feeling. The teacher/learner interaction in the classroom has shifted from imparting knowledge that is reacted to by the use of logic and reason to facilitating a student's discovery of feelings and emotions. "Simply stated, this educational approach requires the teacher, or facilitator as they are now called, to help the students *get in touch with their feelings.*"[21] Certainly there is nothing wrong with helping students express feelings and emotions. However, the objection is the humanistic/New Age theory that if students "can discover their true feelings, they will know what decisions need to be made in any given situation. If the students feel good about themselves and have good self-esteem, they will always make the correct judgment."[22] That ignores the predicament of man's sinful nature, and ultimately it does not work, especially in establishing and maintaining Christian values and morality.

Value clarification relates closely to methods for affective learning. Value clarification "is compatible with New Age thinking on 'confluent education.' This New Age theory posits the equality of individual values because everyone has the wisdom of the universe within."[23] But what is this practice called value clarification? Let's allow an individual who is committed to the use of value clarification to summarize it for us. Father Maury Smith has an earned doctor of ministry in pastoral counseling, is a licensed psychologist, and has written numerous publications in such fields as personal and spiritual growth and human relations training, as well as the book *A Practical Guide to Value Clarification.* Smith comments that values coming out of our Puritan and Victorian past were expressed primarily in moralistic "shoulds" and "should nots." (Presumably, God's values expressed in the Ten Commandments and elsewhere in Scripture would also fit such a description.) Then Smith comments,

136

Value clarification as a methodology considers this moralistic stance to be an imposition upon the individual of predetermined values, and it seeks instead a method whereby individuals can discover their own values. Thus, value clarification does not tell a person what his values should be or what values he should live by; it simply provides the means for him to discover what values he does live by.[24]

According to Smith the goal of value clarification is to enable an individual to arrive at a "full value" which is defined as one that is freely chosen from alternatives after thoughtful consideration of the consequences of each alternative. Further, the individual cherishes his value choice and is willing to affirm it publicly by doing something with his choice repeatedly in some pattern of life. Such a full value "tends to permeate and influence all aspects of one's life."[25]

Again, as with helping students express feelings and emotion, there is nothing inherently wrong with helping a child think through alternatives in a particular situation in order to determine the right response or action. However, Christian parents are concerned when God's love in Christ and the moral absolutes of God's Word (necessarily fundamental for determining values choices) are at best ignored and at worst ridiculed by a teacher "helping" a student clarify a value that will influence all aspects of the student's life.

Aversion to absolutes is a hallmark of the humanistic, affective value clarification process. Smith's book includes readings from value clarification literature. One is "The Clarifying Response," taken from *Values and Teaching* by Louis E. Raths, Merrill Harmin, and Sidney B. Simon, pioneers in value clarification. This reading focuses on teacher responses to student assertions, in order to facilitate the student's clarifying of values. Most important, teacher responses must be value-free: "The clarifying response avoids moralizing, criticizing, giving values, or evaluating. The adult excludes all hints of 'good' or 'right' or 'acceptable,' or their opposites, in such responses."[26]

Marilyn Ferguson displays the same aversion to moral absolutes as she describes the transformation that is necessary to bring about the New Age. She identifies the "open" teacher as one who respects the learner's autonomy and "spends more time helping to articulate the urgent questions than demanding right answers."[27] She further demonstrates her aversion to absolutes: "An educational system that pushes 'right answers' is scientifically and psychologically unsound. And by demanding conformity, in either belief or behavior, it inhibits innovation and asks for scorn in an increasingly autonomous age."[28] In describing the new curriculum that will serve the goals of transpersonal education Ferguson writes,

> A major ambition of the curriculum is autonomy. This is based on the belief that if our children are to be free, they must be free even from us—from our limiting beliefs and our acquired tastes and habits. . . . Maturity brings with it a morality that derives from the innermost self, not from mere obedience to the culture's mores.[29]

Change the word *beliefs* above to *values* and the value clarification process fits quite well into the new educational paradigm for the New Age. Elliot Miller writes,

> Because New Age spirituality flows out of the fountainhead of humanism and subjectivism, the use of values clarification in the schools is just as important to the Aquarian Conspiracy as the use of meditation or mystically oriented guided imagery. In fact, where values clarification becomes established, it will likely be only a matter of time before meditation and guided imagery also appear.[30]

## Occult New Age Techniques in Schools

In addition to humanistic themes in affective learning and value clarification, the NAM has its tentacles reaching into the public schools with occult practices such as self-hypnotism, meditation, guided imagery, and contacting spirit guides. Such practices are to assist students achieve the goal of personal transformation or self-actualization.

Already in 1978, Jack Canfield and Paula Klimek. who were co-directors of the Institute for Wholistic Education in Amherst, MA, wrote an extensive article for *The New Age Journal*, "Education in the New Age." In it they said,

> Within the past five years we have also witnessed the birth of "transpersonal education," the acknowledgement of one's inner and spiritual dimensions, through working with such forms as

dreams, meditation, guided imagery, biofeedback, centering, mandalas, and so forth. . . . Holistic education . . . views the student as being engaged in an integral process of unfoldment under the direction of his/her higher self. This process is perceived as taking place in a universe that is also constantly evolving: each of us is seen as an important part of the larger planetary and universal evolution of consciousness.[31]

The article includes numerous suggestions for integrating transpersonal education into the classroom. Yoga is mentioned as a physical exercise with which children seem to be fascinated. Chanting is recommended as an aid to reach higher consciousness. Meditation can be introduced by asking the children whether they would like to communicate with The Force the way Luke Skywalker did in *Star Wars*. Canfield and Klimek concluded their article,

> We believe that guided imagery is a key to finding out what is in the consciousness of New Age children. . . . Additional emphases in the transpersonal dimension are using nature as teacher, and aligning and communicating with other kingdoms such as the elemental and *devic* [a Hindu word for realm of the gods] realms . . . working with children's psychic capacities (such as seeing auras); working with astrological charts. . . . The souls that are presently incarnating seem to be very special.[32]

Of course, for those supportive of such practices, it is good to avoid using the terminology that describes them, lest those not sympathetic become upset. Canfield and Klimek advise their fellow educators, "Centering can also be extended into work with meditation in the classroom. (Advice: if you're teaching in a public school, don't call it meditation, call it 'centering.' Every school wants children to be relaxed, attentive, and creative, and that's what they will get.)"[33]

Caryl Matrisciana, who was personally involved in Eastern mysticism, writes about the use of Yoga in the classroom under the guise of physical exercise without acknowledging that it is a form of Hindu prayer. She quotes Rabi Maharaj, a former guru: "Any Hindu will tell you that there is *no* Yoga that is purely physical."[34] Both Matrisciana and Kjos refer to *Meditating with Children: The Art of Concentration and Centering* by Deborah Rozman. Rozman is an educational consultant and a transpersonal psychology instructor. One of her exercises has children sitting cross-legged in a circle on the floor to discuss the nature of spiritual energy while the teacher leads the children in a visualization exercise. The children are to sit with their backs straight so that the "energy from the Source within can flow up . . . our spine into our brain."[35] A visualization exercise has this instruction: "Meditate and go into the Source within, and in that One Source feel that you are One with everyone else's Light, Intelligence, Love, and Power. . . . Chant 'Om' softly to fill the whole circle and the whole room with your experience of the Source within."[36]

Matrisciana mentions Rozman's reference to *Education in the New Age* by occultist Alice Bailey. Rozman's book includes meditations with such titles as All is Energy Meditation, White Light Meditation, and Temple of Light Meditation, as well as Hindu symbols, the "third eye," mandalas, and lotuses. Matrisciana comments, "Can you imagine the uproar over a textbook illustrated with crosses, chalices, crown-of-thorns designs, and the Christian ichthus?"[37]

## New Age Programs in Schools

The occult and humanistic New Age is also finding its way into the classroom through various self-esteem and drug education programs. An "Item" in chapter one referred to the Mission SOAR program that educators attempted to introduce into the Los Angeles school system. Many similar programs, perhaps not as occultic but very humanistic, have been introduced into schools across the country. Eric Buehrer reports on the DUSO (Developing Understanding of Self and Others) program. As part of the program, second graders are taken out of the regular classroom setting and run through exercises in guided imagery and self-hypnosis. "Parents who contacted me due to this program were especially concerned because some of their children had difficulty even remembering what occurred during the covert sessions."[38]

The Pumsey the Dragon program uses Pumsey, a dragon with poor self-esteem, and a character called Friend to achieve improved self-esteem for children. Friend speaks to Pumsey about the "Clear Mind," that part of the mind that always thinks positive thoughts and causes good things to happen. The Clear Mind is always there for you whenever it is needed. "It always finds a way to let you feel O.K. *even* if there are walls. . . . Sometimes it just goes right through the wall as if the wall weren't there."[39] (In other words, we can use our mind to create our own reality, one that can escape from the problems of life rather than work at solving them.) How does the Clear Mind go through the walls? One way is to create Mind Pictures using relaxation techniques and deep breathing exercises that follow the pattern in *The Complete Guide to Hypnosis* by Leslie LeCron. LeCron suggests that children are usually the best subjects for hypnotism. Creating a Mind Picture ends with the children opening their eyes and saying with the teacher, *"I am me, and I am enough. I am me, and I am enough. I am me, and I am enough."* Rick Branch comments, "Of course, this is the only possible conclusion to which a student can come, if indeed the Clear Mind is the best friend they can ever have. For, who, besides themselves, can they turn to for help, advice and counsel? The answer is—no one."[40]

The Drug Abuse Resistance Education (DARE) program, another well-intended program, is taught in public schools by police officers. While not occultic, DARE uses non-directive affective education methods that seek to help students clarify values and make their own decisions about drug use. Individual police officers while teaching the material may warn against the dangers of drug use, but the DARE material never once tells the students not to use drugs. To do so, of course, would violate the value clarification process. Unfortunately, studies have not indicated that the DARE program has been successful.

> Ruth Hanson, who has been researching education for 20 years, said there are studies from several major Universities that indicate that the DARE program doesn't live up to all the hype. Hanson cited studies from the University of Illinois and the University of Kentucky in particular. Each devotes at least 30 pages to asserting "the DARE program has no effect or has actually *increased drug use* among students in the program," she said.[41]

## Global Education

A major goal of occult and humanistic methods in public schools is to help create a global community through global education. "Much more than a program for international studies, global education is a method of teaching the humanities and social studies that often either advocates or assumes a New Age ideology of relativism, religious syncretism and one-worldism."[42] Global education takes a variety of forms from peace education to nuclear disarmament to a one-world government.

Not all that is included under the broad heading of global education is necessarily bad. When it promotes a sensitivity to the culture of others, or when it results in students taking an interest in learning a second language, or when it leads to an increase in understanding the interdependence among nations in our world today, then global education can be beneficial. However, global education has some weaknesses.

> Global education has four major weaknesses. These weaknesses, however, form the very foundation for the globalists' New Age, utopian vision. Global education crowds out the study of Western civilization; it teaches that there are no absolutes; it seeks to politically resocialize students into liberal extremism. Some global educators preach a new religion for the world based on Eastern mysticism. In fact, global education is the political side of the New Age coin.[43]

Robert Muller's "World Core Curriculum," mentioned in the previous chapter, is a term that was first used by Dr. Gordon Cawelti, the executive director of the Association for Supervision and Curriculum Development, an association of various educators around the country. In a proposal he made to representative of various Western nations and Japan, Dr. Cawelti indicated that the "world-core curriculum would be extensively based on the ideas in Robert Muller's book *New Genesis: Shaping a Global Spirituality.*" Muller proposed that education should begin to focus on our planetary home, the human family, our place in time, and the miracle of individual human life. On the surface this sounds innocent enough. However, in the context of his book, Muller's ideas for education are blended with such ideas of Eastern and occult mysticism as the law of *karma* and the Hindu concept of *prana (animating principle of the breath of life).*[44] In discussing Cawelti's proposals from Muller's book, Eric Buehrer quotes several passages that demonstrate Muller's New Age thinking. In the context of promoting our planetary home Muller writes,

> We can show children and people that there is something divine,

142

miraculous, and tremendous in being human, that God must have a special design for us, that our evolution makes more and more sense, that it will continue at ever higher levels until this planet has finally become a showcase in the universe, a planet of God.[45]

In the section devoted to our place in time, Muller states that children need to learn they are "universal beings ready to flower." He continues, "In us humans there are divine cosmic elements which will flower to the point that we will become conscious of the total universe and that the universe will become conscious in ourselves.... The incarnated God, or Christ, is in all of us and for all of us to manifest."[46] In summing up the push for global education Elliot Miller writes, "Its advocates claim it is merely an approach to preparing students for responsible participation in the global age in which we live, but its materials are often biased *for* globalism and humanism and *against* nationalism and Christianity.[47]

## A Christian View of New Age Education

As previously indicated, not all of the ideas for improving our educational system are bad or wrong in themselves. Most classroom teachers and school administrators, many of whom are Christian, are trying to do the best they can with the resources they are given in college and at teacher workshops and conferences. Helping students think in more global terms, attempting to have students express feelings, guiding students to make choices out of the many alternatives confronting them, enabling students to make wise decisions with regard to alcohol or drug abuse are all noble endeavors and are to be commended. The sincere Christian has no quarrel with that. The concern is over the methods, techniques, and programs for achieving such worthy goals.

Christians are not only global citizens but also global missionaries. We are to go into all the world and make disciples of all nations (Matt. 28:19) because our Creator God gave his Son to be the Savior of all people (John 3:16). We are to think in global terms, not because we are one with all things, but because in Jesus the Christ "There is neither Jew nor Greek, slave nor free, male nor female, for you are all one" (Gal. 3:28).

Since God's Word teaches us "not to think of yourself more

highly than you ought" (Rom. 12:3), some feel that the Christian should not even speak of self-esteem. However, in Christ we have been made "a new creation" (2 Cor. 5:17), and in the power of the Holy Spirit we are enabled to "be transformed by the renewing of your mind" (Rom. 12:2). Perhaps we should speak in terms of Christ-esteem. Because the Lord Jesus was not esteemed (Is. 53:3) for us, we now have great worth in the kingdom of God. In turn we can now esteem others and "Hold them in the highest regard in love" (1 Thess. 5:13). When such love is shown toward others, their own sense of worth and value in God's eyes is renewed.

Finally, there are moral absolutes that God has commanded people of all times and all places to honor. We are not at liberty to determine our own values independently of God's will. Attempts to do so have contributed greatly to the moral decay of the last decade of the 20th century. Using human wisdom to clarify values for daily life can only lead to destruction. Disciples of Jesus Christ need to stand firmly as did the prophets of old on "This is what the Lord says: . . . The wise will be put to shame; they will be dismayed and trapped. Since they have rejected the word of the Lord, what kind of wisdom do they have?" (Jer. 8:4, 9).

What can Christians do as the NAM continues to infiltrate our schools? We can pray. We can become better informed. We can take an interest in our schools, establishing working relationships with teachers and administrators before problems arise. We can become public school teachers. We can serve on school boards and volunteer our time in parent organizations. Above all, we can give our children sound instruction in God's Word so that they become spiritually discerning and can confront the occultism and humanism of New Age education.

# New Age Business

**Item:** Two car salesmen in the state of Washington refused to participate in a motivational program. Steve Hiatt claimed to have been fired from his job after he walked out of a three-day program designed to prepare him to be an instructor (for fellow car dealership employees) in the Pacific Institute's motivational program called "New Age Thinking to Increase Dealership Profitability." He became particularly upset when the course instructor "began talking about New Age spirituality and life after death." Collin McGinness almost lost his job as a used-car salesmen when the company he worked for required its employees to attend the Pacific Institute program. He had attended a similar program several years earlier and was troubled by the heavy emphasis on "self" in the self-improvement program. Although admitting that there are good things that can be learned in such seminars, McGinness said, "[M]y belief is that God is part of my life and *his* will be done, not your will."[1]

**Item:** A 1986 article in the *New York Times* reported on the growth of both the occult and the humanistic aspects of the NAM. The article referred to the spread of psychological self-help and "human potential" groups such as the Forum, Insight, Actualizations, Silva Mind Control and Lifespring. Robert Lindsey, the author of the article, writes, "These groups' programs for corporate employees attract millions of dollars a year. Borrowing some spiritual concepts from Asian religions, the programs try to transform clients' thought processes and to make them better, more creative people."[2]

**Item:** "But if you doubt that New Age thinking has permeated the highest bastions of American's [sic] business institutions, consider this: The syllabus of Stanford University Graduate School of Business's "Creativity in Business" course taught by Michael Ray lists meditation, chanting, and dream work. Yoga, Zen, and tarot cards are also part of the class."[3]

**Item:** The U. S. Army Corps of Engineers is being transformed into being "a friend of the snail darter and the tidal flat." To aid in this transformation, the Corps consulted with Jim Channon, a former member of the Army's Task Force Delta, a post-Vietnam think tank that developed the Army's human-potential slogan, "Be all that you can be." Channon, a self-described shaman, has also been a consultant to organizations such as AT&T, Du Pont, and Whirlpool. In his opinion, almost all businesses and organizations are lacking in a desire to practice brotherly love, in the inclusion of spiritual values in their work, and in the ability to do something physical together. "On all three counts he thinks modern corporations could learn from tribal cultures."[4]

In the interest of remaining competitive on the world market, American corporations are seeking new methods to stimulate employee productivity. They want employees to be more creative, to maximize their human potential, and to have a better self-image as well as a better image of the corporation. The corporations want workers to feel that they have both the ability and the power to make decisions on their own, while also maintaining a sense of interconnectedness between management and workers. The love and caring that Jim Channon referred to are being considered as motivators in the workplace. Certainly one can not find fault with the goals of increasing employee productivity, improving management-employee relationships, and emphasizing loving and caring in the workplace.

However, as with New Age environmentalism and New Age education, the concern is not with the goals or the desired outcome of a program or emphasis. The concern is with the underlying philosophy and, at times, the techniques used to achieve the goals. The philosophy is the basic New Age concept that personal transformation is needed to achieve the full development of the unlimited potential of the mind and the divinity that resides within each person. The ultimate goal in this case is corporate transformation. The techniques include methods to reshape or transform an individual's beliefs and values with an emphasis on self-image and self-will. The new paradigm that many corporations are buying into is the humanistic themes of the New Age philosophy which state that the mind creates the reality that unlimited human potential can achieve.

The new paradigm might be described as New Age without the

glazed eyes. . . . The new paradigm takes ideas from quantum physics, cybernetics, chaos theory, cognitive science, and Eastern and Western spiritual traditions to form a world view in which everything is interconnected, in which reality is not absolute but a byproduct of human consciousness.[5]

In the fall of 1987, the American Family Foundation, an organization concerned about cults and manipulative forms of control, sponsored a conference on the influence of the New Age philosophy in the world of business. At the conference, Tom Jackson, a business consultant and a board member of the New Age educational center Omega Institute, objected to several critical assessments of New Age influence in the business world. Although downplaying the spiritual dimension of the New Age, "Results in business, he maintained, are not a function of technological know-how but of 'appropriate thinking,' and successful management of human resources is a matter of 'liberating employees' psyches.' "[6]

## The New Paradigm in Business

Already in 1980 Marilyn Ferguson wrote about the need to transform society so that the old paradigm of economics would be replaced with a new paradigm based on inner values. She indicated that, since both capitalism and socialism build upon material values, both are economic paradigms that are inadequate for the transformation of society. The new paradigm of values as envisioned by Ferguson would include positive assumptions such as production that is both qualitative as well as quantitative, ecologically sensitive operations, and the like. However, very New Age sounding assumptions are also included: "Self-actualization . . . . Cooperation with nature, a taoistic, organic view of work and wealth. . . . Spiritual values transcend material gain. . . . Data, logic augmented by hunches, feelings, insights, nonlinear (holistic) sense of pattern."[7]

Almost fifteen years ago Ferguson wrote about a new attitude toward consumerism that was surfacing called voluntary simplicity. Reported by the Stanford Research Institute, it was an attitude that was concerned with thoughtful consumption and was sensitive to the limits of natural resources. An attitude with such a focus is certainly compatible with Christian stewardship. However, the SRI report also indicated that the adherents of voluntary simplicity want

147

to realize "higher human potential, both psychological and spiritual, in community with others."[8] In another SRI report, Willis Harman, who became head of the Institute of Noetic Sciences, an organization founded by New Ager and former Apollo astronaut Edgar Mitchell, said,

> Humanistic and transcendental values aren't a luxury imposed on economic values. They're the measure of the *appropriateness* of economic values. . . . We can choose to understand and move with the tides of history, whatever they may be—or try to resist them.
>
> Upon that choice may rest in great measure the state of business in 1990—and beyond.[9]

Here are some more nuggets from Ferguson about the spread of the New Age philosophy in the world of business:

> One Aquarian Conspirator who works with top management people around the country refers to the new "businessmen-philosophers" who talk to each other until three in the morning about their own changing values and their discoveries of human potential. . . .
>
> Work also becomes a medium through which the individual can express the vision of the Aquarian Conspiracy. . . .
>
> Ron Medved of the Pacific Institute . . . envisioned the coming change: . . . "In a very real way, the New American Working Machine is banking on the sleeping genius in every one of us."
>
> "Sleeping genius," human potential—whatever term they use, new management theorists are interested in the latent capacities that can unfold, given motivation.[10]

## Human Potential Is Big Business

What Ferguson wrote about in 1980 has, in the 1980s and 1990s, become a big business in itself. Let it be said again that there is nothing wrong with the effort to improve employee productivity within the context of a corporation's increased sense of responsibility for the welfare of both employees and society in general. The problem is the philosophy and techniques associated with many human potential seminars. What had begun in many corporations in the 1950s as "Organizational Development" (OD) blended with

148

the human potential movement of the 1970s to produce the concept of "Organizational Transformation" (OT) in the 1980s. The new idea, the new paradigm, is not just to develop corporations but to transform them. "OT's more visionary consultants are avowedly committed to fostering both personal transformation (the spiritual 'awakening' of a corporation's employees) and planetary transformation (the utilization of the corporation's resources and influence for promoting New Age sociopolitical causes)."[11]

In addition to corporations and government agencies already mentioned, Ford Motor Company, Westinghouse, Calvin Klein, Procter & Gamble, Owens-Corning, General Dynamics, IBM, Lockheed, Polaroid, and General Electric have contracted with New Age consultants, transformational technologists, and human potential specialists. "But the philosophies and practices of many of these consultants are rooted in the counterculture movement of the 1960s," a movement that "has come to be known as the New Age movement."[12]

Many individuals have taken advantage of the desire of major corporations to find a new paradigm for unleashing the human potential of their employees. Perhaps none more so than Werner Erhard, the leading guru of both personal and corporate human potential seminars in the 1970s and 1980s. Reference has already been made in chapter one to Erhard's background, his founding of est and the Forum, and his recent personal problems. The extreme and harsh personal encounter techniques of the est seminars of the 1970s were replaced in the 1980s with the Forum's milder approach to personal transformation. The Forum's techniques and methods were in turn repackaged for additional corporate consumption in Transformational Technologies, Inc. However the goal remains the same—the personal transformation of the individual, changing an individual's belief and value systems so that the unlimited potential of the divinity within can be realized.

An example of the bizarre thinking that is at the root of many such human potential seminars is found in a promotional brochure for the Forum.

> Personal effectiveness is thought to be a matter of skill, ability, knowledge or effort. In fact—it is not.
>
> When you get underneath the explanations and opinions, when

you take an honest, no nonsense look at yourself or at people you know who are effective, creative, competent and able—clearly what is happening is simply that you or they are *being* effective, *being* creative, *being* competent, *being* able.

It's as straightforward as that. When you are effective, you are *being* effective.

But what is *being*, really? . . . *Being* is a dimension of ourselves. *Being* is that dimension of ourselves that shapes our actions, our performance and ultimately determines what we accomplish. *Being* limits or expands our creativity, vitality, happiness and satisfaction. *Being* fashions our personality, our character. *Being* literally determines *who you are.*[13]

But what will Erhard and the Forum be able to do for those who participate in its activities? The answer is provided by the publicity brochure:

Your participation in the Forum takes you beyond a mere understanding of *being*, beyond even an occasional, unpredictable experience of *being*, and provides you with direct access to the domain of *being* itself. This is the magic of the Forum. This is the Forum's edge.

By providing access to *being*, the Forum gives you the key to shaping action, performance and results. Here you find the actual source of ability, competence and productivity. It is like putting your hands directly on the levers and dials of personal effectiveness, creativity, vitality and satisfaction. . . .

Out of the Forum, you bring this "magic" to all areas of your life— . . . to your work.[14]

Concerning this mystical philosophy of the Forum, Douglas Groothuis writes,

"The gospel according to Erhard" is a philosophically distilled version of Eastern mysticism and human-potential psychology packaged in a high-pressure group situation. The essence is that we all create our own reality (right and wrong do not objectively exist); we are responsible to no one but ourselves; we become effective not by thinking, but by *being*; and we have limitless potential.[15]

Other individuals have profited along with Erhard in the boom of New Age business seminars. In the early 1970s, John Hanley, a fellow graduate with Erhard of the Mind Dynamics program, founded Lifespring, an eclectic blend of psychological approaches and Eastern religious philosophies. "[I]ts aim is to bring participants in contact with their essential selves and enable them to recognize their own powers. Lifespring terms this process 'getting clear,' and its aim is that students become 'on purpose' with themselves." It provides "a safe environment in which you may experience that you are already perfect—exactly the way you are."[16]

In a critique of the Lifespring program and its publications, Dean Halverson wrote,

> Monistic philosophy is at the core of Lifespring's teachings. The reason one can depend only on oneself is because there is nobody else. We are all one. Only the self exists. The reason each individual is perfect is because there is no standard outside ourselves. The absolute within transcends all dualities, including good and evil. Because the source of reality is within, each person's potential is infinite.[17]

Another human-potential organization, Insight Transformational Seminars, was founded in 1978 by John-Roger, who claims to be the embodiment of the divine Mystical Traveler Consciousness and whose primary organization is the Movement of Spiritual Inner Awareness (MSIA, pronounced Messiah).

The Church of Scientology has two front organizations operating business management and motivational seminars—Sterling Management and World Institute of Scientological Enterprises (WISE).

Life Training, created by two Episcopalian priests in the late 1970s, like est has "a controlled environment in which trainers verbally berate audiences, use of transformational buzzwords, group manipulation, and public exposure of painful past experiences."[18]

# John Naisbitt

The subtle influence of New Age philosophy in the corporate world is illustrated by the popularity of the writings of the guru of prognostication, John Naisbitt. All three of his books, the last two co-authored with his second wife, Patricia Aburdene, have made the best seller lists. While his first book, *Megatrends*, doesn't even use the term New Age, nevertheless an article in *The New York Times* includes Naisbitt's *Megatrends* along with Marilyn Ferguson's *The Aquarian Conspiracy* and Fritjof Capra's *The Tao of Physics* as books "that promote the New Age vision."[19] It is not surprising, therefore, that the New Age magazine *Body, Mind and Spirit* states that *Megatrends'* "conclusions, not surprisingly, coincide directly with projections of New Age thinking."[20]

New Age themes begin to surface more noticeably in the two books co-authored with Aburdene, perhaps because Aburdene, herself a graduate of Werner Erhard's est, introduced Naisbitt to the New Age. "Some of the movement's beliefs and vocabulary—of egalitarian enterprise, human 'networking' and 'peak performance'—pervade Naisbitt's writings and lectures, although he avoids using the 'New Age' label in order to sidestep the more dubious, touchy-feely aspects of the movement."[21] Naisbitt and Aburdene live life "in commendable New Age style" by meditating together each day for 20 minutes, occasionally visiting a psychic for "life readings," and sharing a common belief in reincarnation, the New Age teaching which explains that they get along so well now because they knew each other in a previous life.[22]

New Age philosophy appears in Naisbitt's writings in subtle ways in *Re-inventing the Corporation*, published in 1985. "The book whispers rather than shouts New Age ideas, but it is to the whispers that we listen most carefully."[23] Naisbitt lauds the importance of vision which he describes in terms of "intuitive knowing" and which is found in a person who has "the mental power to create a vision." Who might such people be? Naisbitt approvingly refers to an observation of Peter Senge "that successful entrepreneurs score well above average on tests of intuitive ability such as precognition and remote viewing."[24]

Naisbitt's New Age worldview shows more clearly in his third book, *Megatrends 2000*. He devotes only three paragraphs to a New Age for corporations. However, he spends seven pages on a "theological common ground" between "New Agers and fundamentalists."[25] Again, to identify New Age leanings of an influential author such as John Naisbitt is not to say that there are no positive ideas in his books. Moving corporate executives to elicit democratic input from employees and involve them in decision-making and demonstrating concern for their welfare is commendable. Encouraging

CEOs to think in terms of personal growth for company employees is very positive. However, from a Christian perspective there is real concern. CEOs are being urged to pursue a worldview shaped by Eastern mysticism, and personal growth sessions for employees are primarily human potential seminars based on occult and mystical concepts.

## The Christian Response

No doubt, many in motivational training are promoting the New Age worldview. In a letter to the *Training and Development Journal*, Paul Rondina of Digital Equipment wrote, "I see the training industry being used to proselytize New Age religion under the deceptive marketing of increased productivity, self-actualization and self-improvement. As trainers, we must sound the alarm to this covert missionary work."[26]

Obviously, not all motivational trainers have bought into New Age philosophy and techniques. However, in 1984 Richard Watring, personnel director for Budget Rent A Car Systems, Inc., personally surveyed 9,000 personnel directors, asking whether they had seen or used at least one New Age technique such as meditation, biofeedback, Silva Mind Control, T.M., visualization, est, hypnosis, focusing, dianetics, centering, or yoga. Of more than ten percent who responded, approximately 45 percent had either seen or used one of the eleven techniques.[27]

The potential danger in this is that the person who experiences a change in values and beliefs will eventually adopt the New Age worldview. In a telephone interview with Russell Chandler, Richard Watring commented,

> Meditation techniques are recommended for stress management, and visual imaging for improving intuitive faculties, creativity, and to get employees to accept greater responsibility for themselves. . . . But along with that come some side effects. . . . If you practice a New Age technique often enough with intensity you'll have this mystical experience . . . and accept the worldview beliefs that support it.[28]

What can a Christian do when New Age philosophy and personal transformation techniques are increasingly being adopted and forced upon employees by corporate executives? First would be to pray for the ability to discern when New Age ideas and techniques are used at any personal development seminars an employee is required to attend either as company policy or for implied position advancement. If this produces conflict with one's Christian faith, a 1988 *SCP Newsletter* suggests a three-step approach similar to Matthew 18. First, personally ask the immediate supervisor or other employer representative to be excused from participating. If that brings no results, take along several other employees who share the same concerns. If that fails, the employee can appeal to an Equal Employee Opportunity Commission policy that was adopted in 1988.[29] The policy permits an employee to notify the employer that a particular training program conflicts with the employee's religious beliefs and that "an employer may accommodate the employee's belief by substituting an alternative technique or method not offensive to the employee's belief or by excusing the employee from that particular part of the training program."[30] The policy further states, "That the employer or the sponsor of a 'new age' program believes there is no religious basis for, or content to, the training or techniques used is irrelevant to determining the need for accommodation."[31]

Concerning the New Age influence in business and training seminars Richard Watring said,

> I'm concerned that even strong Christians will look at this training and see nothing wrong with it. They may become conditioned to accept incorrect views of the nature of man and how people are to develop. I think it's the church's responsibility to assist the flock in the formation of a Christian world view so that they will be able to recognize a counterfeit belief system for what it is when it's looking them in the face.[32]

Christian employers and employees must realize that it is not "being" as a dimension of ourselves that shapes our actions and our job performance as the Forum would teach us. We do not have to undergo hypnotic suggestion or practice New Age meditation and visualization techniques in order to be properly motivated to achieve a corporate vision. Being new creations in Christ through baptism and being transformed by the renewing of our minds through the power of the Spirit at work in us motivates Christian employees to do their best (Romans 12). Experiencing the transforming power of God's love produces care and concern for supervisors and fellow workers (1 John 4:19). The Holy Spirit through baptism causes the individual to die to sin and to rise to a new life in Christ (Romans 6) so that he/she strives with integrity to work for the benefit of the company and to "serve wholeheartedly, as if you were serving the Lord, not men." (Eph. 6:7). As Christians search the Scriptures and immerse themselves in the power of God's Word, they find themselves "thoroughly equipped for every good work" (2 Tim. 3:17), including performing to the best of their God-given abilities at their place of employment.

# 10

# New Age Health Care

**Item:** Marilyn Ferguson provides a glowing report on the progress being made toward achieving the new paradigm of the Aquarian Conspiracy when she writes, "The hope for real social transformation need not rest on circumstantial evidence. One major arena, health care, has already begun to experience wrenching change. The impending transformation of medicine is a window to the transformation of all our institutions." She describes the amazing, rapid change taking place in Western medicine: "Within a few short years, without a shot's [sic] being fired, the concept of holistic health has been legitimized by federal and state programs, endorsed by politicians, urged and underwritten by insurance companies, co-opted in terminology (if not always in practice) by many physicians, and adopted by medical students."[1]

**Item:** An advertisement by Bastyr College in the monthly newsletter of the American Holistic Nurses' Association urges, "*Learn the ancient arts and modern science of Oriental medicine.* Accredited 3-year BS/MS program prepares for [sic] you for a career as an acupuncturist. Unique Bastyr education bridges the gap between Western science and traditional Eastern medical practice."[2]

**Item:** A newspaper article reports on a healing seminar in a hotel meeting room. The insignia of the International Human and Universal Energy Research Institute is on the background curtain. It has the symbol of medical practice, a caduceus, topped with the yin-yang symbol and surrounded with lotus leaves. The main presenter is Vietnamese native Dang Minh Luong. He claims to have healed hundreds of people by transferring into their bodies the "universal energy" he has absorbed by practicing yoga and following a strict vegetarian diet. "By meditation and the laying on of hands, Dang and his students claim to be able to open seven chakras, or energy pathways, that they believe run within the human body and regulate organ systems." Dang's literature states, "A person is in

156

optimal health if universal energy is flowing regularly through these channels."[3]

**Item:** Mutual of America, a major insurance company, underwrote the production costs for Bill Moyers' five-part PBS television series, *Healing and the Mind*, and also paid for a 12-page special advertising section in a national news magazine in order to promote a series that ran three consecutive evenings in February 1993. The advertising section begins by asserting that medical experts agree that Obi-wan Kenobi of Star Wars fame was right: " 'May the force be with you' is more than mere movie dialogue. For a few billion Chinese, it's a balance of mind and body within each of us called 'chi.' In *Healing and the Mind*, Bill Moyers journeys with us into the little-explored mind-body connection beginning with this 'enlivening energy' and its implications for healing."[4]

**Item:** In 1986, the Joy Lake Mountain Seminar Center offered a workshop on "Transformational Medicine." It was to focus on the relationship between the "subtle body" and the physical body with an emphasis on "how to anticipate and correct abnormalities in the etheric field before the physical body is affected as a preventative approach to wellness." The use of various transformational tools such as "crystals, crystal shields, radionic devices, color, light, sound and acupressure" would also be examined.[5]

**Item:** An advertisement in a major Midwest newspaper's Sunday magazine promoted a presentation by Deepak Chopra, M.D. on "Quantum Healing—The Mind-Body Connection." In the presentation Dr. Chopra was to "draw on modern science and the ancient wisdom of Ayur-Veda to delve deeply into the quantum level inside each one of us, exploring how the mind directs the body towards sickness or health." Dr. Chopra would develop the premise that we are "minds that have created bodies, thoughts that have created physical matter," in order to discuss "how to use the body's own inner intelligence to invoke the healing response and unfold the secret of perfect health."[6]

**Item:** A 1991 seminar for Navy nurses included a course of instruction titled "Healing Touch for Healthcare Professionals." Among the objectives were that participants would be able to "describe, sense and experience concepts of human energy fields and their relation to modern scientific principles" as well as "develop a daily practice of meditation, energy field expansion, movement, and personal growth." The course included "The basics of Chakra and energy systems ... Meditation for centering and maintaining energy flow ... Therapeutic Touch ... Principles of self-healing."[7]

The above examples show the far reaching effect of New Age ideas on modern health care. From TV specials to training courses for nurses, from seminars to college level degree programs, the New Age paradigm for holistic medicine has spread rapidly and is increasingly accepted by both patients and health care professionals. This general overview of the New Age can only scratch the surface of New Age health care, its positive aspects as well as its physical and spiritual dangers.[8]

## Holistic Health Care: A Definition

While sometimes used as a synonym for New Age medicine, holistic health care in its broadest application is simply the demonstration of care and compassion on the part of a medical professional for the combined well-being of a patient's body, mind, and spirit. It recognizes that emotions, attitudes, and lifestyle have an effect on the origin and course of many diseases, and therefore it is as much preventative in nature as it is curative. Holistic health emphasizes proper nutrition, exercise, and self-discipline in order to maintain good health, perhaps even more than it seeks to provide treatment for illnesses and other malfunctions of body and mind that rob a person of a healthy life. Holistic medicine views a patient not merely as a body with a physical ailment that needs to be excised or a mental problem that needs to be corrected but rather as a total human being with emotions, feelings, hurts, wants and needs. Certainly there is much room for improvement in the American health care system in terms of doctor-patient relationships, an emphasis on a preventive approach to health, and concern for the total well-being of an individual. To the extent that a holistic approach to health care helps to achieve a positive paradigm in the world of medicine, it is to be encouraged.

Unfortunately, much holistic health care has become identified with what is sometimes termed "alternative medicine" and techniques that are based upon the same monistic, pantheistic, all-is-energy principles as is the NAM. To these alternative medicine/holistic health practices Americans are flocking in large numbers.

"A *Time/CNN* poll by Yankelovich Clancy Shulman found that about 30% of people questioned have tried some form of unconventional therapy, half of them within the past year [1991]."[9]

## The New Age in Health Care

The opening examples of this chapter included references to these terms or expressions: traditional Eastern medical practices; universal energy; yin-yang symbol; chakras; "chi" as enlivening energy; the body's own inner intelligence; human energy fields; meditation for centering energy flow. The emphasis on energy is obvious. New Age medicine is based upon the use of techniques and therapies intended to manipulate the mysterious (occult) energy that flows through each human body even as it flows throughout the universe. When this energy flow is blocked or out of balance, disharmony, illness, and disease result. When the alternative medicine therapies restore the energy balance and it is flowing smoothly, health and well-being return. In *New Age Medicine* Paul Reisser, Teri Reisser, and John Weldon devote a chapter to this universal life energy.

> In the New Consciousness and in much of holistic health, it appears under various aliases, such as universal life energy, vital forces, Ch'i, prana, bioplasma, para-electricity, and animal magnetism. We are told that, regardless of its name, this energy pervades everything in the universe, unites each person to the cosmos, and is the doorway to untapped human potential. It is at the root of all healing, all psychic abilities, all so-called miraculous occurrences. It is what religions have called God.[10]

This energy, New Agers believe, is the basic substance of everything in the universe. It is not merely a spiritual form of energy that can otherwise be visibly demonstrated in a nuclear reaction or in the electrical energy so essential to modern life. This universal energy—the prana of Hinduism, the chi of Chinese medicine, the mana of the Polynesian culture, the Force of *Star Wars*—is the foundation of all life. Promoters of New Age medicine have latched on to Einstein's equation, which, they insist, proves that energy and matter are the same. "What we see as material objects (whether living or inanimate) are actually nothing more than congealed energy. Human beings are but one manifestation of universal energy. It does not merely flow through us; it *is* us." Because traditional medicine treats the body as something material it is viewed as old-fashioned and pre-Einsteinian. "The New Medicine, on the other hand, provides us with new ways to heal because it views the body as energy and manipulates energy to change the body."[11]

Since holistic New Age medicine views disease as a blockage or imbalance of the universal energy, alternative New Age therapies claim to restore the proper flow and balance either by direct physical contact (chiropractic, reflexology, shiatsu, rolfing, acupressure) or by an invisible transfer of energy from healer to patient (therapeutic touch, shamanistic healing, the practice of Dang Minh Luong). Some holistic healers believe that this energy is what many have called God and that, therefore, man is God. Rosalyn Bruyere, New Age medium and healer, is one who holds to this foundational principle. She is quoted as saying, "for me, the terms *God* and *energy* are interchangeable. God is all there is, and energy is all there is, and I can't separate the two."[12]

John Ankerberg and John Weldon devote considerable space to this "mysterious energy" in *Can You Trust Your Doctor?* They note that the crucial issue is whether such occult, universal energy really exists. If it doesn't exist as claimed, then there is no energy imbalance, and New Age healers are not manipulating anything. However, while the existence of this universal energy has only been assumed and never demonstrated, some New Age medicine may truly be involved with occult energy.

> What is important to realize is that this energy does not exist or function in the manner *claimed* by new age healers. Divine energy does not circulate within the body through psychic pathways whose imbalance causes disease. Cosmic energy does not connect man's essential nature to "God" or the universe. But if some new age healers legitimately claim to manipulate invisible energies, what then is this energy?
>
> We believe that the energy that does exist is spiritistic or spiritistically-used energy; that is, various natural energies either used by the spirits; or the energy manifestation of the spirits themselves are falsely interpreted as the workings of completely "natural," "human," or divine energies.[13]

160

No one has ever discovered the location or existence of the soul. Yet Christians and other religious people believe it exists. The same could be said for the existence of a "universal energy" that New Agers say is the foundation of all that exists. Some Christians explain their involvement with New Age medicine by arguing that "*chi, prana, mana,* etc., are unknown and unidentified natural components of God's creation which circulate within the body through invisible channels. . . . Christian holistic healers . . . believe that as yet unknown scientific laws will one day explain what is currently unknown or which even seems magic now."[14]

However, the contradictory teachings regarding the nature of this energy, its occult connections, and its association with a monistic and pantheistic worldview point to its demonic origins. The history of spiritism demonstrates that demonic spirits have great power to transfer energy from themselves through a medium or to draw energy from the surrounding environment. It is this occult energy that New Age healers can be manipulating even though they may be unaware of its source and attempt to explain it as the flow of a "neutral" universal energy.

Ankerberg and Weldon describe the characteristics of this "mysterious energy" as unidentifiable; it is not divine, but amoral—that is, it can be used for good or evil; it is not an impersonal or neutral part of nature but can display intelligence (see an introductory item's reference to "the body's own inner intelligence") and cause the development of psychic powers; it is transferable from person to person; it is linked to unbiblical doctrines and associated with the occult.[15]

Ankerberg and Weldon state that New Age medicine takes the natural healing power inherent in the body and attempts to use that to create the idea of an occult, divine energy which, when manipulated by New Age medicine techniques, will bring healing to body and mind.

> This is why so much new age medicine is fundamentally occultic in nature: It associates a natural process with a supernatural one and thereby opens the doors to the occult. . . . The rejection of science and the dependence on manipulating mysterious occultic energies are simply invitations for the spirit world to become involved in new age health practice.[16]

161

## The Growth of New Age Health Care

According to the *Time/CNN* poll referred to previously, by that time the use of alternative medical practices had already become a $27 billion-a-year industry. In recent years, through advances in modern technology, conventional medicine has progressed greatly in its ability to treat a variety of human ailments. Why, then, are people increasingly seeking the services provided by New Age health-care practitioners? There are several parts to the answer.

First, the skyrocketing costs of allopathic (traditional) health care has placed its services and technology beyond the financial reach of many Americans. The increases in health-care costs have far exceeded the rate of inflation as measured by the consumer price index. Another *Time* article states that in 1991 Americans spent nearly twice as much on health care as they did in 1984. "[Medical bills] flow from a surreal world where science has lost connection with reality, where bureaucracy and paperwork have no limit, where a half-hour tonsillectomy costs what an average worker earns in three weeks. The prices, like the system that issues them, are out of control."[17] As a result, in the summer of 1993 a socialistic health care program is being promoted by elected and appointed government officials, a program by means of which the federal government will guarantee health care for every person in the United States. In the meantime, many have looked to alternative and generally less costly forms of treatment.

Second, modern medicine is impersonal. "For all its brilliant achievements . . . conventional medicine, many folks feel, has some serious weak spots, not the least of which is the endless waiting in paper gowns for doctors who view you as a sore back, an inoperable tumor or a cardiac case rather than a person."[18] Holistic medicine offers a strong attraction by focussing on the individual as a whole person—body, mind, and spirit.

Third, many believe that allopathic medicine concentrates on treatment of illness rather than on promotion of health. It is considered crisis oriented, a "pill-and-scalpel" approach that works well for acute conditions, as compared with the person-centered, preventive care approach of holistic medicine. Claudia Wallis writes,

> Sure, doctors know that diet and exercise matter and that stress takes a toll. But medical schools provide little instruction in these

matters. Doctors tend to downplay interactions of mind and body. The patient's state of mind doesn't matter to bacteria, conventional medical thinking goes, so whether the patient is optimistic or anxiety ridden is of little practical concern. In any case, doctors are often too rushed to find out.[19]

The health-consciousness movement of the 1990s is very concerned about diet, exercise, and therapies that will promote well-being and prevent illness. That emphasis is to be commended from the Christian perspective of being good stewards of the life God has given. Unfortunately, this concern has led many to involvement in and acceptance of the occultic philosophy of the New Age. Marilyn Ferguson writes,

> For many Aquarian Conspirators, an involvement in health care was a major stimulus to transformation. Just as the search for self becomes a search for health, so the pursuit of health can lead to greater self-awareness. . . . The proliferating holistic health centers and networks have drawn many into the consciousness movement. A nurse said, "If healing becomes a reality with you, it's a lifestyle. Altered states of consciousness accompany it, increased telepathy. It's an adventure."[20]

The growth in New Age health care has not only been in the number who seek out its therapies and techniques. There has also been significant growth in holistic medicine classes at major medical colleges as well as in the number of medical professionals that have moved partially or totally into holistic health practices. An example has already been given and more will be mentioned later of the spread of energy manipulation techniques in the nursing profession. In 1980, Marilyn Ferguson could already report on numerous seminars and conferences at which holistic health was strongly promoted. She wrote about a 1978 Washington conference sponsored by both government agencies and private organizations. Attendance at the conference on the subject of "Holistic Health: A Public Policy" included representatives of the Department of Health, Education and Welfare, the White House staff, insurance companies, and prepaid health-plan organizations. The presentations included such topics as "crosscultural healing practices, systems theory, the holographic theory of mind and reality, . . . Buddhist meditative techniques, electromedicine,... biofeedback, guided imagery, [and] homeopathy."[21]

Ferguson also referred to conferences organized in 1975 and 1976 near Washington, D.C., that enabled government officials and legislative aides to become better acquainted with holistic concepts of alternative medicine. Those attending could try such psycho-technologies as biofeedback, imagery, and meditation. In 1977, "rap groups" at the National Institute of Mental Health discussed sha-manic healing, meditation, and aura diagnosis. The evidence for a paradigm shift in medical schools was that medical students were beginning to demand courses in psychosomatic medicine, acu-puncture, and other alternative methods of patient treatment.[22]

This shift in medicine, as with other aspects of the NAM, has taken place in a quiet and subtle manner. In describing how the holistic health movement was spreading in the late 1970s, Ferguson wrote,

> The conspirators moved around the country like circuit riders, preaching a perspective, not a dogma; launching an educational program here, a pilot project there, promoting and publicizing the work of others in the network, forging new links. . . .

> The most successful strategies were gentle persuasion and first-hand experience. The wooing of influential policymakers has been an effective way of shaking the status quo. For example, some conferences served a dual purpose, enlightening the paying par-ticipants and *seducing* [emphasis added] partially committed speakers into full alliance.[23]

The growth in New Age health care among medical professionals and in medical schools has continued into the 1990s. The special advertising section promoting the PBS television special on "Healing and the Mind" mentioned several examples of holistic medicine at medical colleges. Dr. Herbert Benson at Harvard University has dem-onstrated how meditation can produce a psychological and physi-ological balance that can lower high blood pressure and decrease the level of chronic pain. At a children's hospital in Cleveland, Dr. Karen Olness has used biofeedback to diminish the severity and frequency of migraine headaches. A program at the University of Massachusetts Medical Center integrates meditation, yoga, and group support. At the Stanford Medical School support groups for women with metastatic breast cancer have combined sharing of feelings about illness and death with self-hypnosis and guided imagery.[23]

## New Age Health Practices

The *Watchman Expositor* identified three general categories of New Age health care. The "Maya" model (*maya* is the Hindu word for illusion) includes those therapies and practices that view sickness and disease as nothing more than an illusion. Since man is God, the universal energy, the reality of health can be created through positive affirmations, meditation, and visualization. The "Energy Balancing" model includes previously mentioned techniques that seek to balance the universal energy flow. The "Psychic Discernment" model includes practices in which alleged illnesses are diagnosed or predicted, based on readings that have no physical connection to the illness.[24] A few examples of the more well-known of New Age therapies and techniques will illustrate the interest in the manipulation of that mysterious, occult energy that has defied description or identification.

## Chiropractic

A brochure of the Logan College of Chiropractic in St. Louis, Missouri, states that of the three recognized systems of health care—allopathic, chiropractic, and osteopathic—chiropractic is the least invasive. It describes the role of the chiropractor as promoting proper function of the nervous system by means of joint manipulation and other specialized techniques. Undoubtedly, a back massage is relaxing. It is understandable that treatments of misaligned vertebrae and joints can relieve pressure on pinched nerves and the corresponding pain. There definitely can be health benefits from some chiropractic applications. If chiropractic treatment would be limited to neuromusculoskeletal conditions so as to relieve pain and improve joint mobility, there would be no connection with New Age health-care concepts. In fact, in 1984 chiropractors interested in reforming chiropractic medicine to keep that focus formed the National Association of Chiropractic Medicine.

The problem in chiropractic is not with reformed-minded chi-

165

ropractors who are attempting to use manipulation in a medically justified manner. Those chiropractors are to be commended. The problem is with those chiropractors who either rely upon classical chiropractic theory, which is scientifically unproven, or who incorporate chiropractic with a wide variety of unsound and potentially harmful new age occultic practices.[25]

The continuing problem for chiropractic (in spite of the fact that it is a rapidly growing field with an estimate of over 25,000 licensed practitioners) is the occultic leanings of its founder and that the basic theory of classical chiropractic has never been scientifically substantiated. Chiropractic's founding can be traced to a misobservation by D. D. Palmer in 1895 that the manipulation of the spine could restore hearing to a deaf man and correct an individual's heart ailment. This led to the formation of the basic chiropractic theory that subluxations (misalignment) of the spinal column create an imbalance in the flow of energy (which Palmer called *Innate*) through the nervous system, which in turn produces disease in the various organs of the body with which the nerves connect.

Both Palmer and his son, B. J. Palmer, the chief promoter of chiropractic after his father's death, were involved in occult practices and beliefs such as phrenology, spiritism, and reincarnation. The occult worldview of chiropractic's founder and chief promoter is evident in their descriptions of the energy they termed *Innate*. D. D. Palmer wrote, "Innate is said to be part of the 'All Wise, Almighty, Universal Intelligence, the Great Spirit, the Greek's *Theos*, the Christian's God, the Hebrew's Helohim [sic], the Mahometan's Allah, [homeopathy founder] Hahnemann's Vital Force, new thot's [sic] Divine Spark. . . .' "[26] B. J. Palmer, who felt strongly that every disease could be traced to "vertebral subluxation," described the Innate in terms of the "fellow within," a personal being living within an individual. He wrote, "Many who read and study our writings re Innate frequently ask, 'HOW can WE contact Innate; HOW can WE get in tune with Innate; HOW can WE reach Innate?' This is equivalent to asking, 'HOW can WE contact God; HOW can WE get in tune with God; HOW can WE reach God?' "[27]

In effect, therefore, the Innate of chiropractic is simply another name for the universal energy (God) which many New Age therapies claim to manipulate. Although modern chiropractic has come a long way from the theories of the Palmers, yet, because of its basic theory of energy manipulation, it has become a gateway way to other occult New Age techniques. Many chiropractors blend iridology, applied kinesiolgy (muscle testing), variations of acupuncture and acupressure, and other New Age health care therapies with their practice. Recently, some chiropractors have been seeking to become a family's primary-care physician particularly for childhood diseases and other pediatric care. "Chiropractors are conducting marketing seminars, holding conventions, distributing pamphlets and coloring books, even publishing telephone-marketing scripts, all with the aim of drawing more children and infants into their practice for basic health care."[28] However, to the extent that modern chiropractors still base their practice on the unscientific and occult concepts of classical Palmer chiropractic or become "mixers" of chiropractic and other New Age therapies, Christians need to be discerning and consult only those chiropractors who follow the practice of manipulation that has been scientifically proven to treat neuromusculoskeletal disorders.

## Acupuncture

Perhaps the most rapidly expanding New Age health care practice is acupuncture and its derivative, acupressure. Of the New Age therapies, acupuncture has the most visible connection to the practice of energy manipulation associated with the Taoistic philosophy of ancient Chinese medicine. "Though literally thousands of years old, Chinese medicine in the form of acupuncture can be said to have 'arrived' in the west at the time of [President] Nixon's visit to China, when the well-known American journalist, James Reston, underwent surgery while under acupuncture anaesthesia."[29]

Previous mention has been made of the *chi* of Chinese medicine. Chi (sometimes spelled ch'i) is the Chinese term for the "vital energy" or "life force" that "is said to flow through the human body along 12 main energy circuits, or *meridians*, which in turn are connected to the 700 or more acupoints spread all over the body's surface."[30] Health is maintained when the energy flow is in balance. Illness and disease result when it is not. To determine the flow and balance of chi, most acupuncturists use pulse diagnosis. However, this is not just simply checking the pulse rate. "Up to twelve pulses must be examined, one for every major meridian, six per wrist. Again, the pulses allegedly provide the acupuncturist with information telling them which meridians are deficient in *chi* energy and whether *yin* or *yang* is dominant."[31] To determine that, the acupuncturist assumes a quiet, meditative position with a mind open and receptive to what the pulses will tell him.

> It is important to *cultivate the ability* to listen to the *vital message* which will become *clearly revealed* to the *calm and RECEPTIVE* mind.

> What is the Life Force doing in each of the Organs and Organ Meridians?

> The human being will tell you through the pulses, the *inmost secrets* of the Life Force animating it—and its message will be a *truthful* message. If the practitioner *is sincere* and genuinely seeks to understand and receive the message, it will be there.[32]

Once the therapist has determined where chi is out of balance and which organs are affected, needles are inserted at the precise acupoints (which can vary from individual to individual) to stimulate energy flow or remove its blockage from the affected meridians. By such treatment acupuncturists claim they can treat all varieties of illness ranging from ulcers to high blood pressure to cancer. Acupressure replaces the use of needles with the application of manual pressure.

Obviously, there is nothing scientific about a practice that manipulates the flow of an unmeasurable, invisible energy through non-physical, invisible meridians. In fact acupuncture is a religious philosophy built upon the metaphysical mysticism of Taoism. There is evidence that acupuncture does act as an analgesic in reducing the sensation of pain. However, even this observable result of acupuncture is most effective when both practitioner and patient believe in the philosophy of Taoism, thereby indicating that a psychic aspect is involved. "Actually, many of the characteristics of acupuncture have been observed in Western medical literature, but given different names."[33]

Many acupuncturists, like many chiropractors, often combine their specialty with other practices such as psychic diagnosis, astrological forecasting, reflexology and others. Because of the occult associations with the true practice of acupuncture, there is the possibility of deeper occult involvement in its basic Taoist philosophy by those who receive acupuncture treatments. Since most acupuncture is not practiced scientifically and there is no regulation of acupuncturists, there are also potential physical hazards such as infection. The best advice is to avoid involvement with any practice that might lead to occult influence.

## Therapeutic Touch

Therapeutic Touch, developed by Dolores Krieger, Ph.D., R.N., is another New Age energy manipulating and energy transfer technique that has been adopted by many in the nursing profession. Estimates are that more than 50,000 nurses, including many in the field of Christian nursing, have been instructed in and use Therapeutic Touch. The occult connections of Therapeutic Touch are obvious. By her own admission, Dolores Krieger was taught this technique by occultist Dora Kunz, a leader in the Theosophical Society (see chapter 2). Krieger herself studied yoga, Ayurveda, Chinese medicine, and other related concepts. As a result, she came to believe in *prana* and the chakra system. In her Therapeutic Touch textbook she writes, "[T]hat prana can be transferred from one individual to another, may not be so readily apparent to us unless we have gotten into the practice and literature of hatha yoga, tantric yoga, or the martial arts of the Orient."[34]

Therapeutic Touch operates on the same basic principles as other universal life energy manipulation practices. It requires that the healer center herself in order to be prepared for the energy transfer. A handout at a Therapeutic Touch workshop describes the centering process for the nurse practitioner: "Take a deep relaxing breath. And breathe in calm energy. . . . Let your body, mind, and spirit be peaceful and in harmony. Fill yourself with universal healing energy. And through you let that healing energy be transmitted." That same handout also has a one-page description, with diagrams of the human body, its major chakra points and the area they nourish. It describes Therapeutic Touch procedure:

> Assessment of the healee, several inches from the body in an effort to locate asymmetries in the energy flow. Feelings of heat, cold, tingling, congestion, or pressure indicate imbalances or obstructions in the field.

Direction and Modulation of the Energy. Once the field has been cleared, then treat areas that have been blocked or congested. Let the hands rest on or near the body area where the block or congestion was detected or in other areas of energy imbalance and direct energy to the area in order to balance or correct the problem.[35]

Therapeutic Touch has become popular because it seems to work, it appears to be safe and natural, it is increasingly accepted in the nursing profession, and, for Christians, it has similarities to the biblical practice of the laying on of hands. However, after extensive quotations from the writings of Krieger and others, Ankerberg and Weldon conclude, "In essence, there is little doubt that Therapeutic Touch is a form of psychic healing."[36] That it seems to work should not be surprising. Occult techniques that transfer energy of a spiritistic nature can have both physical and psychological effects on human beings. The Christian nurse and Christian patient should beware of potential occult involvement in Therapeutic Touch.

## Other New Age Health-Care Therapies

Space prevents a full description of other examples of New Age medicine. Consult the books by Ankerberg and Weldon and by Reisser, Reisser, and Weldon for New Age therapies not mentioned below.[37]

*Iridology.* Although there is some evidence associating iridology with Chinese astrological practices, its modern practice is generally traced to the experience an eleven-year-old Hungarian boy, Ignaz Peczely, had with an owl. He observed what he thought was a connection between the owl's broken leg and a black line in the iris of the owl's eye. Thus was born the theory of iridology which states that through the optic nerve, brain, and nervous system the iris is connected with every organ and tissue of the body. The eye is supposedly a microcosm of the body. Changes in body organs and tissue that signal both physical and mental illness can be read in zones of the iris to which different body organs and corresponding functions are assigned. A change in color of the iris is also considered important. Elaborate charts have been developed which have created somewhat of a diagnostic dilemma for the iridologist because different charts will produce different diagnoses.

"The notion that one small part of the body can reveal or control all of the rest certainly is appealing—but the appeal is to a universal human appetite for shortcuts to knowledge and power."[38] No scientific evidence supports the claims of iridology. Its practitioners often have other associations with the occult, like the rest of New Age medicine. Dr. Bernard Jensen, considered by many the leading exponent of iridology in America, subscribes to such New Age beliefs as reincarnation, astral travel and psychic development. Bibliographies in his books recommend the writings of Helena Blavatsky, Marilyn Ferguson, and the spirit-channeled *A Course in Miracles*.[39] A physical connection between the iris and the rest of the body has never been demonstrated, and, therefore, iridology is not based on physiological information. "Like Astrology, Palm Reading and Crystal Ball gazing, it is based on another principle. That is, the use of a *prop* to *psychically* determine diseases and emotional traits."[40]

*Reflexology.* Also called zone therapy, reflexology teaches "that pressure and stroking of certain parts of the body has a therapeutic effect leading to the normal functioning of other specific parts of the body."[41] While not necessarily limited to the foot, most reflexologists focus on massaging pressure points in the foot which are said to be connected by the nervous system to body organs. Like the iris in iridology, the foot in reflexology is said to be a microcosm of the body, and the feet are divided into various zones to which organs and various body locations are assigned. As in acupressure, massaging pressure points on the foot is said to manipulate the flow of energy that has been blocked so that illnesses can be healed. Reflexologist Mildred Carter in *Body Reflexology: Healing at Your Fingertips* writes, "By massaging reflexes in various places on the body, you not only stop pain but you also send a healing force to all parts of the body by opening up closed electrical lines that have shut off the *universal life force*" (emphasis added).[42]

Here again, there is no scientific evidence to support the claims of reflexology. While massaging the nerve endings in the feet no doubt has a positive effect in temporarily relieving stress and tension, there is no evidence that applying pressure at certain points on the feet can improve the functioning of the kidneys, cure an asthmatic condition, or work any other form of healing. Since there are other occult associations with reflexology, including the promotion of reincarnation (present illnesses can be traced to past lives), it is best to avoid this New Age therapy and let a friend or family member massage your feet.

*Reiki.* An information piece traces the origins of Reiki to ancient Tibet. It took its path through India to Egypt and Rome in the West and to China in the East. The modern practice of Reiki is attributed to the discoveries of Mikao Usui, a Christian minister and teacher in Kyoto, Japan. Challenged by his students regarding healing miracles in the Bible, Usui was eventually led to accept Buddha's reflections about healing as recorded in the sutras (Buddhist scriptures). From Usui's study and eventual practice has come the modern practice of Reiki.[43]

What is Reiki? "[It] is the science and art of activating, directing and applying natural, universal life energy, to promote energy balancing, healing, wholeness; to prevent disorders and to maintain a state of positive wellness no matter what your age." Since its modern development came out of Japan, Reiki literature uses the Japanese *ki* (the equivalent of the Chinese *chi*) as the term for the universal energy Reiki is said to balance. "Ki describes the subtle system of life-sustaining energy circulating in all living things. . . . The amount and the balance of this vital energy, *ki*, within you is essential for your health and well-functioning on a daily basis."[44]

Reiki uses a laying-on-of-hands technique that is taught in a series of workshops. The body is divided into three zones each of which has four points for direct hand placement. Reiki students advance in the workshops through a three-degree program. "The second degree . . . includes further energy activation and the teaching of special techniques for use with deep-seated emotional and mental conditions. The second degree also includes instruction in absent healing (where the person who is ill is spatially separated from the reiki healer.)"[45] It should be obvious that a Christian would want to avoid an involvement in Reiki therapy.

# A Christian Perspective

In a brief but concise article in the *Christian Research Journal*, Elliot Miller reacts to what he identifies as a "growing movement" of Christians in holistic health practices. He particularly responds to the writings of Monte Kline, who is among those who believe that the mysterious "universal energy" is merely, as yet, an unexplainable part of God's creation concerning which man is also to exercise dominion by means of ongoing exploration and discovery. Kline argues for a biblical framework for holistic health practices. However, as Miller points out, not all "energy" is susceptible to exploration and discovery to arrive at a scientific explanation.

The issue Kline ignores, however, is this: If devilish (not to mention divine) supernatural energy is operative in the world (and Scriptures like 2 Thess. 5:7 compel us to affirm that it is), then it is not true that *all* energetic phenomena have a scientific explanation and are among the parts of God's creation that we are to "take dominion" over. We therefore cannot afford to *assume* that all phenomena are spiritually safe for us to explore—even if certain good effects are associated with them (2 Cor. 11:14).[46]

Kline argues that if a particular practice is not condemned by name in Scripture, then it is legitimate for Christians to be involved in a "Christian" application of that "energetic medicine" technique. Miller responds to Kline's argument, "If it [a holistic therapy] can be shown to be a part of or intrinsically related to something that *is* specifically condemned (in this case, *spiritism*—Deut. 18:11), or if it tends to involve or encourage unbiblical (in this case, *occultic*) concepts or behavior, it should still be avoided (1 Thess. 5:22)."[47]

Interest in and use of New Age medicine continues and increases. *Religion Watch*, referring to an article in *Hinduism Today*, reports that practices such as ayurveda, homeopathy, and acupuncture are specifically being found in government health programs. "In the U. S., a new government Office of Alternative Medicines has been set up to make recommendations for testing these various new methods."[48] As has been stated, not all practices and emphases of holistic medicine are to be condemned outright. Again the Christian is urged to practice careful discernment.

Since it is not always easy to detect the New Age presence in medicine, Dr. Reisser suggests the following: Beware of therapies claiming to manipulate "life energies"; beware of psychic diagnosis and healing; beware of practitioners who claim their therapy will cure anything; beware of therapies the explanations of which don't make sense; beware of therapies that rely heavily on altered states of consciousness.[49]

Along with preaching and teaching, healing was a major function of Jesus' ministry (Matt. 4:23). Followers of Christ are to be concerned about their own health as well as the health of others. All God-pleasing preventive measures of a healthy lifestyle are to be actively pursued. We are to thank God for all the advances of medical technology that promote physical health and mental well-being that do not in any way compromise God's sovereignty over life.

> Our God knows how important our physical and mental health is to our happiness and well-being. He reveals His will to us, through His word, the Holy Bible, through His continuous interaction in the world through the Holy Spirit, and through personal relationships with each of us, so that we may experience the joy and peace of mind we all long for.[50]

# New Age "Christianity"

**Item:** A workshop at the Joy Lake Mountain Seminar Center offered the opportunity to arrive at a greater understanding of the Christian heritage that permeates our culture. "How can we be moved by its inner force, rather than operate from rules and intellectual belief? Is there some way in which we can begin to read the Bible from a knowing more like those who wrote the scriptures—rather than from outside?" In other words, is there some as yet unrevealed means by which a person can arrive at the same deep or inner meaning of the Christian Scriptures which the original human authors must have possessed. The workshop would "offer an experience of Christian gnosticism through the body, and will take the form of a continous [sic] liturgy, during which participants will work with the body and with spinal energies in ways that begin to approximate the consciousness from which the gospels were written." The experience of previous participants in the liturgy indicated that "for the first time they really felt the meaning of what they had been hearing and speaking and thinking of as their religion all their lives."[1]

**Item:** A New Age publication for the New England area of the country included articles about feminine spirituality and goddess traditions, about the founder of a network of Buddhist centers, and about the practice of reflexology as a path to good health. It also contained numerous ads promoting New Age practices. The ad for the Independent Catholic Church indicated its purpose was to reach out "to individuals who desire to develop the divine aspect of their nature. We emphasize the Divinity in all of us and offer the celebration of the Holy Eucharist in a spirit of love, peace, and unity." An individual's ad offered his services to help others to open to God. This person "has found a new frequency of Consciousness which can be called a pure I AM." However, this individual has had some assistance in providing such a service. "Since July 1992, Jesus

Christ has been helping to develop the process in the world and randomly enters Michael's consciousness as medium to serve the practice of any individual."[2]

**Item:** In 1990, Berit Kjos attended a mainline church's celebration of Earth Day. As the youth group brought their offerings forward, these words were spoken: "I bring to our Mother, the Earth, the gift of a new beginning. . . . I bring to our Mother, the Earth, the birth of a new consciousness. I bring to our Mother, the Earth, the gift of immortality that you may live forever cherished by your beloved children."[3]

These three examples are but the tiniest tip of the iceberg of New Age "Christianity." Seminars and workshops promote a New Age version of the teachings of Jesus Christ. Channelers claim to receive new revelations from Jesus. The unique messianic title of Jesus, the Christ, is adopted by New Agers who seek to appeal to those living in a culture steeped in Christian tradition. The New Age "Christ" becomes a term describing the divinity resident within every person. The New Age worldview creeps into Christian churches in Earth Day liturgies and in study courses such as "A Course in Miracles."

Russell Chandler writes about New Age motifs finding their way into liberal Christianity while New Age metaphysical groups adapt Christian terminology and practices in order to make "newcomers feel more comfortable in their transition to alternate forms of belief and practice." Writing in the late 1980s he states that "self-improvement, visualization, and guided imagery techniques—including meditational yoga—have percolated into many liberal Protestant denominations, some Roman Catholic circles, and not a few conservative and Pentecostal/charismatic Christian churches.' "[4] Ted Peters comments that in the NAM Jesus Christ can be both a symbol of psychological growth and a teacher of secret wisdom. Late 19th and early 20th-century books detailing Jesus' supposed travels to India are "important because contemporary new age advocates want to draw the connection between Jesus and the Asian spirituality they promote. The use of Jesus' name just may give Hindu and Buddhist doctrines credibility to Western audiences."[5]

What Chandler describes as taking place in the 1980s and what Peters writes about the use of Jesus' name has continued to find even greater application in the 1990s. All of this serves New Agers well in building their network of adherents among disaffected Christians. Marilyn Ferguson reported that among the Aquarian Conspirators surveyed 95 percent indicated at least a token religious background, with 55 percent Protestant and 18 percent Roman Catholic. "Only 19 percent consider themselves active in that tradition in any way, a percentage that includes several clergy, exclergy, and theologians."[6]

Chapter 2 discussed the relationship between the Gnosticism evident at the close of the New Testament period and the Neo-Gnosticism associated with the New Age. In this chapter, New Age "Christianity" (what New Agers describe as *esoteric* Christianity) refers to the creeping influence of the New Age philosophy in Christian churches and the writings of Christian authors as well as a distortion of the person and teachings of Jesus Christ by New Age organizations, by New Age authors, and by the Gnostic gospels, which have great appeal for many New Agers. In his excellent book about the counterfeit Christ of the NAM, Ron Rhodes summarizes what New Agers claim Jesus taught:

1. Jesus taught that all is one, all is God, and man is God.
2. Jesus taught and believed in a unity of the world religions.
3. Jesus taught that he was not uniquely God, but was a human being who became enlightened.
4. Jesus taught that he was a way-shower for humanity, not a Savior.
5. Jesus taught that every human being has the potential and ability to save himself.
6. Jesus taught that esoteric knowledge (gnosis) is all-important to man's self-salvation.
7. Jesus taught that part of man's self-salvation involves a transformation of consciousness.
8. Jesus taught and believed in God the Father and God the Mother.[7]

In what follows, the above statements will be supported with quotations from various authors and writings to indicate the doctrine of New Age "Christianity." This doctrine will either be "from the lips of Jesus," or it will reflect the thinking of those who identify themselves as New Agers, as Christians, or as belonging to a Christian organization. Information about authors and sources will be found in the endnotes.

*1. Jesus taught that all is one, all is God, and man is God.*

"The true self of you, the Christ, the spiritual man, is the individualization of God. You are the Presence of God at the point where you are. Thus, it is true of you as it was of Jesus, 'I and the Father are one.' ... God is in you as the ocean is in a wave"[8]

"I come again to remind you that *all persons must acknowledge the Creator*—that source of power which gives us all our life eternally—and to remind you that a spark of that power is in *you!* God is ... an integral, internal aspect of your own identity!"[9]

"To put it plainly, our unconscious is God. God within us. We were part of God all the time.... I have said that the ultimate goal of spiritual growth is for the individual to become as one with God.... It is for the individual to become totally, wholly God.... We are born that we might become, as a conscious individual, a new life form of God."[10]

*2. Jesus taught and believed in a unity of the world religions.*

"Since you are all one in God ... it matters not which world religion you follow if it takes you to God with clarity and certainty that death is not the end.... Your challenge today is to see the universal message that runs through all world religions and to amalgamate that theme."[11]

"[A]ll the laws, all the truths, all the teachings and all the scriptures [of the different world religions] have but one end, to produce God-man, man self-realized, in which case the self here means the whole self, the one self, the divine self."[12]

[Jesus said,] "All people worship God, the One; but all the people see him not alike.... The nations of the earth see God from different points of view, ... and every nation has a name for God."[13] In other words, the various names for God in the different world religions all refer to the same God.

*3. Jesus taught that he was not uniquely God, but was a human being who became enlightened.*

"And then—one day it happened. Into the consciousness of this thoughtful lad [Jesus] came an idea so great, that He probably didn't catch its full implications at first. It was the concept leading to the full realization of His unity with God."[14]

"The message of the Gospels has been misunderstood. They

178

have been made to appear to say that Jesus was really God taking the form of man.... All this fails to take into account *His great discovery*. It fails to catch the real theme of His teaching: the Truth of the Divinity of Man" (emphasis added)."[15]

"Jesus' unique place in history is based upon his *unprecedented realization* of the higher intelligence, the divinity, the Ground of Being incarnated in him—the ground which is the source of all being (emphasis added).[16]

### 4. *Jesus taught that he was a way-shower for humanity, not a Savior.*

"The significance of Jesus, therefore, is not as a vehicle of salvation but as a model of perfection. That is why the proper attitude toward him is one of reverence, not worship. Jesus showed us the way to a higher state of being and called upon us to realize it, to make it real, actual—individually and as the race."[17]

"And all the people were entranced, and would have worshipped Jesus as a God; but Jesus said, I am your brother man just come to show the way to God; you shall not worship man; praise God, the Holy One."[18]

"Jesus was a great way-shower. We might say that man was earthbound by the law of karma.... Then Jesus made his great discovery of the Divinity of Man. He discovered that man was one with the transcendent Spirit of God and thus, by knowing the Truth of his spiritual unity, man could remove the mountains of human suffering and find abundant life here and now.[19]

### 5. *Jesus taught that every human being has the potential and ability to save himself.*

"That is the human potential—the potential for growth to godhood. That human *potential* is what can change the human *condition* and redeem the world from sinfulness—that alone.... The religion *of* Jesus calls on every human being to take personal responsibility for growing to that same state of cosmic unity and wholeness which Jesus himself demonstrated.[20]

"Jesus believed that Christ in him could save the world and we believe that Christ in him will save the world. But Jesus also believes that Christ in each one of us can and will save the world. He has told me so."[21]

"Watch and pray that you not come to be in the flesh, but rather

179

that you come forth from the bondage of the bitterness of this life. . . . For when you come forth from the sufferings and passion of the body, you will receive rest from the Good One, and you will reign with the King. . . ."[22]

*6. Jesus taught that esoteric knowledge (gnosis) is all-important to man's salvation.*

"Could Jesus be an even greater power and presence than before? I answer, 'YES!' And I will share with you *what you must know* [emphasis added] to free yourself from the past. . . . Let me repeat this for its urgency. *There can be only one basic truth, brought to you over and over again in higher sequence of understanding and application* [emphasis in original]!"[23]

"Both the causes and the effects function in a realm outside the kingdom of God-consciousness. Thus, no matter what the causes or the karmic debt, the effects can be dissolved by 'knowing the Truth,' [esoteric understanding of John 8:32] by raising our consciousness above the level of sin and its atonement."[24]

"These are the secret sayings which the living Jesus spoke and which Didymos Judas Thomas wrote down. And he said, 'Whoever finds the interpretation of these sayings will not experience death.'"[25]

*7. Jesus taught that part of man's self-salvation involves a transformation of consciousness.*

"There is only one way under the sun by which man can achieve his 'Mt. Olympus'—that is to say, achieve the realization and the unfoldment of his own innate divinity (salvation in the truest sense of the word)—and that is by bringing about a radical and permanent change for the better in his own consciousness."[26]

"There is no way to enter the Kingdom except to ascend in consciousness to the Father, to that unconditional love for all creation which Jesus demonstrated. That is what the Christian tradition—and, indeed, every true religion—is all about: a system of teachings (both theory and practice) about growth to higher consciousness."[27]

"The concept of yourself that you now hold would guarantee your function here remain forever unaccomplished and undone. And thus it dooms you to a bitter sense of deep depression and futility. Yet it need not be fixed, . . . Alternatives are in your mind to use, and you can see yourself another way."[28] In other words, alter your conscious thinking to change your perception of yourself.

## 8. *Jesus taught and believed in God the Father and God the Mother.*

"Even I, the Christed One, had many teachers and lessons when I walked upon this tiny planet earth. And it was all part of the Father/Mother's plan so that I could better serve humanity from a place of common experience."[29]

"But my example will not end with death. My body will be laid within a tomb in which no flesh has lain, symbolic of the purity of life in death. And in the tomb I will remain three days in sweet communion with the Christ, and with my Father-God, and Mother-God."[30]

"When we were Hebrews we were orphans and had only our mother, but when we became Christians we had both father and mother. . . . [But] where they will be in their own way, the Holy Spirit [will be, and] her children are many."[31]

The above citations demonstrate that New Age "Christianity" takes an esoteric or mystical view of the person and teachings of Jesus. He is viewed as a mere man in whom the Christ consciousness was more fully manifested than in any other human. Since Jesus was thus enlightened, he becomes an example for us to follow as we work at transforming our consciousness to realize our oneness with God and the fact that, in reality, each person is God.

The teachings of Jesus or about Jesus as recorded in the Bible are given an esoteric interpretation that ignores the larger context of Scripture. One example will suffice. With obvious reference to John 1, Mark and Elizabeth Clare Prophet write, "The only begotten Son of the Father, full of grace and truth, is the Christ whose Image the Lord has reproduced over and over again as the Christ-identity of every son and daughter who has come forth from the infinite Spirit of the Father-Mother God."[32] In addition to giving an esoteric interpretation to biblical teachings, New Agers appeal to secret teachings from the past or newly channeled revelations to give Jesus and the "true" message of Christianity the appearance of being in harmony with New Age doctrine. "New Agers have taken the New Testament sculpture (if you will) of Christ, crafted an esoteric/mystical chisel, and hammered away at this sculpture until a completely new image has been formed."[33] For the unsuspecting and undiscerning Christian, this new sculpture of Christ becomes another deceptive lie of the New Age.

## The New Age in Christian Churches

We have looked at New Age "Christianity" in terms of its distortions of the person and teachings of Jesus Christ found in the Gnostic gospels, New Age organizations, and New Age authors. We now consider the creeping influence of the New Age philosophy in Christian churches and the writings of two self-identified Christian authors.

## Dr. M. Scott Peck

A quotation from Dr. M. Scott Peck earlier in this chapter demonstrates that the New Age concept that man is God is found, in this case, in the writings of someone who claims to be a Christian. In 1990, Dr. Peck granted an interview with *The Door* magazine. While not precisely clear as to the timing, the interview indicates that Dr. Peck had previously become a Christian. He is quoted as being quite approving of the NAM. He states,

> I am and I am not New Age. . . . [T]here are some things about the New Age Movement that are very godly, and some things that are potentially evil.

> The New Age Movement is a reaction to the sins of the Christian Church, the sins of technology, and the excesses of science. . . .

> These sins are very real. I think there is something potentially holy about the New Age movement [sic] because of their openness to new ideas. . . . The New Age Movement, in reaction to the sins of the Christian Church, moved to the *East*—to Oriental philosophy and technology—and attempted to throw all of Christian theology out.[34]

Among Peck's several books, perhaps the one of greatest concern is *The Road Less Traveled,* from which the quote earlier in the chapter was taken. In this book, Peck compares man's spiritual evolution to man's physical evolution, which, it might be added, he also accepts without reservation. Concerning man's spiritual evolution Peck writes,

> For no matter how much we may like to pussyfoot around it, all of us who postulate a loving God and really think about it eventually come to a single terrifying idea: God wants us to become Himself (or Herself or Itself). We are growing toward godhood. God is the goal of evolution. It is God who is the source of the evolutionary force and God who is the destination. This is what we mean when we say the [sic] He is the Alpha and the Omega, the beginning and the end.[35]

While not directly stating at this point that man is God (Peck's writing here would be very compatible with Mormon teaching about man becoming God), Peck's thinking certainly falls in line with the self-deifying, evolution-promoting aspects of the New Age philosophy. In another example, Peck gives the appearance of engaging in Christian reflection when he refers to the account of the Fall in the Genesis 3 in order to explain how he came to accept the teaching of original sin. "So original sin does exist; it is our laziness." This laziness was evident in Adam and Eve who failed "to consult or listen to the God within them, the knowledge of rightness which inherently resides within the minds of all mankind."[36] A major concern is that the writings of Dr. Peck are frequently found on the shelves of Christian bookstores where purchasers of Christian materials become unsuspecting conveyers of Dr. Peck's New Age thinking into their homes and churches.

## Matthew Fox

"One of the most controversial links between Eastern mysticism and Christianity is 'creation spirituality,' developed by Dominican priest Matthew Fox of Oakland, California."[37] On August 8, 1992 the head of the Dominican Order of the Catholic Church in Rome decreed Matthew Fox's dismissal from the Order due to his unwillingness to cease promoting New Age philosophy.

Although Fox is personally critical of some New Age practices, the foundation of his theology, which he has termed creation spirituality, includes variations on many New Age themes even as it denounces the fall/redemption motifs that are the foundation of orthodox Christian theology. Instead of the pantheism (God is all, all is God) of the New Age, Fox claims to teach panentheism (God is *in* all and all is *in* God). Yet his writings sound very pantheistic.

> The absolute, Divine Mind, is all that is in everything that is.... Divinity is the enfolding and unfolding of everything that is. Divinity is in all things in such a way that all things are in divinity.... We are, as it were, a human deity.

> I discover that God and I are one. There I am what I was, and I grow neither smaller nor bigger, for there I am an immovable cause that moves all things.[38]

Fox's creation spirituality builds on his teaching about the Cosmic Christ, an idea similar to the Christ Consciousness of the New Age. Jesus was not the Cosmic Christ. He was only an embodiment of this eternal principle that is also ready to be awakened in all creation. Fox writes, "The divine name from Exodus 3:14, 'I Am who I Am,' is appropriated by Jesus who shows us how to embrace our own divinity. The Cosmic Christ is the I Am in every creature."[39] About this quotation from Fox, Mitchell Pacwa writes, "Again Fox sounds like the Church Universal and Triumphant, claiming that Jesus appropriated His divinity and we can do the same. This makes Jesus no more divine than we are, as New Agers teach."[40]

At the heart of Fox's creation spirituality is an intense concern for the welfare of the earth and the environment. While certainly an important concern, especially to New Agers, Fox's New Age connection can be seen in the individuals he has included on the faculty of his Institute for Culture and Creation Spirituality in Oakland, CA—the witch, Starhawk; a shaman, Buck Ghost Horse; a voodoo priestess, Luish Teish; a representative of Sufism (Islamic mysticism); a gestalt therapist and others. Fox's shift from what he calls "original sin" theology to "original blessing" theology has led to an endorsement of many New Age tenets. "His constant concern with the divinisation of human beings (or, more accurately, with the innate divinity of human beings) and of nature, his monism (panentheism), and his own brand of 'ecumenism' certainly also reflect some measure of congruity with New Age thought."[41] As with M. Scott Peck, the teachings of Matthew Fox are readily available in religious bookstores for consumption by unsuspecting Christians.

# A Course in Miracles

In chapter 3, brief mention was made of *A Course in Miracles*, which claims to be the channeled teachings of the voice of Jesus through the human agent, Helen Schucman. It consists of a student text, an instructor's manual, and a workbook. The work was completed in 1972, and in 1975 Schucman gave the copyright of *A Course* to the Foundation for Inner Peace. It has become extremely popular thanks to media personalities such as Oprah Winfrey, Robert Young, and Robert Schuller being either students or promoters of these newly revealed teachings of Jesus.

Marianne Williamson wrote *A Return to Love: Reflections on a Course in Miracles*. Appearances on TV talk shows helped to catapult her book to the top of the *New York Times* best seller list in 1992. She also made the rounds of the lecture circuit \  ı great success. Her book and lectures based on *A Course* have further increased interest in it. By 1992 over 1,500 groups had been formed for serious study of *A Course*. "More than 800,000 people have bought copies of the 1188-page *Course*, which offers God without guilt, says that love is real and the physical world is illusory, and teaches that inner peace comes from a reoriented view of reality."[42]

What is *A Course in Miracles*? On the surface it seems to be a Christian study course. It implies that the presenter of its teachings is Jesus Christ speaking in the first person. It uses familiar Christian language about God, the Son of God, the Holy Spirit, love, and forgiveness.

> As the work progresses, however, it radically redefines the person of Christ, the meaning of reality, the message of the atonement, and the concept of revelation. None of those redefinitions tallies with the scriptural teachings of Jesus. Taken together, they comprise another gospel, a distinctly gnostic and metaphysical gospel, not a Christian one."[43]

The miracles of *A Course* are not supernatural acts of intervention on the part of God but rather corrections of misperceptions in the minds of people. According to the channeled teachings of Jesus, humankind has become enslaved to many misperceptions. The most serious is that sin has separated man from God. But sin is an illusion; it is not real in the usual understanding of the word. "Actually sin is simply a lack of love, a mistake or error calling for correction,

THE NEW AGE IS LYING TO YOU

not for guilt and punishment."[44] By rising from the dead, Jesus demonstrated that death is also an illusion.

> Now, if the greatest effect of sin in this world is death, demonstrating that death is an illusion simultaneously demonstrated that there is no sin. This also says that the separation never occurred. We therefore need someone to show us that there is no death.
>
> By undoing death that person will also undo sin and will simultaneously show us that there is no separation; the separation never occurred and the only reality, the only true Cause is God. That person was Jesus. And his mission was to show that there is no death.[45]

Obviously, the basic premise of A Course is the New Thought/ Age idea that what we perceive is illusory (Hindu *maya*), while the realm of secret knowledge provides us with reality. How do we correct our misperceptions? We forgive ourselves, and we forgive others by knowing that their sin against us never really happened. We do this when we realize that, like Jesus, each one of us is also the Son of God. Only in my continual remembrance of that fact will my life be free of sin, guilt, fear, and death. "I am as God created me. His Son can suffer nothing. And I am His Son."[46]

William Thetford was involved with Helen Schucman from the beginning in the transcription of A Course. He writes,

> The aim of A Course in Miracles is to lead us from duality to oneness—to the realization of our At-one-ment with God, our Self and all people—our brothers. In this healing is our Salvation— we are *saved* from our misperception of ourselves as separated individuals. When our perception is corrected we remember our true or higher Self, created by God as His Son, and one with Christ. Salvation is really enlightenment, and enables us to accept the Christ within, and see with Christ's vision—love [emphasis in original].[47]

It should come as no surprise that the Unity School of Christianity has for years promoted the study of A Course. Sadly, many mainline Christian churches have also included these channeled teachings of Jesus as part of their education program. The old lies of the New Age are very subtle in their appeal to man's desire to be God and to save himself.

## A Christian Response

Christians need to be very discerning in the selection and use of study materials. A rose by any other name may still be a rose, but study materials and other writings that claim to be Christian and even use Christian terminology may be anything but Christian. The concerned Christian will want to test the spirits to see if they are of God (1 John 4:1). Does a study course in the church maintain a proper distinction between God as Creator and man as creature (Job 38:1–42:6)? Do the writings of certain authors and other study materials that deal with spiritual and eternal matters promote the lordship of Jesus Christ (Phil. 2:10–11)? Do the materials give proper respect to the sovereignty and majesty of God while also acknowledging his personal intervention in the world for the salvation of mankind (Is. 42:8; Phil. 2:6–8)?

Perhaps Mitchell Pacwa's concluding remarks in his article about Matthew Fox could apply to all that has been described in this chapter. "Fox's theology distorts historic Christianity into a crypto-New Age system that leads people away from the real Christ of Scripture. The warning of St. Paul is well-suited for this modern-day wolf in clerical clothing [along with other wolves in other clothing]:"[48]

> See to it that no one takes you captive through hollow and deceptive philosophy, which depends on human tradition and the basic principles of this world rather than on Christ. For in Christ all the fullness of the Deity lives in bodily form, and you have been given fullness in Christ, who is the head over every power and authority (Col. 2:8–10).

# The Biblical Worldview

**Item:** Shirley MacLaine describes a point she had reached in her spiritual journey, "The teachings of the Bible, the Mahabarata, the Koran, and all the other spiritual books that I had tried to understand flooded back to me: *The Kingdom of Heaven is within you. Know thyself and that will set you free; . . . to know self is to know all; know that your are God; know that you are the universe. . . .*" (emphasis and final ellipses in original). She realizes that all the spiritual masters, including Christ, had said and taught the same thing. "They had each taught that the purpose of life was to work one's way back to the Divine Source of which we were all a part. And the karmic events that we encountered along the way were only to be experienced and understood—never to be judged."[1]

**Item:** Russell Chandler describes an interview of Kenneth Wapnick, promoter of the channeled *A Course in Miracles*, by New Age/cult researcher Dean Halverson. In the interview, Wapnick admits that in his interpretation of *A Course* he was very selective in considering some parts of the Bible to be valid while others were considered invalid. "Some parts of the Bible have the Holy Spirit as their source. Other parts are from the ego. Any passage that speaks of punishment or of hell, I understood that as being from the ego. Any passage that speaks of forgiveness and love, the unreality of the body, etc., I took as an expression of the Holy Spirit."[2]

**Item:** Marilyn Ferguson refers to Jacob Needleman's *A Sense of the Cosmos: The Encounter of Modern Science and Ancient Truth* in stating that "Westerners were moving away from the form and trappings of Judaism and Christianity . . . [and] were looking to Eastern traditions to see what they might offer 'our threatened society and our tormented religions.' " She claims that formal religion in the West is in a major state of decline. "If they [churches] cannot find new roles in a rapidly changing society, they may go the way of the railroads—without Amtrak." She describes mystics of all faiths throughout history as being generally treated as heretics. "Now the heretics are gaining ground, doctrine is losing its authority, and knowing is superseding belief."[3]

In a 1987 *Time* article on the NAM, Robert Burrows, at that time with the Spiritual Counterfeits Project organization, says, "Dostoyevsky said anything is permissible if there is no God. But anything is permissible if everything is God. There is no way of making any distinction between good and evil."[4] The New Age concept that all is God has opened the Pandora's box of subjective truth and morality. Since each person is, in essence, his or her own God, truth and morality are relative to each person's perception of the same. Biblical truth is to be reinterpreted so that it agrees with any individual's perception of truth. Authoritative doctrine is out. Mystical experience is in. Personal knowledge (enlightenment) in the realm of spiritual things replaces belief (God-given faith.)

Tal Brooke summarizes the NAM and the spread of its subtle evil by means of what he has termed "The Great Lie." Out of his own personal involvement in the New Age he writes,

> A single thought has danced as a whirling dervish across history, seducing millions in its path. Indeed this very thought seduced the highest created intelligence in the universe. It was also great enough to cause the fall of the entire human race. . . . It is the Great Lie.
>
> The Great Lie is quite simply the belief *that man is God*, that his true identity is the immortal self that is ageless and eternal, and that *as God he will never die*! Death is merely a veil through which we pass—it is not real. Sin and depravity are therefore illusions since this inner divinity is at man's core.[5]

In an article on the New Age for the *Lutheran Theological Review*, John Stephenson (with reference to Dietrich Bonhoeffer) points out that the Christian is concerned with the penultimate (the things of this life, Luther's kingdom of God's Left Hand) as well as with the ultimate (the things of the life to come, Luther's kingdom of God's Right Hand). Stephenson comments that if we only combat the NAM when its tentacles reach into the church (the right-hand realm of the ultimate), "it will still be able to mislead with impunity not only unbelievers but also Christians as it remains impregnably ensconced in the territory of God's Left-Hand kingdom or the sphere of the penultimate."[6] To combat the NAM, Stephenson identifies a two-pronged campaign:

> [T]he Christian struggle should be waged in the kingdom of the Left Hand as well as in the kingdom of the Right Hand; battle should be joined in the area of the penultimate as well as in that of the ultimate; and Christians should fight with all the weapons that God provides, those of right reason as well as those of devout faith. The Christian's calling is not abjectly to cower in the kingdom of the Right Hand, but rather precisely as a subject of the kingdom of God boldly to attest His lordship and His truth in the Left-Hand realm also.[7]

This book has been an attempt to do just that. Following an overview of the basic principles of the NAM, we have considered areas of infiltration of the New Age philosophy into our lives. We have demonstrated that the concerned Christian has to be alert to the NAM's influence both in the realm of the secular (the penultimate/kingdom of God's Left Hand) and in the realm of the spiritual (the ultimate/kingdom of God's Right Hand). Christians have been cautioned to guard against casually yielding to the New Age philosophy wherever they may encounter it in daily living.

As noted, some themes of the New Age can be viewed in a positive way—the emphasis on environmental preservation and renewal; working toward greater harmony among the peoples and nations of the world; a desire to help people become more in touch with their feelings and emotions; the promotion of a holistic approach to health care. The problem is not so much with some of the goals and objectives of the NAM but rather with its man-centered, self-deifying, occult-based, evolution-promoting worldview and with the psychotechnologies used to achieve its goals. Chandler reminds us, "One's worldview determines what one believes, and what one believes has a great influence on individual behavior.... The payload the New Age movement carries is no trivial cosmic joke or magic show; it is the heavy stuff that determines the destinies of men, women, and nations—even the eternal salvation of humanity."[8]

While each chapter has concluded with a brief Christian response, the remaining pages present a biblical worldview as a counterbalance to each of the six fundamental New Age principles outlined in chapter one and offer a final Christian response to New Age thinking.

# A Biblical Worldview

John Stephenson correctly points out, "The starting point and enduring motivation of all resistance to new age encroachments in the sphere of the Right Hand is the realization that the Christian religion commends itself to us . . . in virtue of its truth."[9] Jesus Christ himself is the Truth. When we confront God's revealed word in the Bible, inspired by the Holy Spirit, "that God was reconciling the world to himself in Christ" (2 Cor. 5:19), we meet the truth. Concerning the word of the Heavenly Father, Jesus said, "[Y]our word is truth" (John 17:17). God's word in the Bible is God's truth about him who is the Truth (John 14:6). It is on the basis of that truth that a biblical worldview is set in opposition to the New Age worldview.

## 1. All is not one; all is not God

The basic New Age principle has been identified as a combination of monism (all is one) and pantheism (all is God). In contrast to that, the biblical worldview is expressed in Genesis 1 where the Holy Spirit reveals that God created particular and specific things. He created different life forms—vegetable and animal—each according to its own kind. Creation, the world in which we live, is not an undifferentiated oneness but a plurality and diversity that can be truly appreciated only when one understands that this creation reflects the glory and majesty of God. The Psalmist writes, "Praise the Lord from the heavens. . . . Praise him, sun and moon, praise him, all you shining stars. . . . Praise the Lord from the earth, . . . you mountains and all hills, fruit trees and all cedars, wild animals and all cattle, small creatures and flying birds . . ." (Ps. 148:1, 3, 7, 9–10).

Contrary to the New Age, all is not God. The biblical God is distinct and separate from his creation. God maintains and preserves his creation in love, yet creation does not contain Him. "He [Christ] is the image of the invisible God, the firstborn over all creation. For by him all things were created; things in heaven and on earth, visible and invisible, whether thrones or powers or rulers or authorities; all things were created by him and for him. He is before all things, and in him all things hold together" (Col. 1:15–17). Clearly, the Creator is transcendent and far above His creation. In Rom. 1:25, Paul speaks of those who worship and serve the creature rather than the Creator. Such worship of the creature is possible because the creature is distinct and separate from the Creator. All is not God, and, as Douglas Groothuis reminds us, "To identify what is not God as God is what the Bible calls 'idolatry.' "[10]

Furthermore, the God of the New Age is an impersonal force or energy. In the truth of his inspired word, the true God reveals himself to be both imminent and personal even as he remains transcendent. The most obvious substantiation of this truth is that the transcendent Creator became one with his creatures in the gift of his Son who repeatedly referred in a very personal way to God as Father. Jesus taught his disciples to approach God in prayer as "Our Father" (Matt. 6:9). The resurrected Jesus said, "I am returning to my Father and your Father, to my God and your God" (John 20:17). Ron Rhodes sums up this point, "Clearly, Jesus perceived God not as an 'it' or a 'cosmic force,' but as a person with whom personal relations can be entered."[11]

## 2. Mankind is not divine; his potential is limited.

Satan's old lies—"You shall not die; . . . you shall be like God"— are still lies. It is true that human beings have been created in the image of God (Gen. 1:26). A major discussion of the *Imago Dei* does not fall within the scope of this book. However, one thing the image of God does not mean is that we were given the essential nature of God. Nor does it mean that we are a part of the divine energy source or that this universal energy somehow resides in and imparts divine status to each person. In brief, the image of God means that, like our Creator, we are endowed with intelligence and will and, therefore, we are personal—we think, we feel, and we act. Furthermore, we have the capacity to reflect God's love and righteousness and to do his will. However, the image of God does not mean that we have unlimited potential—we are not infinite, all-knowing, present everywhere, or all-powerful.

In addition, the image of God in man has been seriously distorted ever since man listened to Satan's old lies. If, while being in the perfect image of God, human beings were nothing more than creatures distinct and separate from the Creator, how much less are they God after the image has been flawed and cracked as a result of man's rebellion. The Bible makes it clear that God alone is God, and there is none other beside Him (Deut. 32:29; Is. 45:5–6). The Bible also condemns those who pretend to be God or claim to have a right to the divine throne (Job 38; Acts 12:21–23).

### 3. Mankind's basic flaw is not ignorance; it is sin.

In a sense, the major problem the human race faces is ignorance centered in a lack of understanding. However, it is not ignorance of the divinity resident within a person. Rather it is the ignorance of one's sin and the lack of understanding of mankind's rebellion against God. Mankind's basic flaw is sin, rebellion against a holy God and His holy Law, something which New Agers do not want to admit. Ted Peters describes a time when he invited New Ager Barbara Marx Hubbard to speak to his theology class. When queried by a student about sin, Hubbard replied, "Oh, don't talk about sin! That's negative thinking, and negative thinking is what is blocking our way to spiritual transformation." Peters then addresses a major problem with the New Age. "It is the problem of honestly acknowledging the reality in which we live. . . . In point of plain fact, we live in a sinful world and, what's more, we ourselves are sinful. [Our] spiritual health . . . will have to include an honest appropriation of our own sinful nature, or else it will collapse under the weight of its own naivete."[12]

New Age "truth" tells a person to look within to find the answers and solutions to life's problems. However, looking within does not provide the answer. Rather, it is the problem itself. In Matt. 15:19, Jesus reminds us that it is from within, "out of the heart," that evil comes. Genesis 3 tells how man listened to the lies of Satan and rebelled against his good and gracious Creator. Man's fundamental sin of pride expressed itself by grasping for the forbidden status of being like God. The result of man's original sin is summed up in Eccl. 7:20, "There is not a righteous man on earth who does what is right and never sins." Rom. 3:23 echoes this thought, "For all have sinned and fall short of the glory of God." God's truth throughout the Scriptures testifies that man's basic flaw is not ignorance of his divinity, but rather a transgression of the divine Law—sin.

### 4. Mankind's basic need is not enlightenment, but salvation by grace through faith.

If a person's basic problem is ignorance of the divinity that is within him, then the solution is to remove the darkness of that ignorance by a process of enlightenment. As we have seen, the NAM has many techniques for consciousness raising and increasing one's self-awareness so that eventually an individual will experience personal transformation and realize one's divinity.

Scripture also declares that man needs to be enlightened and transformed. In his sin and rebellion against a holy God, a person is "living in darkness" (Matt. 4:16). He needs to begin to "walk in the light" (1 John 1:7) by coming into a living relationship with the One who is "the light of the world" (John 8:12). He needs to be transformed, to have the divine image in which he was created renewed within him. However, the solution is not in man's effort to achieve enlightenment by raising his consciousness level or increasing self-awareness. Rather, people become transformed by acknowledging sin and entering into a relationship of trust in Jesus Christ. This transformation of confession, repentance, and faith is achieved only by the action of God's grace.

The doctrine of justification is, indeed, the doctrine upon which the church of Jesus Christ stands or falls. This doctrine is a beautiful picture of God's transforming grace. As in a courtroom setting, you and I stand before the Judge of all mankind. We are "as guilty as sin." We deserve nothing but God's eternal punishment. But next to us stands One who knew no sin, yet he was "made to be sin for us, so that in him we might become the righteousness of God" (2 Cor. 5:21). Next to us is the One who made "the atoning sacrifice for our sins, and not only for ours but also for the sins of the whole world" (1 John 2:2). Here is the One who "did not come to be served, but to serve, and to give his life as a ransom for many" (Matt. 20:28). The Judge vents his wrath against our sin by placing it and its penalty of death upon Jesus Christ, the Righteous One. He displays his love for the sinner by pronouncing us not guilty for the sake of his Son, the only Redeemer of all mankind. And we who were nothing but sinners and enemies of God (Rom. 5:8,10) have become saints. Our sin-stained robes have been made white in the blood of the Lamb (Rev. 7:14). We are *simul justus et peccator*, at the same time saint and sinner.

There is no more powerful or enlightening transformation than to be awakened to the forgiving grace of a merciful and loving God. When, through the working of the Holy Spirit in word and sacrament, the light of God's grace in Christ is turned on in a person's life, then, "if anyone is in Christ, he is a new creation; the old has gone, the new has come"(2 Cor. 5:17)! What a transformation! Such a person has been reborn. In his baptism into Christ, he has died with Christ to sin and risen with Christ to live a new life (Rom. 6:1–4). This new life is the sanctified life, a life of loving service to God and to one's fellow man. Ted Peters writes, "The sanctified life is the loving life ... that grows gradually in us, as the indirect yet in some way natural consequence of our commitment to imbibe the love of God expressed in Jesus Christ. Love, more than anything else, is the sign that transformation is under way and wholeness is being embraced."[13] Sinful man does need to be enlightened. However, as Rhodes points out, "True enlightenment ... involves not a growing awareness of divinity but following and believing in a living Christ who himself is the light. True enlightenment is wholly Christ centered, not man centered."[14]

## 5. Not personal transformation but God's creation of a new heaven and a new earth will bring global transformation.

The personal transformation of a critical mass of people by means of consciousness altering techniques will not bring about global transformation. It will come about when people respond to the working of the Holy Spirit who brings them into a right relationship with God in Christ. Then the wolf could live with the lamb and the leopard lie down with the goat (Is. 11:6). However, the Bible indicates that such total global transformation will not happen prior to our Lord's return to judge the living and the dead. Instead, the time before Jesus' return will be marked by the prophecies of many false Christs deceiving and leading many astray from the truth. It will be a period of great tribulation for Christians (Matthew 24).

When Christ returns, as promised, for the final judgment, global transformation will also take place. Peter reminds us that the day of God's judgment "will bring about the destruction of the heavens by fire, and the elements will melt in the heat. But in keeping with his promise, we are looking forward to a new heaven and a new earth, the home of righteousness" (2 Pet. 3:12–13). We do have the assurance that there will be a global transformation, but it will not happen on this planet as it now exists. Instead, it will take place when the One who makes all things new brings this present world to an end and creates a new heaven and a new earth.

## 6. All religions are not one; only one religion leads to the renewal of all creation.

Contrary to New Age teaching, the Bible asserts that all religions are not one at their essential core. All religious teachings do not lead to "at-one-ment" with God. Jesus is not just one among many wise teachers and ascended masters.

As previously noted, the claim of Christianity, based on biblical truth, is exclusive. "Salvation is found in no one else, for there is no other name under heaven given to men by which we must be saved" (Acts 4:12). Jesus' claim concerning himself is exclusive. "I am the way and the truth and the life. No one comes to the Father except through me" (John 14:6). All other religions, also the New Age religion, teach that we are saved by what we do. As Shirley MacLaine stated (the opening item of this chapter), the purpose of life is to work one's way back to the Divine Source. The exclusive teaching of Christianity is salvation by grace through faith. "So we, too, have put our faith in Christ Jesus that we may be justified by faith in Christ and not by observing the Law, because by observing the Law no one will be justified" (Gal. 2:16). The *skandalon* (stumbling block) and foolishness of the cross (1 Cor. 1:23) will ever keep the Christian faith separate from all other religions and will increasingly isolate Christians in a world with people intent on saving themselves.

## A Christian Response to the New Age Movement

The Christian will usually find it necessary to respond differently to New Agers (and non-Christians in general) than to fellow Christians, who ordinarily accept the authority of the Bible in principle if not in fact. Different questions have to be addressed to the New Ager, as well as to anyone who in effect creates his own religion and his own god.

Basic questions, even helpful at times for Christians, are these: If there is a God, what would he be like? Would he not create what he wished and as he wished? Would he retain control of his creation? Would he not reveal himself, yet not exhaustively so as to be *fully* understood? Would his creatures be tempted to become frustrated (as they did when they disobeyed God and listened to Satan in the Garden of Eden)?

Not knowing everything and being resentful, would God's creatures create their own god? In fact, that has been the story of mankind, reaching its peak in the "Age of Reason" a few centuries ago, when great thinkers relied totally on their reason, not believing it had been tainted and corrupted when the first creatures fell for Satan's lie. That feeling of self-sufficiency has been continued by human beings ever since. At times they relied on their intellect. At other times they relied more on their emotions, as they do today in the fantasies of the New Age.

Some of the New Age frenzy is a reaction against the "dead orthodoxy" of the organized church that doesn't seem relevant for today. Therefore, naturally, in an age when nothing seems certain and where there are no absolutes, human beings make their own god or make themselves divine.

What is really *real* is directly related to the concept of God. We soon discover that more than objective things are real. Spiritual powers are seen to be real, particularly for those who dabble with demonic powers and find that they do act.

Other questions bother us. Why be morally upright? Who sets objective standards when each person is god? What is the meaning of life? What happens at death? These questions, too, should be asked of New Agers, and perhaps we should not be too anxious to offer the Christian answer immediately.

The biblical answers to these questions check out when put to the test, but the innate tendency is still there: Create your own standards and your own god! That tendency has become frighteningly popular today. It is at the heart of the New Age.

In the face of such a pervasive, deceptive, and diabolical movement in our society, what can be done? How can an increasing minority of Christians respond to such a man-centered philosophy, especially when some of its terminology and practices have already been accepted by society in general? Walter Martin suggests as guidelines for Christian confrontation with New Agers that we communicate our love, seek common ground, define terminology, study the New Age, define "Jesus," and use the Bible.[15]

In her two books, Berit Kjos urges parents and families to combat the influence of the New Age. One particular suggestion is worth mentioning. The New Age emphasizes various meditation practices, and many Christians are being led into New Age meditation techniques. Kjos would encourage Christians also to meditate, not by emptying one's mind or by concentrating on the repetition of a mantra, but by focusing on "God's love promises." These promises include "I have loved you with an everlasting love" (Jer. 31:3) and "I am convinced that ... [nothing] in all creation will be able to separate us from the love of God that is in Christ Jesus our Lord" (Rom. 8:38–39).[16] I too strongly encourage such Christian meditation and the praying and singing of psalms, hymns, and spiritual songs.

Here are a few additional ideas for a Christian response to the NAM.

1. Perhaps most important for saints in Christ is to follow the exhortation of Peter, "[G]row in the grace and knowledge of our Lord and Savior Jesus Christ" (2 Pet. 3:18). Continually growing in the knowledge and understanding of what God has done in Christ is absolutely essential for sharing the truth of God's Word with others. Now more than ever we need to grow in knowledge and appreciation of all that God has revealed in his holy word so that we may always be prepared to give the reason for the hope within us (1 Pet. 3:15). We need to become wise in the "foolishness" of the cross, not to conquer a New Ager in debate, but rather that through our confident and faithful witness the Holy Spirit may testify to the truth and turn the heart of the New Ager to Christ. Just as important, we need to know the truth God has revealed in Scripture so that we may confront the false teachings of the New Age and not yield to them ourselves.

2. Second, Christians can become informed about the basic ideas of the NAM. Numerous articles about the NAM have been published in Christian and secular magazines. Many books offer a Christian critique of the New Age. It is difficult to speak against error if you are not knowledgeable about it. You cannot detect the pervasive nature of the NAM in society if you are not sensitive to its teachings, techniques, and terminology. You need not become an expert on the New Age before taking a position against it. But the more knowledge you have about the New Age, the more confident you will be and more able to identify its presence.

3. A Christian also needs to be alert and discerning as to how the New Age affects and infiltrates personal circumstances. Life situations will differ, and therefore experiences and exposure to aspects of the NAM will differ. Parents who have children in the public school system may have somewhat similar exposure to the New Age.

A businessman who is required by his company to attend a human potential seminar will have different exposure and experience from the housewife who devotes much time to TV talk shows. Discernment is the key. On the one hand, caution must be exercised in classifying a person as a New Ager simply because he or she uses New Age language or terminology. The same caution is in order when it comes to identifying activities to preserve the environment or certain holistic medical practices. On the other hand, a Christian should not bury his head in the sand and hope that the New Age will go away. The NAM is as old as the original lies of Satan. It has always been around in one form or another, and it will continue until the Lord comes again.

4. Christians need to stand firmly on the truth of the Gospel as it applies to a given situation. We have no authority to add to or subtract from the truth that God has revealed in his Word. The truth is to be applied to whatever situation arises. On this particular subject, Douglas Groothuis writes,

> As J. B. Phillips said, "I am *not* concerned to distort or dilute the Christian faith so that modern undergraduates, for example, can accept it without a murmur. I am concerned with the truth revealed in and through Jesus Christ. Let the modern world conform to him, and never let us dare to try to make him fit into our clever-clever modern world." Christian defenders of the faith should discern the issues at hand and respond to them with the uncompromised, undiluted Word of God.[17]

5. Finally, Christians must pray. Pray that God will lead his redeemed in Christ to grow in the grace and knowledge of their Lord and Savior and pray that he will keep them firm in their faith. Pray that God will provide the words you need to speak when called upon to take a firm stand on the truth of the Gospel in the face of the NAM's pervasive presence. As you grow and witness, "may the God of all grace, who called you to his eternal glory in Christ . . . . make you strong, firm and steadfast. To him be the power forever and ever. Amen" (1 Pet 5:10–11).

# Notes

## Introduction

1. James V. Geisendorfer, *A Directory of Religious and Parareligious Bodies and Organizations in the United States* (Lewiston, NY: Edwin Mellen, 1989), 7–110.
2. "Worldscene: Churches reach out to New Agers," *Faith and Fellowship* (January 20, 1992), 2.
3. "One in Four Aware of 'New Age,' " *PRRC Emerging Trends* (November 1991), 2.
4. "One in Four," 2.
5. A. James Rudin, "Commentary: New Age cults invade the mainstream," Religious News Service (October 14, 1992), 6.
6. Rudin, "New Age Cults," 6.

## Chapter 1: The New Age Worldview

1. Gene Roddenberry, Special Advertising Section, *Time* (April 18, 1988), n.p.
2. "New Age Pilot Program Removed From LA Schools," *Watchman Expositor* (7:8, 1990), 12.
3. Dina Van Pelt, "The Medicine of Mind over Malady," *Insight* (July 16, 1990), 50.
4. Advertisement—"The Crystal Power Ring," *Weight Watchers Magazine* (October 1991), n.p.
5. Phil Linsalata, "Healers, Seers Sell 'New-Age' Wares At Fair," *St. Louis Post-Dispatch* (August 13, 1990).
6. *Ann Arbor Observer* (November 1990), 82.
7. Brooks Alexander, "The Coming World Religion," a four-page critique of the New Age by Spiritual Counterfeits Project (1974, revision 1982), 3.
8. Douglas Groothuis, *Confronting the New Age* (Downers Grove, IL: InterVarsity, 1988), 18.
9. Elliot Miller, *A Crash Course on the New Age Movement* (Grand Rapids, MI: Baker, 1989), 15.
10. *Watchman Expositor* (7:2, 1990), 5.
11. Walter Martin, *The New Age Cult* (Minneapolis: Bethany House, 1989), 25–34.
12. Philip H. Lochhaas, *How to Respond to the New Age Movement* (St. Louis: Concordia, 1988), 7–8.

13. Russell Chandler, *Understanding the New Age* (Dallas: Word, 1988), 26–33.
14. Douglas Groothuis, *Unmasking the New Age* (Downers Grove, IL: InterVarsity, 1986), 18–31.
15. Chandler, *Understanding,* 28.
16. Groothuis, *Unmasking,* 20.
17. Jane Roberts, *The Seth Material* (Englewood Cliffs, NJ: Prentice-Hall, 1970), 237–38. Quoted in Martin, *The New Age Cult,* 25–26.
18. Lochhaas, *The New Age Movement,* 7.
19. Chandler, *Understanding,* 28.
20. "Werner Erhard Flees in the Wake of Tax Liens and Child Abuse Allegations," *Christian Research Journal* (14:1, Summer 1991), 5. The *Christian Research Journal* is the quarterly publication of Christian Research Institute, the counter-cult and Christian apologetic ministry founded by Walter Martin, author of the book that has become a standard work on the subject of the cults, *The Kingdom of the Cults.* "The *Journal* is dedicated to furthering the proclamation and defense of the historic gospel of Jesus Christ, and to facilitating His people's growth in sound doctrine and spiritual discernment."
21. J. Gordon Melton, Jerome Clark, Aidan A. Kelly, eds., *New Age Encyclopedia* (Detroit: Gale Research, 1990), 377.
22. Tal Brooke, *When the World Will Be as One* (Eugene, OR: Harvest House, 1989), 73.
23. Bob Larson, *Straight Answers on the New Age* (Nashville: Thomas Nelson, 1989), 52.
24. Groothuis, *Unmasking,* 24.
25. Groothuis, *Unmasking,* 25–26.
26. Shirley MacLaine, *Dancing in the Light* (New York: Bantam Books, 1985), 111–13.
27. Karen Hoyt and J. Isamu Yamamoto, eds., *The New Age Rage* (Old Tappan, NJ: Fleming H. Revell, 1987), 43.
28. Shakti Gawain, *Living in the Light* (San Rafael, CA: Whatever Publishing, Inc., 1986), 3–4.
29. Chandler, *Understanding,* 33.
30. Miller, *A Crash Course,* 33.
31. Marilyn Ferguson, *The Aquarian Conspiracy: Personal and Social Transformation in the 1980s* (Los Angeles: J. P. Tarcher, 1980), 27–28.
32. Groothuis, *Unmasking,* 28.
33. Groothuis, *Unmasking,* 28–29.
34. Barbara Marx Hubbard, *The Evolutionary Journey* (San Francisco: Evolutionary Press, 1982), 157. Quoted in Groothuis, *Unmasking,* 30.
35. Levi, *The Aquarian Gospel of Jesus the Christ* (Marina Del Rey, CA: DeVorss & Co., Publishers, 1907, 1964), 7–8.

## Chapter 2: A Historical Review

1. Otto Friedrich, "New Age Harmonies," *Time* (December 7, 1987), 62.
2. Chandler, *Understanding,* 44.

3. Melton, Clark, and Kelley, eds., *New Age Encyclopedia,* xxii.

4. Martin, *New Age Cult,* 13.

5. Miller, *A Crash Course,* 19.

6. Brooke, *When the World,* 171.

7. Norman L. Geisler, "The New Age Movement," *Bibliotheca Sacra* (January—March 1987), 91.

8. Douglas Groothuis, *Revealing the New Age Jesus* (Downers Grove, IL: Inter-Varsity, 1990), 73.

9. Robert G. Hoerber, Horace D. Hummel, Walter R. Roehrs, and Dean O. Wenthe, eds., *Concordia Self-Study Bible* (St. Louis: Concordia, 1986), 1925.

10. Ronald H. Nash, *Christianity and the Hellenistic World* (Grand Rapids, MI: Zondervan), 222. Quoted in Ron Rhodes, *The Counterfeit Christ of the New Age Movement* (Grand Rapids, MI: Baker, 1990), 18.

11. Rhodes, *Counterfeit Christ,* 18.

12. Rhodes, *Counterfeit Christ,* 19.

13. The Christ, *New Teachings for an Awakening Humanity* (Santa Clara, CA: Spiritual Education Endeavors, 1986), 45.

14. J. Gordon Melton, ed., *The Encyclopedia of American Religions,* Second Edition (Detroit: Gale, 1987), 113.

15. Melton, ed., *Encyclopedia of American Religions,* 113.

16. Melton, Clark, and Kelly, eds., *New Age Encyclopedia,* xxiii.

17. Melton, Clark, and Kelly, eds., *New Age Encyclopedia,* 287.

18. Melton, Clark, and Kelly, eds., *New Age Encyclopedia,* xxiii.

19. Hoyt and Yamamoto, eds., *New Age Rage,* 21.

20. Marcus P. Manthey, "Testing the Spirit of the New Age," *Lutheran Synod Quarterly: Theological Journal of the Evangelical Lutheran Synod* (March 1992), 21.

21. Melton, Clark, and Kelly, eds., *New Age Encyclopedia,* xxiv.

22. *Constitution and Bylaws* (Washington, DC: National Spiritualist Association, 1930), 7. Quoted in Melton, *Encyclopedia of American Religions,* 114.

23. Michel P. Richard and Albert Adato, "The Medium and Her Message: A Study of Spiritualism at Lily Dale, N.Y.," *Review of Religious Research* (December 1980), 186.

24. Melton, Clark, and Kelly, eds., *New Age Encyclopedia,* xxv.

25. Rhodes, *Counterfeit Christ,* 117.

26. Geisler, "New Age Movement," 85–6.

27. Martin, *New Age Cult,* 15.

28. Joseph P. Gudel, Robert M. Bowman, Jr., and Dan R. Schlesinger, "Reincarnation—Did the Church Suppress it?" *Christian Research Journal* (10:1, Summer 1987) 8.

29. Rhodes, *Counterfeit Christ,* 120.

30. Brooke, *When the World,* 173.

31. Hoyt and Yamamoto, eds., *New Age Rage,* 24.

32. Brooke, *When the World,* 172–73.

33. Rhodes, *Counterfeit Christ,* 126. The quote from Alice Bailey is from her book *The Externalisation of the Hierarchy* (New York: Lucis Trust, 1957), 222.

34. Rhodes, *Counterfeit Christ,* 128.

35. Melton, Clark, and Kelly, eds., *New Age Encyclopedia,* 327.

36. Mary Baker Eddy, *Science and Health with Key to the Scriptures* (Boston: The First Church of Christ Scientist, 1934), 25, 468.

37. Madame Helena P. Blavatsky, *The Secret Doctrine* (Los Angeles: Theosophy, 1925), Vol. 3, 386.

38. Blavatsky, *Secret Doctrine,* Vol. 2, 132.

39. Blavatsky, *Secret Doctrine,* Vol. 3, 246.

40. Won Yong Ji, "Challenge of Eastern Spiritualities to the West," *Concordia Journal* (April 1991), 131.

41. Won Yong Ji, "Eastern Spiritualities," 133.

42. Philip H. Lochhaas, *How to Respond to the Eastern Religions* (St. Louis: Concordia, 1979), 11.

43. Lochhaas, *Eastern Religions,* 12.

44. Lochhaas, *Eastern Religions,* 23.

45. Won Yong Ji, "Eastern Spiritualities," 134.

46. Bob Larson, *Larson's Book of Cults* (Wheaton, IL: Tyndale House, 1983), 98.

47. Larson, *Book of Cults,* 99.

## *Chapter 3: New Age Occultism*

1. "What's New in the Headlines," *Christian Research Newsletter* (September/October 1991), 3.

2. *Spring Catalog of Pyramid Books and the New Age Collection* (n.d.), 4, 7, 22, 34.

3. "Group seeking writings it says can save world," *The Columbus Dispatch* (October 19, 1991), 8D.

4. Julia Duin, "American religion changing: outsiders moving in," Religious News Service (November 11, 1991), 6.

5. George W. Cornell, "Survey: Religion Changing," *The Leaf-Chronicle,* Clarksville, TN (September 7, 1991), 5A.

6. Lochhaas, *The New Age Movement,* 5.

7. Miller, *A Crash Course,* 108.

8. Hoyt and Yamamoto, eds., *New Age Rage,* 48.

9. Hoyt and Yamamoto, eds., *New Age Rage,* 48.

10. Caryl Matrisciana, *Gods of the New Age* (Eugene, OR: Harvest House, 1985), 16.

11. Matrisciana, *Gods of the New Age,* 16–17.

12. Shirley MacLaine, *Out on a Limb* (New York: Bantam Books, 1983), 181.

13. Alice A. Bailey, *The Reappearance of the Christ* (New York: Lucis, 1948), 116–17. Quoted in Martin, *New Age Cult,* 33.

14. F. LaGard Smith, *Out on a Broken Limb* (Eugene, OR: Harvest House, 1986), 13.

15. Smith, *Broken Limb,* 13.

16. Mark Albrecht, *Reincarnation: A Christian Appraisal* (Downers Grove, IL: InterVarsity, 1982), 11–12.

17. Smith, *Broken Limb,* 72.

18. Albrecht, *Reincarnation,* 20.

19. Matrisciana, *Gods of the New Age,* 44.

20. Smith, *Broken Limb,* 76.

21. Gudel, Bowman, and Schlessinger, "Reincarnation," 10.

22. Albrecht, *Reincarnation,* 100.

23. Merrill F. Unger, *Demons in the World Today* (Wheaton, IL: Tyndale House, 1971), 11.

24. Kurt E. Koch, *Christian Counseling and Occultism* (Grand Rapids, MI: Kregel Publications, 1972), 13. Koch's work is viewed by some as a definitive work on the subject of occult bondage and oppression. His presentation of over 100 pastoral cases from the field of occultism clearly demonstrates the demonic powers at work in the world.

25. Melton, Clark, and Kelly, eds., *New Age Encyclopedia,* 101.

26. Chandler, *Understanding,* 81.

27. Miller, *A Crash Course,* 166. Miller devotes two chapters to spiritistic channeling and a Christian analysis of it.

28. MacLaine, *Out on a Limb,* 182.

29. Paul Zuromski, ed., *The New Age Catalogue* (Island Publishing Company, 1988), 7.

30. Anne and Arthur Cataldo, eds., *Channels: Newsletter of the Center for Transformation* (Summer 1988), 1–2.

31. John Klomo, "Channeling," *The New Age Journal* (December 1987), 38. Quoted in Brooke, *When the World,* 23.

32. Brooks Alexander, "Theology from the Twilight Zone," *Christianity Today* (September 18, 1987), 24.

33. Melton, Clark, and Kelly, eds., *New Age Encyclopedia,* 429.

34. Melton, Clark, and Kelly, eds., *New Age Encyclopedia,* 140.

35. Linda Moran Evans, "Crystal Power: Fad ... or Health Tool?" *Beauty Digest* (June/July 1988), 24.

36. Martha Smilgis, "Rock Power for Health and Wealth," *Time* (January 19, 1987), 66.

37. Larson, *Straight Answers,* 70.

38. Gawain, *Living,* xiv-xv.

39. Melton, Clark, and Kelly, eds., *New Age Encyclopedia,* 133.

40. Larson, *Straight Answers,* 44–45.

41. David Hunt and T. A. McMahon, *The Seduction of Christianity* (Eugene, OR: Harvest House, 1985), 146.

42. Nathaniel Lande, *Mindstyles/Lifestyles* (Los Angeles: Price/Stern/Sloan Publishers, 1976), 317.

43. David Hoover, *How to Respond to the Occult* (St. Louis: Concordia, 1977), 15. Hoover's booklet in the Response Series deals with the occult apart from the context of the New Age. However, as indicated in the text, New Agers have extensively adopted and adapted many occult practices to assist them in their personal transformation. Hoover devotes several pages to such divination practices as palmistry, dowsing, and cartomancy.

44. Larson, *Straight Answers*, 138.

45. "Defining the 'New Age,'" *PRRC Emerging Trends* (November 1991), 5.

46. *Dallas Morning News* (November 19, 1985), 1-C. Quoted in Rick Branch, "Looking to the Creation for Answers," *Watchman Expositor* (8:1, 1991), 7.

47. Larson, *Straight Answers*, 145.

48. Quoted in *Watchman Expositor* (8:1, 1991), 10.

49. Lande, *Mindstyles/Lifestyles*, 321.

50. Roger Sonnenberg, "God's Message in the Stars," *Teacher's Interaction* (December 1991), 2–4, 18–20; *Teacher's Interaction* is a magazine for Lutheran church school teachers. Sonnenberg suggests Christian interpretations that could be given to the constellations and their individual stars—for example, "Gemini is perhaps one of the more confusing signs of the Zodiac.... The Hebrew word for this constellation is *Thaumim*, meaning *joined together*. Some say it is a starry picture of the Messiah as being both the Son of God and the Son of Man. Others imagine that it foretells the day when Christ and His people will be forever united in eternity (1 Thess. 4:17)."

51. Lochhaas, *The New Age Movement*, 10.

52. Chandler, *Understanding*, 92–93.

53. William M. Alnor, "UFO Cults Are Flourishing in New Age Circles," *Christian Research Journal* (Summer 1990), 5. Alnor himself has written *UFOs in the New Age* (Baker Book House, 1992).

54. John Ankerberg and John Weldon, "UFO Encounters," *SCP Journal* (17:1–2, 1992), 17–18. The *SCP Journal* is the quarterly publication of Spiritual Counterfeits Project, a cult research/Christian apologetic organization that seeks "to provide a biblical perspective on new religions and spiritual trends." In 1992, SCP devoted an entire double issue of the *SCP Journal* to UFOs.

55. William M. Alnor, *Christian Research Journal* (Summer 1991), 37, a book review of *Something's Going On Out There* (Fleming H. Revell, 1990) by David Wimbish. Concerning the book, Alnor writes, "This book . . . . is the first responsible evangelical book on UFOs to have been published in more than ten years." Alnor also says, "Wimbish . . . exposes the occult links behind the Urantia Book, and tells us there is little difference between ET messages and Joseph Smith's revelations that led to Mormonism."

56. William M. Alnor, "Of Gods and Aliens," *SCP Journal* (17:1–2, 1992), 43.

57. Whitely Strieber, *Communion* (New York: Avon Books, 1987), 5.

58. Brooks Alexander, "Machines Made of Shadows," *SCP Journal* (17:1–2, 1992), 10.

59. William M. Alnor, "The Alien Obsession . . . with Repudiating Christianity," *SCP Journal* (17:1–2, 1992), 32.

60. Melton, Clark, and Kelly, eds., *New Age Encyclopedia*, 278.

61. John Chesterman and others, eds., *An Index of Possibilities: Energy and Power* (New York: Pantheon Books, 1974), 236–37.

62. Lande, *Mindstyles/Lifestyles,* 193–94.

63. B. J. Oropeza, "Should a Christian Practice the Martial Arts?," *Christian Research Newsletter* (4:1, January/February 1991), 6.

64. Larson, *Book of Cults,* 300.

## Chapter 4: New Age Entertainment

1. Dr. John Eidsmoe, *Basic Principles of New Age Thought* (Green Forest, AR: New Leaf Press, 1991), 31–32

2. *Teenage Mutant Ninja Turtles,* 1990. Quoted in Manthey, "Testing the Spirit," 8.

3. Melton, Clark, and Kelly, eds., *New Age Encyclopedia,* 95.

4. Marc Shulgold, "Heavenly Music . . . ," *Rocky Mountain News* (September 23, 1992), 62–63.

5. Brooke, *When the World,* 146.

6. Eidsmoe, *Basic Principles,* 49.

7. Berit Kjos, *Your Child & the New Age* (Wheaton, IL: Victor Books, 1990), 83.

8. *Time* (May 19, 1980), 73. Quoted in Geisler, "New Age Movement," 90.

9. *Star Wars,* 1983. Quoted in Manthey, "Testing the Spirit," 8.

10. Groothuis, *Unmasking,* 19.

11. Kjos, *Your Child,* 88.

12. Kjos, *Your Child,* 87.

13. Ron Rhodes, "What's New in the Headlines," *Christian Research Newsletter* (4:1, January/February 1991), 3.

14. *Indiana Jones and the Last Crusade,* 1990. Quoted in Manthey, "Testing the Spirit," 8.

15. Woodrow Nichols, "Indiana Jones: Screen Superhero or Amoral Avatar," *SCP Newsletter* (10:4, July/August 1984), 9.

16. "Indiana Jones and the Holy Grail," *Watchman Expositor* (6:10, 1989), 2.

17. MacLaine, *Dancing in the Light,* 404.

18. Tal Brooke, "Myths—Adhesive for a Generic Religion," *SCP Journal* (9:2, 1990) 8.

19. Groothuis, *Revealing,* 73–74.

20. Kjos, *Your Child,* 103.

21. Groothuis, *Confronting,* 185.

22. Marlys Harris, "Shirley's Best Performance," *Money* (September 1987), 162.

23. *St. Louis Post-Dispatch* (July 1, 1987), 9W.

24. Craig V. Anderson, "Pruning Time for Shirley MacLaine?" *The Christian Century* (February 25, 1987), 182.

25. Anita Manning, "Earth Notes," *USA Today* (August 13, 1991), 6D.

26. Melton, Clark, and Kelly, eds., *New Age Encyclopedia,* 28–29.

27. John Denver, "You and Me . . . ," *New Realities* (November/December 1986),

9–10, 12–13. Quoted in Melton, Clark, and Kelly, eds., *New Age Encyclopedia,* 94.

28. Kathleen A. Hughes, "As New Age Books Prosper, Publishers Squeeze All They Can Into the Category," *The Wall Street Journal* (March 10, 1988), 23.
29. Chandler, *Understanding,* 133.
30. Hughes, "New Age Books," 23.
31. Marvin H. Scilken, ed., *The U\*N\*A\*B\*A\*S\*H\*E\*D Librarian* (74, 1990), 9.
32. Scilken, *Librarian,* 9–12.
33. Miller, *A Crash Course,* 191.
34. Meg Cox, "'New Age Music' Wins Wider Following As Many People Grow Too Old for Rock," *The Wall Street Journal* (April 1, 1987), n.p.
35. Groothuis, *Confronting,* 191.
36. Groothuis, *Confronting,* 191.
37. *Master of Life* (Issue 35), 8. Quoted in Groothuis, *Confronting,* 192.
38. F. LaGard Smith, "New Age Prayer," *New Covenant* (June 1989), 14.
39. Larson, *Straight Answers,* 188.
40. Miller, *A Crash Course,* 191.
41. Terry Mattingly, "'Star Trek' worldview rooted in mystic East," *Rocky Mountain News* (February 6, 1993), n.p.

## Chapter 5: New Age Neo-Paganism

1. Melton, Clark, and Kelly, eds., *New Age Encyclopedia,* 297.
2. Gary Massaro, "Teacher comes to grips with neo-paganism," *Rocky Mountain News* (October 1992), n.p.
3. Derk Roelofsma, "Inside the Circle of Witches, Modern," *Insight* (June 8, 1987), 59.
4. Sallie Han, "Members of area group try to dispel image of paganism," *Kansas City Star* (December 26, 1992), n.p.
5. Tami Simon, *Sounds True* (1:1, 1988–1989), 13. The publisher's (Tami Simon's) introductory remarks to this first issue of the catalog note that the purpose of the catalog "is to distribute tapes that remind us of who we are and how to create the world we want . . . . We *can* create a world that works for everyone if we are properly informed, and inspired to claim our role in this process of personal and planetary transformation."
6. Alan Morvay, ed., *Joy Lake Mountain Seminar Center 1986 Catalog of Events,* 20.
7. Melton, Clark, and Kelly, eds., *New Age Encyclopedia,* 311.
8. Chandler, *Understanding,* 125.
9. Margot Adler, *Drawing Down the Moon: Witches, Druids, Goddess Worshippers and Other Pagans in America Today,* 2nd Edition (Boston: Beacon Press, 1986), xi.
10. Brooks Alexamder, "Neo-Witchcraft's Charter Myth and Its Variations," *SCP Journal* (16:3, 1991), 41.
11. For a brief but rather thorough overview of the development of pre-Christian paganism into the European witchcraft of the Middle Ages and later, see the special report, "Witchcraft and Neo-Paganism: From the Dark Ages to the New Age," by Brooks Alexander in the *SCP Journal* (16:3, 1991). The entire issue

is devoted to witchcraft. For a more extended treatment see Adler's *Drawing Down the Moon*.

12. Craig S. Hawkins, "The Modern World of Witchcraft: Part One," *Christian Research Journal* (12:3, Winter/Spring 1990), 11. This and the succeeding issue of the *Christian Research Journal* include two extensive articles by Hawkins on modern witchcraft. The second article includes a thorough critique of witchcraft from a Christian theological perspective.
13. Alexander, "Witchcraft and Neo-Paganism," 30.
14. Adler, *Drawing Down the Moon,* 547–48.
15. Hawkins, "Modern Witchcraft: Part One," 11.
16. Dave Bass, "Drawing Down the Moon," *Christianity Today* (April 29, 1991), 18–19.
17. Adler, *Drawing Down the Moon,* ix.
18. Adler, *Drawing Down the Moon,* ix.
19. Bass, "Drawing Down the Moon," 15.
20. Hawkins, "Modern Witchcraft: Part One," 12.
21. Melton, Clark, and Kelly, eds., *New Age Encyclopedia,* 314.
22. Hawkins, "Modern Witchcraft: Part One," 13.
23. "Religious Requirements and Practices of Certain Selected Groups, A Handbook for Chaplains," Department of the Army Pamphlet No. 165–13 (April 1978), VII–7.
24. Bass, "Drawing Down the Moon," 16.
25. Norman Geisler, "Neopaganism, Feminism, and the New Polytheism," *Christian Research Journal* (14:2, Fall 1991), 12. In this article Geisler provides a philosophical evaluation of Neo-Paganism's polytheism and its particular feminist emphasis.
26. Groothuis, *Unmasking,* 135.
27. Chandler, *Understanding,* 122. Interior quote is from Chandler's interview with Robert Ellwood, Los Angeles, December 14, 1987.
28. Melton, Clark, and Kelly, eds., *New Age Encyclopedia,* 302.
29. Melton, Clark, and Kelly, eds., *New Age Encyclopedia,* 302.
30. Melton, Clark, and Kelly, eds., *New Age Encyclopedia,* 445.
31. Chandler, *Understanding,* 112–13.
32. Adler, *Drawing Down the Moon,* 431.
33. Groothuis, *Unmasking,* 137.
34. Frederick and Mary Ann Brussat, "Native American Spirituality," *Values & Visions* (23:3, 1992), 2–4.
35. Melton, ed., *Encyclopedia of American Religions,* 639–61.
36. Adler, *Drawing Down the Moon,* 107–08.
37. Melton, Clark, and Kelly, eds., *New Age Encyclopedia,* 313.
38. Hawkins, "Modern Witchcraft: Part One," 12.
39. Adler, *Drawing Down the Moon,* 14–16.
40. Adler, *Drawing Down the Moon,* 23.

41. Hawkins, "The Modern World of Witchcraft: Part Two," *Christian Research Journal* (Summer 1990), 23–24.

## Chapter 6: New Age Environmentalism

1. Brussat, "Native American Spirituality," 3.
2. Loren Wilkinson, "Earth Summit: Searching for a Spiritual Foundation," *Christianity Today* (July 20, 1992), 48.
3. Mike Samuels, M.D. and Hal Zina Bennett, *Well Body, Well Earth* (San Francisco: Sierra Club Books, 1983)), 68–69. Quoted in Berit Kjos, *Under the Spell of Mother Earth* (Wheaton, IL: Victor Books, 1992), 32–33.
4. *New Age Journal* (January/February 1992), 54. Quoted in "Sacred Fires to Mother Earth," *Watchman Expositor* (9:3, 1992), 8.
5. Chandler, *Understanding,* 120.
6. Adler, *Drawing Down the Moon,* 152.
7. Kjos, *Under the Spell,* 23–24.
8. Tal Brooke, "The Ecological Great Awakening—Earthcrisis and Eco-Purges," *SCP Journal* (17:3, 1992), 7.
9. Quoted in Michael Coffman and Brooks Alexander, "Eco-Religion and Cultural Change," *SCP Journal* (17:3, 1992), 16.
10. John B. Cobb, Jr., "Biblical Responsibility for the Ecological Crisis," *Second Opinion* (18:2, 1992), 13. Cobb's article presents, I believe, a fair analysis of White's thesis and is a call to Christians everywhere to pursue a biblical approach to caring for God's creation.
11. Loren Wilkinson, "How Christian Is the Green Agenda?" *Christianity Today* (January 11, 1993), 16.
12. Brooke, "The Ecological Great Awakening," 10.
13. Brooke, "The Ecological Great Awakening," 11. As part of Brooke's article, Stuart Chevre, in a sidebar, raises some interesting questions about the global warming theory. He points out that all current estimates of average global temperatures are produced by computer models and that even minute faulty assumptions about initial conditions "can drastically alter estimates of predicted temperature" with the result that the "temperature estimates produced are therefore meaningless." 9.
14. Brooke, "The Ecological Great Awakening," 14.
15. Wilkinson, "Earth Summit," 48
16. Senator Al Gore, *Earth in the Balance* (New York: Houghton Mifflin Company, 1992), 1.
17. Douglas Groothuis, "America's Ecological Millennium: Al Gore in the Balance," *SCP Journal* (17:3, 1992), 27.
18. Gore, *Earth in the Balance,* 258.
19. Gore, *Earth in the Balance,* 260.
20. Groothuis, "America's Ecological Millennium," 29–30.
21. Tod Connor, "Is the Earth Alive?," *Christianity Today* (January 11, 1993), 22.
22. James Lovelock, *Gaia: A New Look at Life* (Oxford: Oxford University Press,

1987), 11. Quoted by Stuart Chevre in "The Gaia Hypothesis: Science, Mythology, and the Desecration of God," *SCP Journal* (16:1, 1991), 24.

23. Gore, *Earth in the Balance,* 28.

24. Chevre, "The Gaia Hypothesis," 28.

25. Brooks Alexander, "Gaia: Sects and Squabbles," and "Deep Ecology," *SCP Journal* (16:1, 1991), 8, 10.

26. Elliot Miller, "A Summary Critique" of Warwick Fox's *Toward a Transpersonal Ecology: Developing New Foundations for Environmentalism, Christian Research Journal* (14:4, Spring 1992), 36.

27. Alexander, "Deep Ecology," 11.

28. Alexander, "Deep Ecology," 13.

29. Adler, *Drawing Down the Moon,* 4, 6.

30. "Statement of Philosophy," *Women of Power* (18, Fall 1990). Quoted in Alison Lentini, "The Goddess Comes of Age," *SCP Journal* (16:1, 1991), 20.

31. Carl Sagan, "Science on Parade," *Parade Magazine* (March 1, 1992), 12.

32. Frances Schaeffer, *Pollution and the Death of Man—the Christian View of Ecology* (Wheaton, IL: Tyndale House, 1970). Quoted in *SCP Journal* (16:1, 1991), 33–34.

33. Connor, "Is the Earth Alive?," 25.

## Chapter 7: New Age Politics/Globalism

1. Richard P. Cimino, ed., *Religion Watch* (8:3, January 1993), 1.

2. Hilary F. French, "Hidden Success at Rio," *World Watch* (September/October 1992), 7–8.

3. Chandler, *Understanding,* 194.

4. Much of the comparison/contrast in this paragraph is taken from Philip Lochhaas, *How to Respond to the New Age Movement,* 14–15. For a concise summary of the anti-God, anti-Christian philosophy of secular humanism, the reader is referred to Lochhaas' book on that subject listed in the bibliography.

5. *Humanist Manifestos I* and *II* (Buffalo: Prometheus Books, 1973), 8.

6. *Humanist Manifestos,* 16.

7. *Humanist Manifestos,* 9.

8. *Humanist Manifestos,* 23.

9. "New Age People: We Are a Political Force," *New Age Harmonist* (1:1), 2. Quoted in Miller, *A Crash Course,* 108.

10. Groothuis, *Unmasking,* 111.

11. Gore, *Earth in the Balance,* 269, 277.

12. Ferguson, *Aquarian Conspiracy,* 191.

13. Ferguson, *Aquarian Conspiracy,* 190.

14. Ferguson, *Aquarian Conspiracy,* 231.

15. Melton, Clark, and Kelly, eds., *New Age Encyclopedia,* 323–24.

16. Ferguson, *Aquarian Conspiracy,* 202.

17. Ferguson, *Aquarian Conspiracy,* 203.

18. Ferguson, *Aquarian Conspiracy,* 205.

19. Miller, *A Crash Course,* 112.

20. Ferguson, *Aquarian Conspiracy,* 214.

21. Chandler, *Understanding,* 196.

22. Cimino, ed., *Religion Watch* (6:1, November 1990), 4.

23. Fritjof Capra and Charlene Spretnak, *Green Politics: The Global Promise* (New York: E. P. Dutton, 1984), 198. Quoted in a review by Ronald Sider, *SCP Newsletter* (11:3, 1985), 7.

24. Fritjof Capra and Charlene Spretnak, "Who Are the Greens?" *New Age* (April 1984), 77. Quoted in Groothuis, *Unmasking,* 123.

25. Hoyt and Yamamoto, eds., *New Age Rage,* 94.

26. Melton, Clark, and Kelly, eds., *New Age Encyclopedia,* 351–52.

27. Groothuis, *Unmasking,* 121–22.

28. Ferguson, *Aquarian Conspiracy,* 232.

29. Ferguson, *Aquarian Conspiracy,* 234.

30. Ferguson, *Aquarian Conspiracy,* 236.

31. Gore, *Earth in the Balance,* 302.

32. Hoyt and Yamamoto, eds., *New Age Rage,* 104.

33. Melton, Clark, and Kelly, eds., *New Age Encyclopedia,* 357.

34. *Humanist Manifestos,* 21.

35. Melton, Clark, and Kelly, eds., *New Age Encyclopedia,* 357.

36. Brooke, *When the World,* 201.

37. Brooke, *When the World,* 203.

## *Chapter 8: New Age Education*

1. Ferguson, *Aquarian Conspiracy,* 295, 315.

2. Chandler, *Understanding,* 156–57.

3. Rick Branch, "SRA Reading Program: Occultism for Elementary Students," *Watchman Expositor* (8:8, 1991), 1.

4. Cimino, ed., *Religion Watch* (8:5, March 1993), 2–3.

5. John Dunphy, "A Religion for a New Age," *The Humanist* (January/February 1983), 26.

6. Brooks Alexander, "The Rise of Cosmic Humanism: What Is Religion?" *SCP Journal* (Winter 1981–82), 4. Quoted in Miller, *A Crash Course,* 95.

7. Kjos, *Your Child,* 15.

8. Groothuis, *Confronting,* 131.

9. Kjos, *Your Child,* 20.

10. Eidsmoe, *Basic Principles,* 141–42.

11. Tal Brooke, "Education: Capturing Hearts and Minds for a New World," *SCP Journal* (16:4, 1992), 14–15.

12. Ferguson, *Aquarian Conspiracy,* 287.

13. Ferguson, *Aquarian Conspiracy,* 281–82.

14. Kjos, *Your Child,* 20.
15. Eric Buehrer, *The New Age Masquerade: The Hidden Agenda in Your Child's Classroom* (Brentwood, TN: Wolgemuth & Hyatt, Publishers, Inc., 1990), 102.
16. Ferguson, *Aquarian Conspiracy,* 297.
17. Ferguson, *Aquarian Conspiracy,* 79–80.
18. Ferguson, *Aquarian Conspiracy,* 81.
19. Ferguson, *Aquarian Conspiracy,* 293.
20. Miller, *A Crash Course,* 96–97.
21. Rick Branch, "Affective Education: What Is It Teaching Our Kids?" *Watchman Expositor* (9:5, 1992), 1.
22. Branch, "Affective Education: What Is It Teaching?" 1.
23. Chandler, *Understanding,* 154.
24. Maury Smith, *A Practical Guide to Value Clarification* (La Jolla, CA: University Associates, Inc., 1977), 5.
25. Smith, *Value Clarification,* 7, 12.
26. Smith, *Value Clarification,* 210.
27. Ferguson, *Aquarian Conspiracy,* 292.
28. Ferguson, *Aquarian Conspiracy,* 302.
29. Ferguson, *Aquarian Conspiracy,* 316.
30. Miller, *A Crash Course,* 98.
31. Jack Canfield and Paula Klimek, "Education in the New Age," *The New Age Journal* (February 1978), 28. Quoted in Brooke, *When the World,* 112.
32. Canfield and Klimek, "Education in the New Age," 39. Quoted in Brooke, *When the World,* 113.
33. Canfield and Klimek, "Education in the New Age," 36. Quoted in Miller, *A Crash Course,* 96.
34. Matrisciana, *Gods of the New Age,* 174.
35. Deborah Rozman, *Meditating with Children: The Art of Concentration and Centering* (Boulder Creek, CA: University of the Trees Press, 1975), 32. Quoted in Kjos, *Your Child,* 24.
36. Rozman, *Meditating with Children,* 42. Quoted in Kjos, *Your Child,* 24.
37. Matrisciana, *Gods of the New Age,* 172.
38. Buehrer, *New Age Masquerade,* 83–84.
39. Rick Branch, "Pumsey the Dragon, Not a Friend," *Watchman Expositor* (9:3, 1992), 1.
40. Branch, "Pumsey the Dragon," 6.
41. *Empire-Tribune*, Stephenville, Texas (October 20, 1991), 5. Quoted in Rick Branch, "Doing Damage: DARE Verses [sic] Drugs," *Watchman Expositor* (9:8, 1992), 12 (emphasis his). As mentioned in the third "Item" in this chapter, in 1990 the *Watchman Expositor* began to run a series of articles on the influence of New Age humanism and occultism in public schools. Other articles in this series not referred to in the text included evaluations of the Quest program (8:3, 1991); New Age programs for the gifted child (8:4, 1991); general relaxation techniques (8:5, 1991); and non-directive education (8:6, 1991).
42. Groothuis, *Confronting,* 135.

43. Buehrer, *New Age Masquerade,* 29.
44. Buehrer, *New Age Masquerade,* 70–74.
45. Robert Muller, *New Genesis: Shaping a Global Spirituality* (Garden City, NY: Image Books, Doubleday and Co., Inc., 1984), 145. Quoted in Buehrer, *New Age Masquerade,* 75.
46. Muller, *New Genesis,* 152. Quoted in Buehrer, *New Age Masquerade,* 76.
47. Miller, *A Crash Course,* 125.

## *Chapter 9: New Age Business*

1. Bill Dietrich, "Pacific Institute Called 'Anti-Christian'," *The Seattle Times* (February 25, 1987), n.p.
2. Robert Lindsey, "Spiritual Concepts Drawing a Different Breed of Adherent," *New York Times* (September 29, 1986), n.p.
3. John Naisbitt and Patricia Aburdene, *Megatrends 2000* (New York: William Morrow and Company, Inc., 1990), 295.
4. Frank Rose, "A New Age for Business?" *Fortune* (October 8, 1990), 160, 162.
5. Rose, "A New Age for Business?" 157.
6. Robert Burrows, "Corporate Management Cautioned on New Age," *Eternity* (February 1988), 33.
7. Ferguson, *Aquarian Conspiracy,* 328–29.
8. Ferguson, *Aquarian Conspiracy,* 338.
9. Ferguson, *Aquarian Conspiracy,* 339–40.
10. Ferguson, *Aquarian Conspiracy,* 340, 346, 349–50.
11. Miller, *A Crash Course,* 102.
12. Karen Cook, "Scenario for A New Age," *The New York Times Magazine* (September 25, 1988), 26.
13. The Forum (1985), n.p. A promotional brochure.
14. Forum, n.p.
15. Groothuis, *Unmasking,* 154.
16. Lande, *Mindstyles/Lifestyles,* 152.
17. Dean C. Halverson, "Lifespring and the Sovereignty of Subjectivism," a publication of Spiritual Counterfeits Project (1981, revised 1984), 3.
18. Larson, *Straight Answers,* 25. In his book Larson provides a concise summary of a number of human potential programs.
19. Lindsey, "Spiritual Concepts," n.p.
20. Zuromski, ed., *The New Age Catalogue,* 217.
21. David Gelman, "The Megatrends Man," *Newsweek* (September 23, 1985), 60–61.
22. Gelman, "The Megatrends Man," 61.
23. Groothuis, *Confronting,* 158.
24. John Naisbitt and Patricia Aburdene, *Re-inventing the Corporation* (New York: Warner Books, 1985), 20–21, 70.
25. Naisbitt and Aburdene, *Megatrends 2000,* 280–87, 293–95.

26. Richard Watring, "New Age Training in Business: Mind Control in Upper Management?" *Eternity* (February 1988), 30.
27. Watring, "New Age Training," 32.
28. Quoted in Chandler, *Understanding,* 149.
29. "New Age in Business: What You and Your Employer Should Know," *SCP Newsletter* (14:1, 1988), 8.
30. *Insight* (May 16, 1988), 26.
31. "New Age in Business," 1.
32. "Karma for Cash: A 'New Age' for Workers?" *Christianity Today* (June 17, 1988), 74.

## Chapter 10: New Age Health Care

1. Ferguson, *Aquarian Conspiracy,* 241–42.
2. *Beginnings: The Official Newsletter of the American Holistic Nurses' Association* (11:2, February 1991), 5.
3. Christine Bertelson, "Believers Are Drawn Here," *St. Louis Post-Dispatch* (November 24, 1991), 13A.
4. Special Advertising Section, "Healing and the Mind," *Newsweek* (February 22, 1993), A2.
5. Morvay, ed., *Joy Lake,* 24.
6. Advertisement in *St. Louis Post-Dispatch Magazine* (November 1, 1992), 23.
7. Information piece describing the course "Healing Touch for Healthcare Professionals."
8. For a detailed study of New Age medicine from a Christian perspective the reader is referred to two books. John Ankerberg and John Weldon, *Can You Trust Your Doctor?: The Complete Guide to New Age Medicine and Its Threat to Your Family* (Brentwood, TN: Wolgemuth & Hyatt, Publishers, Inc., 1991) and Paul C. Reisser, M.D., Teri K. Reisser and John Weldon, *New Age Medicine: A Christian Perspective on Holistic Health* (Downers Grove, IL: InterVarsity Press, 1987).
9. Claudia Willis, "Why New Age Medicine Is Catching On," *Time* (November 4, 1991), 68.
10. Reisser, Reisser and Weldon, *New Age Medicine,* 33–34.
11. Reisser, Reisser and Weldon, *New Age Medicine,* 36.
12. Quoted in Ann Nietzke, "Portrait of an Aura Reader," *Human Behavior* (February 1979), 31. In turn quoted in Reisser, Reisser and Weldon, *New Age Medicine,* 39.
13. Ankerberg and Weldon, *Can You Trust,* 68–69.
14. Ankerberg and Weldon, *Can You Trust,* 69, 73.
15. Ankerberg and Weldon, *Can You Trust,* 72–77.
16. Ankerberg and Weldon, *Can You Trust,* 78–79.
17. Janice Castro, "Condition: Critical," *Time* (November 25, 1991), 34.
18. Wallis, "New Age Medicine Catching On," 68.
19. Wallis, "New Age Medicine Catching On," 69.
20. Ferguson, *Aquarian Conspiracy,* 257–58.

21. Ferguson, *Aquarian Conspiracy,* 259–60.

22. Ferguson, *Aquarian Conspiracy,* 259–69.

23. "Healing and the Mind," A6.

24. James Walker, "Shopping for New Age Health Care," *Watchman Expositor* (9:7, 1992), 1, 5.

25. Ankerberg and Weldon, *Can You Trust,* 206.

26. D. D. Palmer, *Textbook of the Science, Art, and Philosophy of Chiropractic for Students and Practitioners* (Portland, OR: Portland Publishing House, 1910), 493. Quoted in Ankerberg and Weldon, *Can You Trust,* 212.

27. B. J. Palmer, *The Bigness of the Fellow Within* (Spartanburg, SC: Sherman College of Straight Chiropractic, 1949), 67–68. Quoted in Ankerberg and Weldon, *Can You Trust,* 213.

28. "A New Market: Chiropractors Seeking to Expand Practices Take Aim at Children," *The Wall Street Journal* (March 18, 1993), A1.

29. Chesterman and others, eds., *Index of Possibilities,* 153.

30. Chesterman and others, eds., *Index of Possibilities,* 153.

31. Ankerberg and Weldon, *Can You Trust,* 119.

32. Mary Austin, *The Textbook of Acupuncture Therapy* (New York: ASI Publishers, Inc., 1978), 50. Quoted in Ankerberg and Weldon, *Can You Trust,* 121.

33. Reisser, Reisser, and Weldon, *New Age Medicine,* 70. The authors provide several pages of information about scientific medical observations such as counterirritation, referred pain, trigger points, and the "gate control" theory of pain that explain similar forms of pain control or relief associated with acupuncture.

34. Dolores Krieger, *The Therapeutic Touch: How to Use Your Hands to Help or to Heal* (New York: Prentice Hall, 1986), 13. Quoted in Ankerberg and Weldon, *Can You Trust,* 393.

35. Quotations are from "Therapeutic Touch," a handout provided at a workshop for Navy nurses. On file in the office of the Commission on Organizations of the Lutheran Church—Missouri Synod.

36. Ankerberg and Weldon, *Can You Trust,* 397. The reader is referred to this book, pages 390–406, for a detailed analysis of Therapeutic Touch. Almost an entire issue of the *SCP Newsletter* (14:3, 1989) is devoted to the subject of "Nursing's New Age."

37. In addition to the New Age practices described in the body of the text, *Can You Trust Your Doctor?* includes extensive treatments of altered states of consciousness, applied kinesiology, attitudinal healing, channeling, crystal healing, herbal medicine, homeopathy, and New Age meditation. *New Age Medicine* describes several of the above and also gives consideration to Touch for Health (chiropractor John Thie's popularized form of applied kinesiology), Jin Shin Do, psychic healing, and biofeedback. Although not quoted in the text, another book that devotes several pages to each of a variety of topics associated with the occult aspects of the New Age in general and New Age medicine in particular is *Occult ABC* by Kurt E. Koch. See the bibliography for complete information. Koch covers such topics as acupuncture, anthroposophy, astrology, color diagnosis and color therapy, iris diagnosis, meditation, and peditherapy, along with many other topics related to the occult.

38. Reisser, Reisser, and Weldon, *New Age Medicine,* 143.

39. Ankerberg and Weldon, *Can You Trust,* 342–43.

40. Rick Branch, "Iridology: Studying the Body's Television," *Watchman Expositor* (9:7, 1992), 15.

41. Melton, Clark, and Kelly, eds., *New Age Encyclopedia,* 379.

42. Quoted in Rick Branch, "Reflexology: The Sickness Is All in the Foot!" *Watchman Expositor* (9:7, 1992), 7.

43. Melton, Clark, and Kelly, eds., *New Age Encyclopedia,* 382.

44. Quotations are from a one-page information piece in the files of the office of the Commission on Organizations of the Lutheran Church—Missouri Synod.

45. Melton, Clark, and Kelly, eds., *New Age Encyclopedia,* 383.

46. Elliot Miller, "The Christian, Energetic Medicine, and 'New Age Paranoia,' " *Christian Research Journal* (14:3, Winter 1992), 25.

47. Miller, "Energetic Medicine," 25.

48. Cimino, ed., *Religion Watch* (8:8, June 1993), 7.

49. Reisser, Reisser, and Weldon, *New Age Medicine,* 147–52.

50. Stuart Chevre, "Visualization, Guided Imagery, and the Holistic Health Movement," *SCP Journal* (9:3, 1990), 27.

## Chapter 11: New Age "Christianity"

1. Morvay, ed., *Joy Lake,* 25.

2. L. Masterson Badger, ed., *Earth Star: Whole Life New England* (February/March 1993), 48, 57.

3. Kjos, *Under the Spell,* 14.

4. Chandler, *Understanding,* 207–08.

5. Ted Peters, *The Cosmic Self: A Penetrating Look at Today's New Age Movement* (San Francisco: Harper Collins Publishers, Inc., 1991), 88.

6. Ferguson, *Aquarian Conspiracy,* 367 (footnote).

7. Rhodes, *Counterfeit Christ,* 91–92.

8. Eric Butterworth, *Discover the Power Within You* (San Francisco: Harper & Row, Publishers, 1968, 1989), 33–34. Eric Butterworth is an ordained minister of the Unity School of Christianity, the New Thought organization founded in 1889 by Charles and Myrtle Fillmore. While not directly identified as New Age, Charles Fillmore described Unity as drawing on the best of all religions (including Eastern). Much of the teaching of Unity is a precursor of and a present parallel to New Age principles. In *Megatrends 2000,* John Naisbitt identified Unity as "about the closest thing to organized religion in which the eclectic modern New Ager could feel comfortable (p. 283)." As of the late 1980s Butterworth was preaching at the Avery Fisher Hall in the Lincoln Center of New York City. The flyleaf of the jacket cover of the 20th-anniversary edition of Butterworth's book includes the following statement: "Eric Butterworth believes that the greatest discovery of all time was of the divine dimension of every human being. Christianity has emphasized Jesus' divinity, but Jesus himself taught the divinity of man."

9. The Christ, *New Teachings,* 2. This volume was referred to in chapter 2. The book is written in the form of a channeled revelation by one who is only

identified as The Christ and who was resident in the earthly Jesus. The revelation is given for this New Age because of the negativity rampant throughout the earth and because the warring of humankind threatens not only to destroy the earth but to upset the peace of the surrounding universes. The following quote is from the book's dedication page: "This book is dedicated to God and to peace and the preservation of all life everywhere . . . to every soul on the planet earth . . . and to our guides, friends and teachers from the heavenly realms who lead us lovingly back to full spiritual awareness and manifestation."

10. M. Scott Peck, M. D., *The Road Less Traveled* (New York: Simon and Schuster, 1978), 281, 283. An evaluation of Dr. Peck's New Age leanings is provded in chapter 11.

11. The Christ, *New Teachings,* 116, 123.

12. David Spangler, *Reflections on the Christ* (Forres, Scotland: Findhorn Publications, 1981), 73. Quoted in Rhodes, *Counterfeit Christ,* 79. In the early 1970s, David Spangler was the head of the education department at Findhorn, a prototype New Age community in Scotland that has served as a pattern for many New Age organizations in the United States, including Spangler's own Lorian Association. Spangler has written over 15 New Age books in which he details his views of the "Cosmic Christ" resident within every human being.

13. Levi, *The Aquarian Gospel of Jesus the Christ* (Marina Del Rey, CA: DeVorss & Co., Publishers, 1964, 1991), 48. Levi Dowling was a Civil War Army chaplain. He claimed to transcribe *The Aquarian Gospel* from the Akashic Records, an occult "memory bank" which contains a record of every human thought and action. Levi's gospel is an account of the education and travels of Jesus including his supposed travel to India where he then studied with the Hindus and Buddhists.

14. Butterworth, *Discover the Power,* 7.

15. Butterworth, *Discover the Power,* 7–8.

16. John White, "Jesus and the Idea of a New Age," *The Quest* (Summer 1989), 14. A New Age author and a leading figure in the field of consciousness research, John White has served as director of education for the Institute of Noetic Sciences and as president of Alpha Logics, a school for self-directed growth in body, mind, and spirit.

17. White, "Jesus and . . . a New Age," 18.

18. Levi, *Aquarian Gospel,* 46.

19. Butterworth, *Discover the Power,* 137.

20. White, "Jesus and . . . a New Age," 17.

21. Mark C. Prophet and Elizabeth Clare Prophet, *The Lost Teachings of Jesus, 3: Masters and Disciples on the Path* (Livingston, MT: Summit University Press, 1988), 239. Quoted in Rhodes, *Counterfeit Christ,* 83. Mark and Elizabeth Prophet founded what has become the Church Universal and Triumphant. Its theology is an eclectic blend of Christian terminology and Eastern mysticism. Prior to Mark's death the Prophets coauthored four volumes titled *The Lost Teachings of Jesus.* The front jacket of volume one includes the following statement: "Many of Jesus' teachings were altered, deleted, or never recorded. Here's the evidence—and a reconstruction of his message" (Quoted in Rhodes, *Counterfeit Christ,* 82).

22. James M. Robinson, ed., *The Book of Thomas the Contender* in *The Nag Ham-*

*madi Library: In English* (San Francisco: Harper and Row, Publishers, 1977), 194. Elaine Pagels, a member of the translating team of the Coptic Gnostic Library Project wrote a book titled *The Gnostic Gospels*. Douglas Groothuis says that Pagels' book "arguably did more than any other effort to ingratiate the Gnostics to modern Americans." Pagels was one of the first to translate the Nag Hammadi texts (13 leather-bound papyrus books dating from about the year A.D. 350) from Coptic into English. "Her central thesis was simple: Gnosticism should be considered at least as legitimate as orthodox Christianity because the 'heresy' was simply a competing strain of early Christianity" (Groothuis, *Revealing the New Age Jesus,* 78).

23. The Christ, *New Teachings,* 78, 124.

24. Butterworth, *Discover the Power,* 136.

25. Robinson, ed., *The Gospel of Thomas* in *The Nag Hammadi Library*, 118. The quotation is the opening statement of perhaps the best known and most often commented upon of the Nag Hammadi texts.

26. Butterworth, *Discover,* 16.

27. White, "Jesus and . . . a New Age," 19.

28. Julius J. Finegold and William M. Thetford, eds., *choose once again: Selections from A Course in Miracles* (Millbrae, CA: Celestial Arts [The Foundation for Inner Peace], 1981), 66. More about A Course in Miracles and the infiltration of its New Age theology into the Christian church is provided later in Chapter 11.

29. The Christ, *New Teachings,* 32.

30. Levi, *Aquarian Gospel,* 173.

31. Robinson, ed., *The Gospel of Philip* in *The Nag Hammadi Library*, 132, 136.

32. Mark and Elizabeth Prophet, *Climb the Highest Mountain* (Los Angeles: Summit University Press, 1974), 228. Quoted in Rhodes, *Counterfeit Christ,* 143.

33. Rhodes, *Counterfeit Christ,* 15.

34. *The Door* (May/June 1990), 5–15. Quoted in Rick Branch, "New Age Teacher: M. Scott Peck," *Watchman Expositor* (7:10, 1990), 8.

35. Peck, *The Road,* 269–70.

36. Peck, *The Road,* 273.

37. Chandler, *Understanding,* 209.

38. Matthew Fox, O.P., *The Coming of the Cosmic Christ* (San Francisco: Harper and Row, Publishers, 1988), 126, 164. Quoted in Mitchell Pacwa, S.J., "Catholicism for the New Age: Matthew Fox and Creation-Centered Spirituality," *Christian Research Journal* (15:2, Fall 1992), 29. The reader is referred to the article by Pacwa for a thorough critique of Fox's New Age spirituality.

39. Fox, *Cosmic Christ,* 154. Quoted in Pacwa, "Matthew Fox," 29.

40. Pacwa, "Matthew Fox," 29.

41. David Rankin, "The New Age and the Old Gnosticism," *Lutheran Theological Journal* (26:2, August 1992), 102.

42. Steve Rabey, "New Book No 'Course in Miracles,'" *Christianity Today* (May 18, 1992), 49.

43. Frances Adeney, "'Re-visioning' Reality," *SCP Newsletter* (7:2, June/July 1981), 1.

44. Finegold and Thetford, eds., *choose once again,* 2. Page 2 is part of the intro-

duction to this book of excerpts from *A Course in Miracles*.

45. Kenneth Wapnick, "A Talk Given on A Course in Miracles," 65. Quoted in Rick Branch, "A Course in Miracles Denies All," *Watchman Expositor* (7:10, 1990), 10. This issue of *Watchman Expositor* also includes a "Biblical Response to the Course."
46. Finegold and Thetford, eds., *choose once again,* 96.
47. Finegold and Thetford, eds., *choose once again,* 2–3.
48. Pacwa, "Matthew Fox," 31.

## Chapter 12: The Biblical Worldview

1. MacLaine, *Dancing in the Light,* 350.
2. Dean Halverson, "A Matter of Course: Conversation with Kenneth Wapnick," *SCP Journal* (7:2, 1987), 16–17. Quoted in Chandler, *Understanding,* 307–08.
3. Ferguson, *Aquarian Conspiracy,* 367–71.
4. Friedrich, "New Age Harmonies," 72.
5. Brooke, *When the World,* 233–34.
6. John R. Stephenson, "Giving a Twofold Response to the Ancient Errors of the 'New Age,'" *Lutheran Theological Review* (III:2, Spring/Summer 1991), 51.
7. Stephenson, "A Twofold Response," 51.
8. Chandler, *Understanding,* 320.
9. Stephenson, "A Twofold Response," 53.
10. Groothuis, *Unmasking,* 21.
11. Rhodes, *The Counterfeit Christ,* 188.
12. Peters, *Cosmic Self,* 172.
13. Peters, *Cosmic Self,* 185.
14. Rhodes, *The Counterfeit Christ,* 191.
15. Martin, *New Age Cult,* 97–108.
16. Kjos, *Under the Spell,* 107.
17. Groothuis, *Confronting,* 65. The quote from J. B. Phillips is from his book *The Ring of Truth* (New York: Macmillan, 1967), 9–10.

# Bibliography

Adler, Margot. *Drawing Down the Moon: Witches, Druids, Goddess-Worshippers, and Other Pagans in America Today.* 2nd Edition. Boston: Beacon Press, 1986.

Albrecht, Mark. *Reincarnation: A Christian Appraisal.* Downers Grove, IL: InterVarsity Press, 1982.

Alexander, Brooks and Tal Brooke, eds. *SCP Journal* (16:1, 1991): 4–34; (16:3, 1991): 5–44; (17:1–2, 1992): 4–64; (17:3, 1992): 4–56.

Ankerberg, John and John Weldon. *Can You Trust Your Doctor?: The Complete Guide to New Age Medicine and Its Threat to Your Family.* Brentwood, TN: Wolgemuth and Hyatt, Publishers, Inc., 1991.

Bass, Dave. "Drawing Down the Moon." *Christianity Today* (April 29, 1991): 14–19.

Brooke, Tal. *When the World Will Be as One.* Eugene, OR: Harvest House Publishers, Inc., 1989.

Buehrer, Eric; *The New Age Masquerade: The Hidden Agenda in Your Child's Classroom* (Brentwood, TN: Wolgemuth & Hyatt, Publishers, Inc., 1990).

Butterworth, Eric. *Discover the Power Within You* (San Francisco: Harper & Row, Publishers, 1968, 1989),

Fritjof, Capra and Charlene Spretnak, *Green Politics: The Global Promise* (New York: E. P. Dutton, 1984).

Fritjof, Capra and Charlene Spretnak, "Who Are the Greens?" *New Age* (April 1984)

Chandler, Russell. *Understanding the New Age.* Dallas: Word Publishing, 1988.

Christ, The. *New Teachings for an Awakening Humanity.* Santa Clara, CA: Spiritual Education Endeavors Publishing Company, 1986.

Connor, Tod. "Is the Earth Alive?" *Christianity Today* (January 11, 1993): 22–25.

Eidsmoe, Dr. John. *Basic Principles of New Age Thought.* Green Forest, AR: New Leaf Press, 1991.

Ferguson, Marilyn. *The Aquarian Conspiracy.* Los Angeles: J. P. Tarcher, Inc., 1980.

Finegold, J. Julius. and William M. Thetford, eds., *choose once again: Selections from A Course in Miracles* (Millbrae, CA: Celestial Arts [The Foundation for Inner Peace], 1981)

Friedrich, Otto. "New Age Harmonies," *Time* (December 7, 1987): 62–72.

Gawain, Shakti. *Living in the Light.* San Rafael, CA: Whatever Publishing, Inc., 1986.

Geisendorfer, James V. *A Directory of Religious and Parareligious Bodies and Organizations in the United States.* Lewiston, NY: The Edwin Mellen Press, 1989.

Geisler, Norman L. "The New Age Movement." *Bibliotheca Sacra* (January—March 1987): 79–104.

Gore, Senator Al. *Earth in the Balance.* New York: Houghton Mifflin Company, 1992.

Groothuis, Douglas R. *Confronting the New Age.* Downers Grove, IL: InterVaristy Press, 1988.

———. *Revealing the New Age Jesus.* Downers Grove, IL: InterVarsity Press, 1990.

———. *Unmasking the New Age.* Downers Grove, IL: InterVarsity Press, 1986.

Gudel, Joseph P., Robert M. Bowman, Jr., and Dan R. Schlesinger. "Reincarnation—Did the Church Suppress It?" *Christian Research Journal* (Summer, 1987): 8–12.

Hawkins, Craig S. "The Modern World of Witchcraft: Part One." *Christian Research Journal* (12:3, Winter/Spring 1990): 8–14.

———. "The Modern World of Witchcraft: Part Two." *Christian Research Journal* (13:1, Summer 1990): 22–27.

Hoover, David W. *How to Respond to . . . the Occult.* St. Louis: Concordia Publishing House, 1977.

Hoyt, Karen, and J. Isamu Yamamoto, eds. *The New Age Rage.* Old Tappan, NJ: Fleming H. Revell Company, 1987.

Hunt, David, and T. A. McMahon. *The Seduction of Christianity.* Eugene, OR: Harvest House Publishers, 1985.

Ji, Won Yong. "Challenge of Eastern Spiritualities to the West." *Concordia Journal* (April 1991): 128–40.

Kellogg, Bill, ed. *SCP Journal* (9:2, 1990): 6–44.

Kjos, Berit. *Under the Spell of Mother Earth.* Wheaton, IL: Victor Books, 1992.

———. *Your Child & the New Age.* Wheaton, IL: Victor Books, 1990.

Koch, Kurt E. *Christian Counseling and Occultism.* Grand Rapids, MI: Kregel Publications, 1972.

221

———. *Occult ABC.* Germany: Literature Mission Aglasterhausen, Inc., 1978. American printing and distribution by Grand Rapids International Publications.

Lande, Nathaniel. *Mindstyles/Lifestyles.* Los Angeles: Price/Stern/Sloan Publishers, Inc., 1976.

Larson, Bob. *Larson's Book of Cults.* Wheaton, IL: Tyndale House Publishers, Inc., 1983.

———. *Straight Answers on the New Age.* Nashville: Thomas Nelson Publishers, 1989.

Levi. *The Aquarian Gospel of Jesus the Christ.* Marina Del Rey, CA: DeVorss & Co., Publishers, 1964, 1991.

Lochhaas, Philip H. *How to Respond to . . . the Eastern Religions.* St. Louis: Concordia Publishing House, 1979.

———. *How to Respond to . . . the New Age Movement.* St. Louis: Concordia Publishing House, 1988.

———. *How to Respond to . . . Secular Humanism.* St. Louis: Concordia Publishing House, 1990.

MacLaine, Shirley. *Dancing in the Light.* New York: Bantam Books, 1985.

———. *Out on a Limb.* New York: Bantam Books, 1983.

Manthey, Marcus P. "Testing the Spirit of the New Age." *Lutheran Synod Quarterly: Theological Journal of the Evangelical Lutheran Synod* (March 1992): 8–76.

Martin, Walter. *The New Age Cult.* Minneapolis: Bethany House Publishers, 1989.

Matrisciana, Caryl. *Gods of the New Age.* Eugene, OR: Harvest House Publishers. 1985.

Melton, J. Gordon, ed. *The Encyclopedia of American Religions,* Second Edition. Detroit: Gale Research Company, 1987.

Melton, J. Gordon, Jerome Clark, and Aidan A. Kelly, eds. *New Age Encyclopedia.* Detroit: Gale Research Inc., 1990.

Miller, Elliot. *A Crash Course on the New Age Movement.* Grand Rapids, MI: Baker Book House, 1989.

Pacwa, Mitchell, S. J. "Catholicism for the New Age: Matthew Fox and Creation-Centered Spirituality," *Christian Research Journal* (15:2, Fall 1992): 14–19, 29–31.

Peck, M. Scott M. D., *The Road Less Traveled* (New York: Simon and Schuster, 1978)

Peters, Ted. *The Cosmic Self: A Penetrating Look at Today's New Age Movement* (San Francisco: HarperCollins Publishers, Inc., 1991)

Reisser, Paul C., M. D., Teri K. Reisser and John Weldon. *New Age Medicine:*

# BIBLIOGRAPHY

*A Christian Perspective on Holistic Health.* Downers Grove, IL: InterVarsity Press, 1987.

Rhodes, Ron. *The Counterfeit Christ of the New Age Movement.* Grand Rapids, MI: Baker Book House, 1990.

Richard, Michael P. and Albert Adato. "The Medium and Her Message: A Study of Spiritualism at Lily Dale, N.Y." *Review of Religious Research* (December 1980): 186–97.

Robinson, James M., ed. *The Nag Hammadi Library: In English.* San Francisco: Harper and Row, Publishers, 1977.

Smith, F. LaGard. *Out on a Broken Limb.* Eugene, OR: Harvest House Publishers, 1986.

Smith, Maury. *A Practical Guide to Value Clarification* (La Jolla, CA: University Associates, Inc., 1977)

Spangler, David. *Reflections on the Christ* (Forres, Scotland: Findhorn Publications, 1981),

Stephenson, John R. "Giving a Twofold Response to the Ancient Errors of the 'New Age,'" *Lutheran Theological Review* (III:2, Spring/Summer 1991)

Unger, Merrill F. *Demons in the World Today.* Wheaton, IL: Tyndale House Publishers, Inc., 1971.

Wallis, Claudia. "Why New Age Medicine Is Catching On," *Time* (November 4, 1991): 68–76.

*Watchman Expositor* (9:7, 1992): 1, 5–12, 14–15.

White, John. "Jesus and the Idea of a New Age," *The Quest* (Summer 1989).

Wilkinson, Loren. "How Christian Is the Green Agenda?" *Christianity Today* (January 11, 1993): 16–20.

Zuromski, Paul, ed. *The New Age Catalogue.* Island Publishing Company, Inc., 1988.

For many years the Rev. Eldon K. Winker has been engaged in research and in providing counsel and information to pastors concerning the New Age, cults, Satanism, the occult, and similar groups. He has written and spoken widely on the subject of this book and has taught at Concordia Seminary, St. Louis. He recently completed a four-year term as Executive Secretary of the Commission on Organizations of The Lutheran Church–Missouri Synod, a position that provided unusual opportunities for examining and understanding New Age and parallel organizations.

Pastor Winker has served as a parish pastor for 20 years in Illinois, Arkansas, and Missouri. He holds a master of divinity degree from Concordia Seminary in St. Louis. He and his wife, Judith, have three children, Carrie, Kristin, and Joyce.